ARSINOË OF EGYPT AND MACEDON

WOMEN IN ANTIQUITY

Series Editors: Ronnie Ancona and Sarah B. Pomeroy

This book series provides compact and accessible introductions to the life and historical times of women from the ancient world. Approaching ancient history and culture broadly, the series selects figures from the earliest of times to late antiquity.

Cleopatra
A Biography
Duane W. Roller

Clodia Metelli
The Tribune's Sister
Marilyn B. Skinner

Galla Placidia
The Last Roman Empress
Hagith Sivan

Arsinoë of Egypt and Macedon
A Royal Life
Elizabeth Donnelly Carney

ARSINOË OF EGYPT AND MACEDON

A ROYAL LIFE

Elizabeth Donnelly Carney

OXFORD
UNIVERSITY PRESS

OXFORD
UNIVERSITY PRESS

Oxford University Press is a department of the University of Oxford.
It furthers the University's objective of excellence in research,
scholarship, and education by publishing worldwide.

Oxford   New York

Auckland   Cape Town   Dar es Salaam   Hong Kong   Karachi
Kuala Lumpur   Madrid   Melbourne   Mexico City   Nairobi
New Delhi   Shanghai   Taipei   Toronto

With offices in

Argentina   Austria   Brazil   Chile   Czech Republic   France   Greece
Guatemala   Hungary   Italy   Japan   Poland   Portugal   Singapore
South Korea   Switzerland   Thailand   Turkey   Ukraine   Vietnam

Oxford is a registered trade mark of Oxford University Press
in the UK and in certain other countries.

Published in the United States of America by
Oxford University Press
198 Madison Avenue, New York, NY 10016

Library of Congress Cataloging-in-Publication Data
Carney, Elizabeth Donnelly, 1947–
Arsinoë of Egypt and Macedon : a royal life / Elizabeth Donnelly Carney.
p. cm.—(Women in antiquity)
Includes bibliographical references and index.
ISBN 978-0-19-536551-1—ISBN 978-0-19-536552-8—ISBN 978-0-19-971101-7
1. Arsinoe II, Queen, consort of Ptolemy II, King of Egypt, ca. 316–270 B.C.
2. Egypt—History—332–30 B.C. 3. Egypt—Kings and rulers—Biography.
4. Greece—History—Macedonian Hegemony, 323–281 B.C.
5. Macedonia—History—Diadochi, 323–276 B.C.
6. Thrace—Kings and rulers—Biography.
I. Title. II. Series: Women in antiquity.
DT92.C37   2013
932.021092—dc23   2012023599

Printed in the United States of America
on acid-free paper

In Memoriam
John Francis Oates

Contents

Acknowledgments

I OWE SPECIAL thanks to the editors of the Women in Antiquity series, Ronnie Ancona and Sarah Pomeroy, for encouraging me to return to the topic of Arsinoë II. Stefan Vranka, Oxford University Press's editor for Classics, Ancient History, and Archaeology was a close reader of the original manuscript and made many helpful suggestions, and his editorial assistant, Sarah Pirovitz, proved invaluable time and again.

Since I spend most of my scholarly time in ancient Macedonia, embracing a project that involved Ptolemaic Egypt as well put new demands on my knowledge and understanding of people and events, and I owe a debt to many people who helped me. Let me start with the man to whom this volume is dedicated, John Francis Oates, my beloved teacher (and dissertation director) who first acquainted me with Arsinoë II. My last conversation with him was about her since, at the time, I had just refocused on her and was writing a paper that dealt with her and other royal women for the first Edinburgh Hellenistic conference in 2006. Indeed, I owe a special debt to the conveners of that conference, Andrew Erskine and Lloyd Llewellyn-Jones, for their helpful comments (as well as those of Stephanie Winder). The second (2011) Edinburgh conference on Hellenistic Courts helped me to understand Arsinoë's court life better than before and also enabled me to meet many scholars I had previously known only from their work. Sylvia Barbantani has been immensely helpful in acquainting me with scholarship dealing with Alexandrian poetry, as has Kathryn Gutzwiller. Sabine Müller and Branko von Oppenheim saved me from chronological confusion and illuminated many aspects of Ptolemaic Egypt. My visit to the University of Waterloo, as part of the program for its Institute for Hellenistic Studies, enabled me to pick the brains of all there, but Craig Hardiman and Sheila Ager were particularly helpful. Daniel Ogden listened to numerous complaints about the problem of Ptolemy the Son and helped me to come up with a title for the present volume. Conversations with Stan Burstein, Jenny Roberts, and Olga Palagia contributed to the completion of this work.

As always, I am indebted to my colleagues and especially to my husband, Bill Aarnes, and my daughter, Emma Aarnes, both of whom have listened to my numerous rants about Ptolemaic chronology and, writers both, tried to keep me centered on the story of this particular royal woman.

Abbreviations

ActaArchHung	*Acta archaeologica Academiae scientiarum Hungaricae*
AHB	*Ancient History Bulletin*
AJA	*American Journal of Archaeology*
AJAH	*American Journal of Ancient History*
AJP	*American Journal of Philology*
AJN	*American Journal of Numismatics*
AncW	*Ancient World*
AncSoc	*Ancient Society*
ANSMN	*American Numismatic Society Museum Notes*
ArchPF	*Archiv für Papyrusforschung und verwandte Gebiete*
ARF	*Appunti romani di filologia: studi e comunicazioni di filologia, linguisticae letteratura greca e latina.* Pisa: Istituti Editoriali e Poligrafici Internazionali.
BCH	*Bulletin de correspondance hellénique*
BICS	*Bulletin of the Institute of Classical Studies,* University of London
BIFAO	*Bulletin de l'Institut français d'archéologie orientale de Caire*
ChrÉg	*Chronique d'Égypte*
CJ	*Classical Journal*
ClAnt	*Classical Antiquity*
CP	*Classical Philology*
CQ	*Classical Quarterly*
CW	*Classical World*
FGrH	F. Jacoby et al. (eds.) 1923–. *Die Fragmente der griechischen Historiker.* Multiple volumes and parts. Berlin and Leiden.
G&R	*Greece and Rome*
GRBS	*Greek, Roman, and Byzantine Studies*
HSCP	*Harvard Studies in Classical Philology*
JEA	*Journal of Egyptian Archaeology*
JHS	*Journal of Hellenic Studies*
JNES	*Journal of Near Eastern Studies*

JÖAI	*Jahreshefte des Österreichischen Archäologischen Institutes* in Wien
JRS	*Journal of Roman Studies*
MDAI(A)	*Mitteilungen des Deutschen Archäologischen Instituts, Athenische Abteilung.* Berlin: von Zabern.
OGIS	W. Dittenberger. 1903–05. *Orientis Graeci inscriptiones selectae.* 2 vols. Leipzig.
PP	*La Parola del Passato*
RDAC	*Report of the Department of Antiquities, Cyprus*
RE	Pauly-Wissowa, *Real-Encyclopädie der klassischen Altertumswissenschaft (1893–)*
RendIstLomb	*Rendiconti. Istituto lombardo,* Accademia di scienze e lettere
RhM	*Rheinisches Museum für Philologie*
RivFil	*Rivista di filologia e d'istruzione classica*
SyllClass	*Syllecta Classica*
TAPA	*Transactions of the American Philological Association*
ZfN	*Zeitschrift für Numismatik*
ZPE	*Zeitschrift für Papyrologie und Epigraphik*

Timeline

Note: Virtually all dates are approximate and most are disputed.

318–14	Arsinoë II is born
300	Arsinoë marries Lysimachus
298–93	Arsinoë bears three sons
293	Lysandra, Arsinoë's half-sister, marries Agathocles
285	Lysimachus becomes king of Macedonia
	Ptolemy II made coregent with Ptolemy I
283/2	Death of Agathocles
281(February)	Lysimachus dies at Corupedium; Arsinoë returns to Macedonia
(fall)	Seleucus invades Thrace; Ptolemy Ceraunus murders him and is proclaimed king
281/80	Arsinoë marries Ptolemy Ceraunus
	Ptolemy Ceraunus murders her two younger sons
	Arsinoë flees to Samothrace
	Ptolemy son of Lysimachus battles Ceraunus
280/79–277/76	Arsinoë returns to Egypt
279 (spring)	Gauls invade Macedonia
	Ptolemy Ceraunus dies confronting the Gauls
277/6	Antigonus Gonatas defeats Gauls and becomes king of Macedonia
276–273/2	Arsinoë II marries Ptolemy II, probably 275
272/1	Cult of *theoi adelphoi*
?	Cult of Arsinoë Aphrodite at Zephyrium
270(68)	Arsinoë dies
	Cult of *thea philadelphus*
268/7	Decree of Chremonides
268/7–259	Ptolemy the Son coregent of Ptolemy II
259	Ptolemy son of Lysimachus at Telmessus

Family Tree of Lysimachus

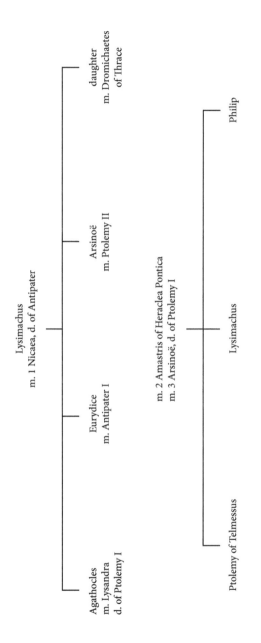

Lysimachus
m. 1 Nicaea, d. of Antipater

Agathocles
m. Lysandra
d. of Ptolemy I

Eurydice
m. Antipater I

Arsinoë
m. Ptolemy II

daughter
m. Dromichaetes
of Thrace

m. 2 Amastris of Heraclea Pontica
m. 3 Arsinoë, d. of Ptolemy I

Ptolemy of Telmessus

Lysimachus

Philip

Simplified Family Tree of the Early Ptolemies

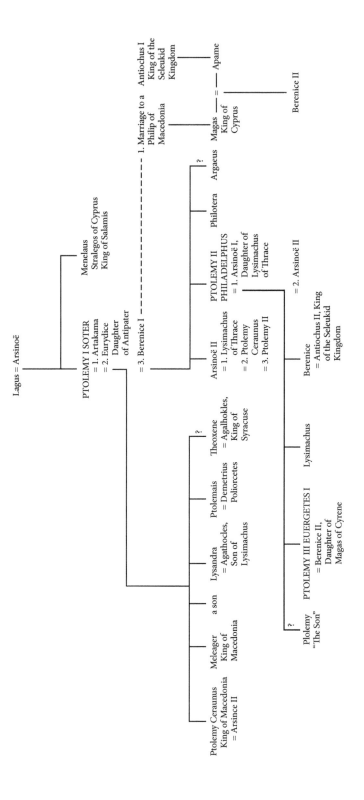

MAP 1 Map of eastern Mediterranean.

ARSINOË OF EGYPT AND MACEDON

Introduction

ARSINOË (II) LIVED a dramatic and adventurous life (ca. 316–ca. 270 or 268 BCE), full of extreme highs and lows. In its course, she played a part in the courts of four kings, married three times (twice to a sibling or half sibling), saw two of her sons murdered, fled two kingdoms because her life was in danger, yet ended her days in great wealth and security and ultimately was deified. Born in Egypt, she departed as a teenage bride for marriage to Lysimachus, ruler of Thrace, parts of Asia Minor, and Macedonia. After her husband died in battle, she tried to protect the claims of her three sons to rule in Macedonia against the attempts of others to seize the kingdom. In support of this effort, she married one of these rivals (her half brother Ptolemy Ceraunus), only to have this marriage alliance end in a bloodbath that compelled her to return to Egypt, where her brother Ptolemy II had succeeded their father (Ptolemy I) as king. Once back, Arsinoë married her brother (the first full brother-sister marriage of a dynasty that would make such marriages an institution). She died in Egypt, having spent her last years playing a prominent role in the kingdom. Throughout much of her life, Arsinoë controlled great wealth and exercised political influence, but domestic stability characterized only her last few years.

Bitter and sometimes violent struggles for the throne marked nearly her entire career. During all but her final years, Arsinoë lived with the more or less constant fear of death or exile at the hands of dynastic rivals. Her childhood experience coping with life in a court divided by succession politics colored virtually all the major decisions of her life. She played the roles of both victim and victimizer: Arsinoë likely had a hand in one murder but endured the slaughter of her younger sons. She possessed some political acumen and considerable drive, but boldness and the willingness to take risks were her most salient personality traits, the ones that led to her most dramatic successes and failures. Like most of the members of the Macedonian elite, male and female alike, Arsinoë single-mindedly and sometimes violently pursued *kleos* (fame, renown) for herself, her sons, and her dynasty. Royal women of Arsinoë's era and earlier periods aggressively pursued goals similar to hers, and some employed brutal means more frequently than she, although Macedonian males much more often killed for political gain.

Political violence—assassination plots, conspiracies, murders both secret and public—recurred again and again in Macedonian history; if anything, the level of political violence increased after the death of Alexander the Great as his empire fragmented and the gradual demise of his dynasty expanded the number of potential candidates for the throne.

Arsinoë coped with the complex and rapidly changing political world of the Hellenistic period (the era from the death of Alexander until the death of the last of the descendants of Alexander's successors, Cleopatra VII in 30 BCE).[1] Alexander the Great's death in Babylon in 323 BCE caused disarray, disunity, and uncertainty in the vast territories he had so recently conquered: some level of stability did not return to all the regions of his former empire until two generations after his death. In theory, his posthumous son (Alexander IV) and his mentally limited half brother (Philip Arrhidaeus) served as kings. In practice, Alexander's generals—known as the Successors, or Diadochi (the men who had left with him on his expedition of epic conquest, among them Arsinoë's father, Ptolemy), ignored the nominal rulers and divided up the empire among themselves. The Successors fought each other nearly constantly, forming rapidly changing alliances. By about 309, both Alexander IV and Philip Arrhidaeus had been murdered, though none of the Diadochi employed a royal title until 306. After they had begun to use a royal title, the aging Macedonian warriors acted to legitimize not only their own rule, but that of their descendants.[2]

Ptolemy I, father of Arsinoë, had been part of the small inner circle around Alexander. After Alexander's death, he acquired Egypt as his satrapy (province), a country with a long history as a unified kingdom with a centralized monarchy.[3] Ptolemy, like most of the Successors, imitated the polygamy of Macedonian kings. The struggles of his two families by two different wives (Eurydice and Berenice, Arsinoë's mother) to gain the upper hand in terms of the succession divided his court. Arsinoë grew up against this backdrop of dynastic strife.

Arsinoë negotiated her way through three different monarchic traditions: Macedonian monarchy, Hellenistic monarchy in its early stages (what had happened since the death of Alexander, in the period when the Diadochi were establishing their rule and their sons the Epigoni institutionalizing it), and pharaonic Egyptian monarchy (whose origins went back before the third millennium BCE). We need to consider each, highlighting the role of royal women, if we are to understand the context of her life and decisions. Arsinoë after all had to cope with these varying, interlocking, and sometimes contradictory monarchic traditions.

The Argead kings ruled Macedonia from its origins as a kingdom until the death of Alexander IV, the son of Alexander the Great.[4] Macedonian kings stood out only a bit from the rest of the Macedonian elite and led their people in battle, in some religious rites, and in the administration of justice. Kingship in Macedonia evolved against a background of internal strife and external threat. The Argeads claimed descent from Heracles and thus from his father, Zeus, and during the reigns of Philip II and his son Alexander III (the Great), the kings flirted with divinization. Still, little ceremony surrounded the kings until Alexander's encounter with the Persian court. Despite their semisacred role, kings were often assassinated or driven from the throne, primarily because no clear rules of succession to the throne developed and because of royal polygamy.[5] Consequently, royal wives functioned as succession advocates for their sons, especially if their husbands died while their sons were still young. Mother and son formed a succession unit and usually the other full siblings of that son functioned as part of the unit as well. Succession struggles often pitted the children of one wife against the children of another.[6]

Although a royal woman might take center stage while her son or sons were minors and she acted to support their succession, the institutional role of royal women in Macedonian monarchy was minimal and many royal wives and daughters remained obscure. They probably did play a part in the public religion of the kingdom, likely as priestesses, and they certainly functioned as tokens in political alliances. By the later Argead period, some royal women acted as patrons of shrines and cults, demonstrating and increasing their own *kleos* as well as that of their male kin.[7] Argead kings, however, had no titular chief wife; indeed there was no title for royal women of any sort.[8]

Hellenistic monarchy developed within the tradition of Argead/ Macedonian kingship but was dramatically affected by Alexander the Great's career and by his attempts to change the form of monarchy he had inherited by borrowing from monarchic tradition in the lands he conquered, particularly Persia.[9] By the late fourth century, the Successors began to receive cult worship; somewhat later kings established cults for themselves and their dynasties.[10] Unable to claim the right to rule on hereditary grounds, Alexander's former generals initially claimed it on the basis of military success. The new kings moved rapidly, however, to transform their individual claims of excellence into dynastic ones.[11] They manufactured genealogies linking themselves to the Argeads and the Argead ancestor Heracles, and other heroic ancestors. The Diadochi and the Epigoni gradually shaped a new kind of monarchy, though one that varied from kingdom to kingdom. Projecting the dynastic image was vital in all the Hellenistic kingdoms. Images of dynastic continuity acted to legitimize current rulers and dynastic images—for instance, statue groups that included ancestors, the current ruler and his wife, and other family members—made the literally remote king and court seem real and approachable.[12] He and his family functioned as a kind of "symbolic cement" that held together the various ethnicities of kingdoms with disparate populations.[13]

Each of the dynasties established itself in a region with a distinctive history, and over time, each developed a distinctive image and tradition, one in which royal women played varying roles.[14] Certain commonalities did, however, affect all the dynasties founded by the Successors, thanks to their common Macedonian past, the exchange of women between dynasties, patronage of common Panhellenic shrines, and political competition.

Polygamy dominated in the first generation after Alexander, but as the third century began, new royal marriage and succession patterns gradually emerged. Endogamy grew more common and polygamy less so. During this same period, a number of the Successors chose not only to select an heir to throne but to formalize the position by making the heir their co-king.[15] Consequently, though rivalry between sons by different wives persisted, these struggles now happened during the lifetime of the royal father, rather than after his death. Potential heirs now contended not only with rival brothers but might become involved in disputes with their fathers as well. These dynastic struggles often turned bloody. Sometimes losers (the candidate for the throne himself, his mother, and his full siblings) simply fled, but often the winning side killed them.

Since a series of succession battles darkened the life of Arsinoë II, it is important to understand their dynamics. Ancient sources, in this area, can provide only modest assistance. Because dynastic murders were usually done in private, our sources rarely depend on certain knowledge, more often on speculation. At best, they preserve court gossip or the propaganda of rivals. Moreover, ancient and modern historians tend simply to assume that the person who most benefitted (the one who seems to have won), initiated a conspiracy.

We should avoid choosing villains and heroes in dynastic disputes. Some of these men and women may actually have been sadistic, but most simply focused on guaranteeing their personal and political survival and that of those closest to them. Many dynastic confrontations began not so much because a person on one side wished to kill someone on the other but because combatants feared that if they did not act first, they would themselves be killed or, at the very least, exiled. In that belief, they were likely often correct. Indeed, on a number of occasions, both sides were plotting against each other at the same time. We should not assume that the loser in a dynastic dispute (whether the loss involves actual murder or simply exile or loss of prestige) was an innocent victim; the loser could just as well be a guilty but less effective or less lucky schemer. Another reason it is wise to resist moralistic judgments about dynastic vendettas is that the participants often had few alternatives, only a choice of lesser evils. That is particularly true of royal women. One reason royal women had few alternatives is that the Successors used the women of their own families as instruments of legitimization.

Like the Argeads, the Successors arranged marriage alliances. Marriage alliances generated conflicting loyalties, particularly for royal women: the family of birth might expect the royal daughter to function as its ambassador to the family into which she had married; women not infrequently returned to their original family when husbands died or rejected them, thus reinforcing the view of their birth families that they were, in effect, only loaned out; fathers and husbands could have conflicting views of where a royal woman's loyalty should lie; brides tended to bring with them a group of people, attendants and aids who re-created a miniature version of the court of origin; exiled family members might arrive at the married woman's court, importing into the new court the dynastic strife of the court they had left.

In addition to marriage alliances, the Successors expanded previous Argead practices related to the women of the dynasty but also developed new ones. Philip II and Alexander had founded cities and named them after themselves; the Successors made eponymous foundations as well but also named them after their mothers, wives, and daughters. Royal women had long acted as patrons of cults and as benefactors, but now they tended to do so more overtly in service of the dynasty and, in some kingdoms, dynastic cults. Cults—private, civic, dynastic—developed not only for male rulers, but also for many royal women, often in a way that associated the women with Aphrodite, the goddess who epitomized conventional femininity and was increasingly a patron of marriage. Soon after the first of the Successors took a royal title in 306, a female title, *basilissa*, began to be used by royal women.[16] Royal wives and even unmarried daughters employed the title.[17] Royal women also often wore the diadem, the symbol of the Hellenistic ruler. Neither the diadem nor the title meant that these women ruled, but both suggested that they were somehow part of rule and the monarchy.[18]

Even though more than one royal woman in a kingdom might be called *basilissa*, granted the decline of polygamy already noted, an imagery that paired the king with one woman, usually his consort, developed. In many dynasties, the focus was on these male and female images, not on the heir to the throne, though dynastic statue groups might include the ruler, the mother of the heir, the heir, and other siblings.[19] The royal pair, functioning sometimes as personifications of male and female virtues and/or deities, appears primarily in Ptolemaic Egypt, but not clearly before Ptolemy II and Arsinoë II.

Generally speaking, the role of royal women seems to have been more institutionalized in the Hellenistic period than earlier. Royal women had always played out conventional domestic roles for women and now they came to act out, in religious rites and gestures, many of the values and needs of the new dynasties in terms of conventional women's roles, writ large: prayers for the safety of husbands and sons; thanksgiving for triumphal returns and the birth of potential heirs; attendance at weddings and funerals. Many of these things royal women did in tandem, or at least in parallel, with their husbands. Royal women played a public role in the ceremonies of the kingdoms, but how accessible and visible they were at court is less clear.[20]

Despite their role in the public life of the kingdom, it is not always easy to tell, as we shall see with Arsinoë, how much actual influence as opposed to mere prominence a given royal woman had. Even within the same dynasty, much may have depended on the character of the individual woman, the chances of her circumstance, and the era.[21] Still, Hellenistic royal women did seem to be able to intercede on behalf of others with their husbands, sons, and brothers, a practice that therefore more or less institutionalized the idea of female influence.[22] They were peculiarly connected to the female population of their kingdoms and their religious activities and roles often related to critical points in the lives and experiences of women.[23] Moreover, as Arsinoë's own career demonstrates, the divide between the idealized consort pictured in official representations and the reality of court life and succession politics was often extreme; the two should not be conflated.[24]

Ptolemaic monarchy had, in the context of other Hellenistic dynasties, a distinctive feature that certainly affected royal women. Ptolemaic kingship had a double personality: Graeco-Macedonian and Egyptian. In order to gain and retain the support of their Egyptian subjects, particularly the powerful priestly class, the Ptolemies portrayed themselves not only as *basileis* (kings) but also as pharaohs. We must, therefore, also consider pharaonic monarchy and the role of women in that tradition of kingship.[25]

Egyptian pharaohs were in some sense divine; while living they embodied aspects of various gods, and when dead, they became Osiris, god of the afterlife.[26] They maintained *maat* (the order of the universe), reconciled the gods with men, and interceded with the divine powers for their people. The king also personified the unity of his kingdom, often, for instance, wearing the double crown, combining the crowns of upper and lower Egypt. The pharaoh was the source of law, and in theory, his power was unchecked. Elaborate ritual surrounded him, much of it connected to the need of the king to preserve *maat*.[27]

Discussing the role of women in pharaonic kingship is daunting: the extraordinarily long period of time during which pharaonic monarchy persisted (at least twenty-five hundred years) inevitably meant considerable change over time, however masked by Egyptian conventions that denied such change; much of the evidence consists of images, the interpretation of which is problematic;[28] Egyptian tradition did not generally show anything negative, untraditional, and disorderly; and terms indicating kinship were not only vague by our standards but sometimes blurred with those indicating status or rank.[29] As with any other human system, events and circumstance sometimes generated situations that empowered royal women, but often the power lasted only as long as the situation; they did not have authority in their own right but rather only through sons.[30]

The role of royal women was directly tied to the nature of pharaonic monarchy; the power of royal women was increased by the power and endurance of the monarchy.[31] By her union with the king,[32] the king's wife had a role in sacred sovereignty and represented the female element in monarchy; dualism was central to Egyptian monarchy.[33] The "mother of the king" appears as a title well before "wife of the king."[34] A title that singles out one wife as more important, "great wife of the king," does not appear until the Middle Kingdom (2055–1650 BCE) and is not well established till the eighteenth dynasty (1550–1295 BCE).[35] Occasionally, usually when a royal clan had run out of males, female kings ruled. The most famous female king, Hatshepsut, however, became senior co-king with her stepson.[36] Brother-sister marriage was not an essential or even a particularly regular part of pharaonic monarchy, though some pharaohs did marry sisters or half sisters.[37]

Royal women were represented with symbols borrowed both from the gods and from the king. The king maintained *maat* by sacrificing to the gods, and the queen might be represented behind him as part of this effort to maintain order.[38] Was there some understanding of "queens" (kings' mothers and kings' principal wives) as divine like kings? Yes. As early as the Old Kingdom (2686–2184 BCE), royal women began to wear the vulture headdress, originally worn by the goddess Nekhbet.[39] The uraeus (representation of a rearing cobra worn on forehead) was perhaps the best-known symbol of kingly power, yet by the fifth dynasty (2494–2345), queens wore the uraeus as part of their headdress; it too was also worn by various deities. During the Old Kingdom, a period when pyramids constituted a distinctively royal burial, a number of royal women were given pyramid burials.[40] New Kingdom (1550–1069 BCE) royal women, as individuals and institutionally, had far greater power than in previous Egyptian periods, particularly during the eighteenth dynasty, by which point many symbols once unique to the king belonged to the royal wife or mother as well,[41] and royal women functioned in some sense as doubles of the king, helping him maintain *maat*, thus leading to the increasing prominence of royal pairs in iconography. This tendency reached a height in the reign of the religious revolutionary king, Amenhotep IV or Akhenaten (1352–36).[42] By the eighteenth dynasty, royal women often wore a double uraeus—worn by goddesses too—perhaps associated with rule and/or protection of Upper and Lower Egypt. The cow horns and sun disk of Hathor (a goddess associated with sexuality and motherhood) began to appear in their headdresses. In short, symbols once associated with kings and/or deities were worn by these women, indicating a certain tendency to understand power as dual, male and female.[43] In addition, a few royal wives and mothers had individual cults, some of which endured for considerable periods.[44]

Motivation is a central issue in any biography. Arsinoë was rarely on her own for long periods of time, making it difficult to determine when she herself shaped events and when her male kin did so. This limitation is particularly relevant to the period after her return to Egypt, during her marriage to Ptolemy II, when it sometimes seems that Arsinoë the individual disappears into the institution of Ptolemaic monarchy. Even before her return, however, though we can establish a context for events in her life, we cannot always know what or who triggered them. Because of this problem, we will pay particular attention to those episodes in her career when Arsinoë clearly functioned independently. On the other hand, we will need to recognize that people do not necessarily act in a consistent fashion throughout their lives; what was compelling to a young mother of potential heirs to a throne might not have been to a middle-aged woman with only one problematic son and a much more secure personal base.

Assessing her political importance at various stages in her life proves difficult because of two problems that often arise when one looks at the lives of individual women. Sources on her career are unusually spotty: a grab bag of much later literary sources of dubious quality, sometimes hostile references by contemporary writers and poets, and some inscriptions and papyri. A narrative source is lacking for the period of her marriage to Ptolemy II. Royal women had access to rulers; did they use that access to influence events and decisions? Arsinoë was a prominent public figure, but was she influential? Influence is hard to demonstrate, even harder to quantify. Perhaps because of these difficulties, in the last century, analysis of her career has ricocheted between an extreme of wishful (or fearful) thinking about the great extent of Arsinoë's power and influence and an equally extreme reaction against this point of view, one that denies that she had any meaningful role at all in the public life of Macedonia or Egypt, except, perhaps, a negative one. (On sources and assessment of Arsinoë, see the Appendix.)

This study will chart a middle course in considering the degree and sort of influence Arsinoë wielded with her various husbands. It will put her career in the context of her Argead and early Hellenistic predecessors, not simply in the context of Ptolemaic Egypt. Too often, aspects of her life have been seen as unique because only Ptolemaic material has been examined and, on the other hand, there has been a rejection of some possibilities about her life and actions because similar actions of other royal women have not been sufficiently considered. Arguments from silence are always dubious and when the silence is about women particularly so; putting Arsinoë in the context of the actions and careers of other royal women helps to solve this problem.

Looking at Arsinoë's life is a bit like trying to meet someone at a big party, but somehow always missing them though, perhaps, getting a whiff of their perfume and hearing a lot of stories about them. In a sense, Arsinoë is always in the other room.

CHAPTER ONE

Arsinoë's Background and Youth
318/14—300

NOTHING SURVIVES THAT tells us anything directly about Arsinoë's life before her first marriage about the turn of the third century BCE. In fact, it is the approximate date of her marriage that provides the basis for the guess that she was born between 318 and 314.[1] Still, we do know something about her parents, where she grew up, what her cultural and educational background likely was, and about events during her early years that affected not only her childhood but her later years as well.

Parents play critical roles in most people's lives. In the case of Arsinoë, the character, status, and identity of her parents had especially great importance, if anything greater importance later in her life than earlier. Developments in Egypt after she had left her father's court for marriage had a dramatic impact on her adult life. By the time Arsinoë had reached middle age, it mattered even more than it had when she was a young woman that she was the daughter of Ptolemy I Soter ("the savior") and Berenice I.

Ptolemy I Soter

Ptolemy came from the region of Eordaea in Macedonia (Arr. 3.28.4, *Ind* 18.5).[2] His father was Lagus, likely a Macedonian noble of neither particular distinction nor notoriety,[3] yet Ptolemy's mother—Arsinoë was her namesake—was somehow related to the royal house of Macedonia.[4]

Although the Roman historian Justin implied (13.4.10) that Ptolemy did not come from the Macedonian elite and Plutarch (*Mor.* 458a–b) employs the term *dusgeneia* (low birth) in terms of Ptolemy, his close early association with Alexander signifies that at least one of his parents had important court connections. Later Ptolemaic propaganda probably fabricated the stories (Paus. 1.6.2, 8; Curt. 9.8.22; Aelian frg. 285; *Suda s.v.* "Lagos") that made Ptolemy a son of Philip II (the father of Alexander the Great) and his mother a cast-off royal mistress in order to connect Ptolemy to the most glorious figures of the recent Macedonian past.[5]

Ptolemy belonged to the small group of Alexander's *hetairoi* (companions) whom Philip II exiled late in his reign because he blamed them, in part, for Alexander's involvement in an attempt to substitute himself as groom in place of his brother Philip Arrhidaeus in a marriage alliance with the daughter of Pixodarus, satrap of Caria (Plut. *Alex.* 10.4; Arr. 3.6.5). This group of intimates around Alexander was made up of men somewhat older than Alexander, chosen by Philip to advise his son.[6] The only direct evidence (Ps. Lucian *Macrob.* 12) about Ptolemy's age indicates that he was born ca. 367/66, making him about seven or eight years older than Alexander. At a relatively early age Ptolemy had acquired a position of power and prestige in Macedonia and had demonstrated his personal loyalty to the future Alexander the Great.

After Philip's death, Alexander naturally recalled Ptolemy and the others exiled for his sake. Though we hear nothing about Ptolemy's role in the early stages of Alexander's invasion of the Persian Empire, he and the others in Alexander's inner circle probably took part in the campaign from the start, though they did not initially hold high office. Once Alexander had demonstrated his brilliance in military matters, his father's general Parmenio was eliminated in 330 and the members of Alexander's circle then began to gain more important commands.[7] Although Ptolemy was somewhat slower to move up than some of the others,[8] after the fall of Parmenio, Alexander made Ptolemy one of the seven (later eight) royal bodyguards (Arr. 3.27.5). In keeping with that role, it was Ptolemy in fall of 328 who tried (and failed) to prevent Alexander's embarrassing and terrifying drunken killing of Cleitus the Black, an officer who had saved Alexander's life in battle (Arr. 4.8.9; Curt. 8.1.45, 48). In spring of 327, Ptolemy played a critical role in the revelation of the "Pages Conspiracy," a plot to assassinate Alexander (Curt. 8.6.22; Arr. 4.13.7). When, in 324, Alexander finally married the daughter of Darius, the last Persian king, and arranged for the marriages of many of his most important officers to women of the Persian elite, Ptolemy married a daughter of Artabazus (Arr. 7.4.6; Plut. *Eum.* 1.7). Artabazus was the most important member of the Persian elite and another of his daughters was Alexander's mistress. The unexpected death of Alexander's closest companion, Hephaestion, late in that same year inevitably changed the existing pecking order within the king's inner circle and seemed to benefit Ptolemy.[9]

When Alexander sickened and died at Babylon in June 323, Ptolemy, as one of the bodyguards, was present. Since Alexander's half brother Philip Arrhidaeus was not mentally competent and Alexander IV (Alexander the Great's son by his first wife, Roxane) had not yet been born, there was no obvious heir. Apparently Alexander, on his deathbed, had given his signet ring to Perdiccas (another member of the circle around Alexander, like Ptolemy a royal bodyguard, someone who had held more important military commands than Ptolemy), but debate raged about what to do about the succession and administration of Alexander's empire.[10] While Perdiccas wanted to wait to see if Roxane's child would be male and the infantry favored Alexander's half brother, Ptolemy wanted the inner circle to function as a kind of executive committee, meeting in the presence of Alexander's throne (Curt. 10.6.13–16). This debate makes it clear that Ptolemy and Perdiccas were already opponents. In the end, after some violence, a combination of all of these proposals happened: there were two kings, neither competent, Perdiccas was regent, and the rule of Alexander's empire was allotted to various satraps (governors). Ptolemy, whether because of his own contriving, that of Perdiccas, or simple luck came away with the region that would become the heart of his kingdom and that of his descendants, Egypt.[11]

During the wars of the Successors, Ptolemy not only managed to retain Egypt and defend it against invasion, but to increase his territory on the east and west, creating buffers that added to the natural protections Egypt had always enjoyed.[12] Egypt was rich in grain, a source not only of wealth but also power in the Mediterranean basin, and it produced or controlled a number of other valuable goods as well, including a monopoly on papyrus, the material from which books were made. This wealth would make possible the cultural patronage for which Ptolemy and his descendants became famous.[13]

Ptolemy, though officially only a satrap until 304, made himself the heir to the pharaohs (see Introduction). At the same time Ptolemy was staking his claim to this Egyptian tradition of monarchy, he was building a connection to Macedonian monarchy as well. He probably manufactured the story about Philip II being his father during the period while he was still merely a satrap.[14] Early in that same period, in 321 or 320, Ptolemy pulled off a propaganda coup that also linked him to Argead monarchy. He managed to wrest control of the corpse of Alexander, which was en route for burial in Macedonia, from Perdiccas' forces, and instead entomb it in Egypt, first in Memphis and later in Alexandria (Paus. 1.6.3; Diod. 18.28.2–4). Ptolemy used Alexander's remains as the basis for a state cult that would ultimately, under his heirs, become a dynastic cult. Although he initially took up residence in Memphis, capital of Egypt during much of the pharaonic period, at some point (between 320 and 311)[15] he moved his primary residence to the new city on the coast that Alexander had founded in 331, Alexandria.

Each of the Successors, unable to claim kingship by right of descent, instead claimed the royal title on the basis of a military victory. Ptolemy did wait for his great victory against Demetrius Poliorcetes, when he raised the siege of Rhodes, to claim the royal title (ca. 304); this incident was probably the origin for the epithet—Soter—that came to identify him.[16] With the exception of Rhodes, his greatest military success was defensive; he prevented attempts to invade Egypt. The founder of the Ptolemaic dynasty never managed to be a charismatic commander in the field (this in an era characterized by an entire generation of gifted and often showy field commanders), and he certainly suffered defeats, although he had a knack for the politics of command. It is worth noting, however, that a famous passage on kingship and how you get it does not connect rule to military success alone, but also to astute policy: kingdoms go to those "who are able to lead an army and to handle affairs intelligently; such as Philip was, and the successors of Alexander."[17] Military prowess was somewhat less critical for Ptolemy than for the other generals. His foundation of the cult of Alexander, his cultural patronage, his dual role as Egyptian ruler as well as Macedonian, all were arguably more critical to the foundation of his monarchy than his military exploits.[18] In practice, the dynasty was from its start less grounded in military glamour and success than most of the other Hellenistic ruling families. This trend would intensify in the reign of Ptolemy I's son, Ptolemy II.

The Successors tried to build a bridge to power for their sons, but it was their sons, the second generation, who really created most dynastic institutions, primarily because they claimed right to rule by descent, whereas their fathers claimed it on the basis of their own actions. Certainly that is true of Ptolemy I's heir, Ptolemy II. Nonetheless, even as early as the first Ptolemy, certain critical decisions were made, many of them ones that would shape the life of Arsinoë.

One of the hallmarks of her dynasty would be its endlessly self-replicating nature (see chapter 4). Each king was Ptolemy; at first, epithets clearly distinguished one Ptolemy from another, but after a time even these doubled back on themselves. Ptolemy I began this distinctive dynastic pattern; he named his oldest sons by two different wives "Ptolemy" (Ptolemy Ceraunus ca. 319/18 and Ptolemy II in 309)[19] rather than the conventional Lagus (Hellenic practice was to name the first son born after the paternal grandfather, the second after the maternal grandfather).[20] In addition, he created a female version of the same name—"Ptolemais"—and gave it to a daughter by Eurydice (Plut. *Demetr.* 46.5). These name choices, all made after he had become satrap and perhaps hoped to be more, are suggestive. By these unconventional choices, Ptolemy deemphasized his father, Lagus, and gave his sons names that imply they replicated him rather than his ancestors. The name choice, in other words, parallels his monarchy, self-created and not inherited. He made himself the founder of his line but also made sure that his sons and descendants had to allude to their descent from him.

Ptolemy I made several other decisions with long-term impact for Arsinoë and the entire dynasty. He established an enduring aspect of Ptolemaic foreign policy, support for the freedom of Greek cities. By making the cult of Alexander a state cult and tying it directly to the monarchy he was building, he created the foundation for what would become the dynastic cult.[21] Soter invented the dual or double monarchy, both Egyptian and Graeco-Macedonian that would characterize Ptolemaic rule to the end, one that would quickly involve royal women as well as men. Although Alexander himself had founded the most famous of all the Alexandrias and perhaps marked out the walls and major temples (Arr. 3.1.5; Diod.17.52.3–4), the Roman historian Tacitus (*Hist.* 4.83) claims that Ptolemy Soter actually built the first walls and sanctuaries, and created the first religious rites.[22] Ptolemy I may also have planned and begun construction on the famous Pharos lighthouse (*Suda s.v.* "Pharos")[23] and the mole that connected it to the mainland, built the first structures in the palace area, and decided to implement the idea of the Library[24] and Museum,[25] although the physical reality of these institutions may not have appeared until the reign of his son Ptolemy II, who at the very least completed his father's construction plans (see further chapter 5).[26] Ptolemy I took the old Argead practice of royal patronage of artists and intellectuals and transformed it into patronage of a collective institution that would pass from father to son.[27] Ptolemy I turned his dynasty into the greatest of cultural patrons and Alexandria into the center of Hellenistic culture, one able to exercise a kind of cultural imperialism.[28]

Arsinoë's Upbringing and Education

We know nothing specific about Arsinoë's childhood and maidenhood,[29] but a few things seem fairly certain. Ptolemy, while still a satrap, moved his primary residence from Memphis to the new Greek city of Alexandria; even if Arsinoë was born before the royal family had left Memphis, her memories would have been of Alexandria.[30] She grew up in the primarily Greek but somewhat Egyptian new city, not in Memphis, the original capital of pharaonic Egypt.

The dynasty always identified as Macedonian, not simply as generically Hellenic. Court poetry, for instance, stressed the Macedonian roots of the Ptolemies (see chapter 5), and the Ptolemies themselves spoke Macedonian. This identity may have had comparatively little to do with memories of Macedonia itself, but more to do with Macedonian court life. Ptolemy had not been back to Macedonia since 334, though Arsinoë's mother, Berenice, only left around 320. Neither Ptolemy nor his wives could have been certain in his early years in Egypt that he and they were there to stay. He had spent many years on the move, and after all, many of the Successors and their families moved multiple times, changing countries. Life at the royal court, even as the splendid buildings grew in number and the institutions we associate with Ptolemaic Egypt were planned, may still have seemed more like life in the moving court that Alexander had maintained than something geographically fixed.

Granted, our poor information about this formative period of the city, reconstructing the kind of material culture in which Arsinoë grew up is difficult, but it seems likely that the court grew more splendid as she grew older, though she would have found the Alexandria she returned to after her long absence to be almost unrecognizable as the city she had left. Arsinoë did not really grow up in Ptolemaic Egypt but rather in a place that was becoming Ptolemaic Egypt. The wealth and luxury that would characterize the Ptolemaic court had begun to develop but could not yet have been as marked as they would become.

As we have seen, Ptolemy I made cultural patronage a hallmark of the dynasty. He himself wrote a history of Alexander's campaign and reign, one that glorified himself and downplayed his enemies. If Ptolemy wrote his history soon after the death of Alexander, during his struggles with Perdiccas,[31] then Arsinoë's father established his personal intellectual credentials long before he took the royal title.

What sort of education did he arrange for Arsinoë? Education for women increased throughout the Hellenistic period.[32] Earlier Macedonian royal women seem to have been literate and Ptolemaic royal women, including Arsinoë, were much celebrated in poetry and may have functioned as patrons themselves (see chapter 5). Ptolemy Soter inaugurated the Ptolemaic tradition of inviting distinguished intellectuals to serve as tutors to royal sons,[33] following the model of Philip II's choice of Aristotle as a tutor for his son. Philetas of Cos (*Suda s.v.* "Philetas didaskalos") and Zenodotus of Ephesus (*Suda s.v.* Zenodotus) tutored Arsinoë's brother Ptolemy II (Zenodotus, a scholar of Homer, eventually became the head of the Library). Ptolemy I had already established a close tie to the Peripatetics (the philosophical school founded by Aristotle) by his patronage of Demetrius of Phalaerum. Another major Greek intellectual who tutored Ptolemy II was Strato of Lampsacus, the Peripatetic philosopher who later directed the Lyceum, the institution Aristotle had founded.[34] In the Hellenistic period, the sons of kings were given an excellent education. Ptolemaic daughters may have shared this education and been tutored along with their brothers or by the same people who tutored their brothers. Indeed, Strato apparently had a correspondence with Arsinoë (Diog. Laert. 5.4), quite possibly because he had originally been her tutor.[35] All of this implies that Arsinoë could have had an unusually good education.

Polygamy, Royal Women, and Succession in
Argead and Early Ptolemaic Monarchy

Before we examine the career of Berenice and its impact on her daughter Arsinoë, we need to look at the context of Berenice's marriage to Ptolemy I. The marriage practices and succession policy of Ptolemy I affected Arsinoë's life (as well as the lives of her mother and her full and half siblings). Like the other Successors, Ptolemy imitated Argead polygamy (Plut. *Pyrrh.* 4, 4; *Dem. and Ant.*4.1) and had children by many women. In terms of the succession, the most important and successful of the Successors were more innovative than in their marriage practices. As we have already noted, they determined the succession by choosing a son as co-king. Essentially, what governed the early life of Arsinoë and her siblings was that the lack of rules about succession in traditional Macedonian kingship was now compounded by the innovations and uncertainty that the creation of new dynasties generated.

Wives

Women and their children filled the court in which Arsinoë grew up. Some were wives, some not. The legal situation of their mothers may not have had much effect on the pecking order of sons and daughters within the dynasty. Their mothers' rank and connections as well as their personal relationship with Ptolemy mattered more. Any kind of relationship to Ptolemy, by blood or marriage, could lead to a position of power or a position that could be used to acquire power.

Thaïs, the *hetaira* (courtesan) who supposedly urged Alexander to burn the palace at Persepolis, had sexual relationships with both Alexander and Ptolemy.[36] Cleitarchus (*ap.* Ath. 576d = *FGrH* 137 F11) asserted that Ptolemy married Thaïs after the death of Alexander. Judging by the apparent ages of Thaïs' children, the relationship (and possibly marriage) predated the death of Alexander:[37] Thaïs and Ptolemy had two sons, Leontiscus and Lagus, and a daughter, Eirene. That Thaïs' oldest son was named after his paternal grandfather strongly suggests that Ptolemy had, at the time, no other sons.[38] Even years later, when Ptolemy certainly did have other sons, his sons by Thaïs apparently accompanied him on campaign (Leontiscus was captured during Ptolemy's great defeat at Salamis in 306; Just. 15.12) and in peacetime as well. Lagus won a victory in the chariot race at the Lycaean games of 308/7 (*SIG*³ 314 + *IG* V.2.250); presumably he had accompanied his father on his trip to Greece in that year. Eirene married Eunostus, king of Soli in Cyprus. Her marriage, though not on a par with the more prestigious marriages of Ptolemy's daughters by Eurydice and Berenice nonetheless constituted a marriage alliance.

For some years after Ptolemy took the royal title in ca. 305, his younger sons were not old enough to succeed him and rule on their own or run a campaign. Legitimate or not,[39] these half brothers of Arsinoë would initially have functioned as her father's heirs. Since they did not figure in the succession struggle that developed much later in Ptolemy I's reign, Thaïs' sons did not apparently present serious competition to their father's sons by more famous (and less notorious) wives once, that is, those younger sons had reached adulthood. They must, however, have been real contenders when the future Ptolemy Ceraunus was a young child and the future Ptolemy II not yet born.

Another and more notorious *hetaira*, Lamia, also had a relationship with Ptolemy. It ended when Demetrius Poliorcetes defeated Ptolemy at Salamis in 306 and she became part of his plunder (Plut. *Demetr.* 16).[40]

Two more respectable but exotic women may have been present at court when Arsinoë was growing up. As we have noted, at Susa in 324, Ptolemy married a daughter of Artabazus, a half sister of Alexander's mistress Barsine, called Artacama (Arr. 7.4.6) or Apama (Plut. *Eum.* 1.3).[41] Perhaps Ptolemy abandoned his Persian wife soon after Alexander's death,[42] but Artacama/Apama may have lived out her life in comparative obscurity in Alexandria.[43] There might also have been an Egyptian wife, a member of the last native Egyptian dynasty.[44] Whether or not Arsinoë would have had personal contact with Thaïs, Lamia, or Artacama—as we shall see, not much is known about the physical location of the women connected to Ptolemy's court—she would certainly have heard stories about the first two—Lamia in particular was a colorful and ribald character—and perhaps also about the exotic Persian wife.

The woman who would have loomed much larger—not in a good way, probably—in Arsinoë's childhood was Eurydice, daughter of Antipater.[45] Antipater had served as general and diplomat for Philip II and administered Macedonia during Alexander's long absence on the Asian campaign.[46] Ptolemy Soter, like Perdiccas before him, wanted to ally himself with this grand old man of the Macedonian political world. Ptolemy married Eurydice (Paus. 1.6.8; App. *Syr.* 62.30) around the time (ca. 322–20) that the surviving Successors renegotiated the distribution of power in Alexander's former empire at Triparadisus, after the elimination of Perdiccas. Eurydice had at least four children by Ptolemy I. Two were sons: Ptolemy (App. *Syr.* 62) and a son of unknown name. This Ptolemy acquired the epithet Ceraunus (thunderbolt) and would later become king of Macedonia and marry his half sister Arsinoë. Ptolemy II killed Eurydice's other son for fomenting revolt among the Cyprians (Paus. 1.7.1). There were also two daughters: Lysandra,[47] who would marry one of Cassander's sons and then Agathocles, son of Lysimachus; and Ptolemais,[48] one of the last of the many brides of Demetrius Poliorcetes ((Plut. *Demetr.* 46.5). Eurydice may have borne two more sons to Ptolemy. Meleager, though not said to be a son of Eurydice by any source, briefly succeeded Ceraunus as king in Macedonia, suggesting that he had fled Egypt at the same time as Ceraunus and accompanied him on his travels, almost certainly because he was his full brother.[49] Argaeus may also have been a child of this marriage; he too was eliminated by Ptolemy II (Paus. 1.7.1).[50] As we shall see, Eurydice and Berenice, Arsinoë's mother, were having children by Ptolemy at the same time.[51]

However many wives and mistresses Ptolemy kept about him at court, Eurydice would long have had the most prestige. Initially, this prestige would have stemmed from her father's reputation, later from her brother Cassander's role (after 316) as the ruler of Macedonia, and from the impressive marriages of her sisters. What must have seemed decisive, however, was that Ptolemy named the first son she bore him after himself. By this stage, as his name choice suggests, Soter had begun to think like a dynast. He may have hoped that the son who shared his name, once he was old enough, would be his heir, replacing his sons by Thaïs.

When Eurydice arrived in Egypt, a sort of lady-in-waiting, a young widow named Berenice (I) accompanied her (Paus. 1.6.8).[52] Berenice's mother was Antigone, the daughter of a brother of Antipater (Schol. Ad Theoc. 17.61), making Antipater Berenice's great-uncle.[53] Berenice's father was apparently a man named Magas,[54] about whom nothing is known. Intriguingly, thanks to Posidippus (AB 88), we now know that Berenice, like her second husband Ptolemy I, may have been from Eordaea too.[55] Berenice had first married a man named Philip, by whom she had a son called Magas (Paus. 1.7.1–3),[56] a daughter Antigone (and possibly another daughter, Theoxene).[57] Berenice's first husband, Philip, had apparently died and Pausanias (1.6.8) says that Antipater sent this widowed poor relation (she was Eurydice's second cousin) to Egypt with his daughter Eurydice. The children of Berenice's first marriage demonstrably benefited by her subsequent marriage to the ruler of Egypt. Magas became governor of Cyrene but later, attempting independent rule, rebelled during the reign of his half brother Ptolemy II. Antigone married Pyrrhus, king of Epirus (Plut. *Pyrrh.* 4).

According to Pausanias (1.7.1) Berenice I's first husband was obscure and of low birth; the names of two of Berenice's children by this first marriage—since they refer to their maternal grandparents—seem to confirm Pausanias. Theocritus (a poet under Ptolemaic patronage), rather than employing the usual patronymic, refers to Berenice as the daughter of Antigone; the matronymic not only stresses her ties to Antipater but again confirms that her maternal ancestry was more distinguished than her paternal, much as was the case with her husband Ptolemy.[58] One wonders if this background—more distinguished female ancestry and consequent stress by descendants on the female line of descent—helps to explain the role of women in Ptolemaic monarchy, even early on, at the beginning of the dynasty. These were, after all, two families where the mother's identity was important, perhaps decisive, in terms of status.[59]

Berenice became Ptolemy I's wife, possibly as soon as she caught his eye.[60] Was she his mistress first?[61] The line between wife and mistress was not a very clear one,[62] as we have seen in terms of Thaïs. At the very least, by the time Berenice began to have children by Ptolemy, she was his wife, just as we know Thaïs was.[63] Their relationship, whether originally a marriage or not, must have begun comparatively soon after Berenice's arrival in Egypt. The evidence for the length of their relationship is the marriage date of their oldest child, Arsinoë, around 300 BCE, implying, as we have noted, that Arsinoë was born between 318 and 314. Thus her parent's relationship dated, at the very least to 315, but may well have begun several years earlier. Berenice had another daughter by Soter, Philotera (Strab. 16.4.5; Callimachus Fr. 228), whose date of birth is unknown and hard to surmise since she apparently never married and died before Arsinoë.[64] In 309/8 on the island of Cos, Berenice gave birth to the future Ptolemy II Philadelphus.[65] It is surely significant that Ptolemy I chose to name a second son after himself; indeed the name choice itself implies that these two Ptolemies literally became rivals at birth.

Berenice was, more or less, in Anne Boleyn's position and managed a similar rise to prominence, though she was able to improve rather than lose her status (not to mention her head) as Boleyn did. Ptolemy I had no worldly reason to marry Berenice. Despite the fact that kings virtually always married for policy, as part of some sort of alliance, ancient authors almost always claim that kings married for love. Ptolemy I is the exception who actually did. Pausanias (1.6.8), discussing Ptolemy's preference for Berenice, speaks of his being *epimanēs* (mad for women). Ptolemy, after all, already had an aristocratic and well-connected wife who was producing children, apparently more than one son, and Berenice had no powerful relatives who were not closer kin of Eurydice. Berenice resembles that staple of Victorian fiction, the poor relative dependent for a living on her more well-to-do kin, who manages to find a rich and distinguished husband. Theocritus' celebration of Ptolemy's love for Berenice (*Id.* 17.38–39) is entirely justified in the sense that theirs was actually a unique royal marriage, based, so far as one can tell, on *eros*.[66] The scholiast (someone who wrote comments in the margin of a manuscript) for Theocritus 17.34 implausibly proclaimed that Berenice was the most chaste of Soter's wives. Had she really been so chaste, she might not have become his wife.[67] True, Ptolemy I did marry Thaïs as well, but Thaïs' sons did not become contenders for the throne. The really remarkable thing about Berenice is not simply that Ptolemy married her but that, in the end, her son would become king.

Rivalry and the Succession before Arsinoë's Marriage

Apparently for many years, Eurydice and her son Ptolemy Ceraunus expected him to succeed his father. Lagus, Thaïs' son, never attracted much attention and no source mentions him as involved in contesting succession. Two other sons of Ptolemy I tried for the throne or rebelled during the reign of Ptolemy II (Paus. 1.7.1) but not during their father's reign. The real competition during the lifetime of Ptolemy Soter was between his two sons named Ptolemy.

The future Ceraunus had two advantages over his half brother of the same name; his mother was more prestigious and far better connected than his rival's mother,[68] and perhaps even more important, he was about ten years older than his half brother. Ptolemy I turned out to live until, by ancient standards, extreme old age, but no one could have predicted that in the fourth century BCE. Berenice's son could easily have been still a child at the time of his father's death. Justin (16.2.7; 17.2.9–10) seems to believe that some rule or practice existed that somehow promised the succession to Ceraunus. As we have seen, this was certainly not the case, but as a practical matter, the expectation of the court and certainly of Eurydice and her children must have been that Ceraunus would be his father's heir. In Argead times, internal and external bonds of *philia* (friendship or alliance) had been critical to reaching the throne and then to keeping it;[69] *philoi* (friends or allies) were also vital in Hellenistic courts, for kings and other members of the royal family and powerful *philoi* apparently favored Ceraunus.[70] The career of Demetrius of Phalerum, philosopher and Athenian tyrant, who fled to the court of Ptolemy Soter ca. 297, confirms this. Demetrius, whom Plutarch terms "the first" of Soter's friends (Plut. *Mor.* 601f) and who played a pivotal role in the foundation of the library of Alexandria, also advised Soter to give the succession to Ceraunus (Diog. Laert. 5. 79). Demetrius, with his considerable political experience, doubtless gave his advice in terms of which son he thought would win the struggle.

This rivalry between the two Ptolemies did not, in all likelihood, develop immediately. While Eurydice and Berenice may have vied for Ptolemy's personal favor, the succession struggle that developed between them, their sons, and the full siblings of each could not have predated the birth of Berenice's son in 309/8 and probably did not become a serious issue until about the end of the fourth century, by which point the young boy would have passed the most dangerous years of early childhood and have begun to show some signs of character and indications of ability. As the 290s progressed and Berenice's son approached adulthood, the rivalry doubtless intensified.

Thus most of Arsinoë's childhood and adolescence happened in a circumstance where her father's other wife and children were more important than her own mother and siblings. Her brother's improved situation in terms of the succession would ultimately have dramatic affect on her position as the wife of Lysimachus and on her hopes for her own sons, but his success was a feature of her adulthood, not her childhood. Arsinoë would have grown up in the shadow of Ptolemy's other family. Especially in her early childhood, her mother's position must have appeared quite insecure. Even after the birth of Arsinoë's brother, it must have seemed a long shot indeed that he would triumph over her half brother, that her mother would defeat Eurydice. Arsinoë's childhood memories would probably have been of a mother who fought hard for Ptolemy's attention without, for many years, much hope of more than his personal favor.

When Ptolemy I, for reasons we will consider shortly, finally made Berenice's son his co-king in 285, Berenice's side of the Ptolemaic line had triumphed.[71] The continuing rivalry between Eurydice and Berenice and their two sets of children helps us to understand Arsinoë's background and was almost certainly a model for Arsinoë's full and half siblings in terms of their understanding of how monarchy and courts worked, what policies succeeded, and what failed.[72]

Typically, in polygamous situations, some ranking develops among the various wives, even when no institutionalized office of chief wife exists nor any recognizably institutionalized position of heir to the throne. Instead, the king's treatment of wives and sons, gestures of approval or disapproval, gave them indications of where they stood in the court pecking order. For instance, the fact that Philip II chose Alexander to take care of Macedonia when he was only sixteen and gave him command of the cavalry charge at Chaeronea (the victory that enabled Philip to control the Greek peninsula) when he was eighteen certainly led Alexander, his mother Olympias, and the rest of the court to believe Philip considered him his heir, but events a few months after that seemed to reverse this situation for both Alexander and Olympias. Although Olympias would have been the dominant woman at Philip's court for many years, her position was suddenly thrown into jeopardy by the threat to her son's potential succession.[73]

Which of Ptolemy I's wives was the functionally dominant one? Before the end of the fourth century, there are few signs to guide us in answering that question, though, as we have seen, there seems to have been a widespread presumption that Eurydice's son would inherit and that, in turn, implies that she was considered the dominant wife, even if she were not the king's personal favorite. Nothing we know about events before 300 indicates that Berenice was the dominant wife. True, in 309/8, she accompanied Ptolemy I on his naval expedition to Greece (we know this since the future Ptolemy II was born in Greece, on Cos, during the expedition). On the other hand, Thaïs' son Lagus also accompanied his father. Lamia must have been part of Ptolemy's entourage as well, since Demetrius seized her after Ptolemy's defeat at Salamis in 306. Nothing much can therefore be made of Berenice's presence in Greece, other than that it suggests that Ptolemy wanted her with him, possibly because of concern about her pregnancy.

The first hint of change in the status of Berenice and her children came after the defeat of Antigonus at the battle of Ipsus in 301 by an alliance of four of the other Successors (Cassander, Seleucus, Ptolemy, and Lysimachus). The victory of the allies led to the arrangement of a series of marriage alliances (not all of them actually accomplished immediately) in the next year or two, the majority apparently involving Ptolemy. Earlier critical moments (the departure of Alexander's Asian campaign, the death of Alexander, the meeting at Triparadisus) had also produced a spate of marriage alliances among elite Macedonians. Whereas before Ipsus, the Successors had not generally arranged marriages with each other, now they rushed to do so, suggesting that Ipsus, perhaps more than the assumption of the royal title by the Successors in 306 and 305, signaled the real recognition of separate new monarchies.[74] Ptolemy's marriage arrangements after Ipsus were therefore important in terms of what he understood the future of his dynasty to be. (As we have seen, Ptolemy had presumably arranged a marriage much earlier for his daughter by Thaïs, Eirene, to a minor Cypriot king.)

At this point, Ptolemy I arranged the marriages of Theoxene (probably Berenice's daughter) to Agathocles, king of Sicily; of Berenice's daughter Arsinoë to Lysimachus; of Eurydice's daughter Lysandra, first, probably to Alexander son of Cassander, and then, after his death, to Agathocles, son of Lysimachus; of Ptolemais (Eurydice's daughter) to Demetrius Poliorcetes (though the marriage did not actually take place till years later); and of Antigone (Berenice's daughter by her first husband, Philip) to Pyrrhus. Judging by the relative prestige of the grooms and the potential for the brides to become mothers of heirs, the daughters of Eurydice and Berenice all made better marriages than Thaïs' daughter (of course, Ptolemy's prestige and power was greater by the time of these later marriages). If anything, one could conclude that Ptolemy carefully balanced the interests of his two families, perhaps consciously avoiding making one seem more important than the other.[75] Arsinoë's marriage to Lysimachus, a man whose son Agathocles was already adult, could have been seen as something of a dead end for an ambitious royal woman whereas Lysandra's marriages were either to adults or near adults who seemed to be heirs to thrones. Ptolemy I, however, may not have viewed the situation that way: Arsinoë, after all, married a man who was already king whereas Lysandra married two men who hoped to be king (assuming that her first marriage, to Cassander's son, was arranged while Cassander was still alive and so also his eldest son).[76] In any event, Lysandra's marriages (let alone Ptolemais') proved even less successful than Arsinoë's (see chapter 2).

Antigone, though only Ptolemy's stepdaughter, did very well in the marriage market; indeed her marriage could indicate that Berenice now had greater clout, but in 299 or 298, at the time of Antigone's marriage, Pyrrhus was only a twice-exiled king, in the court of Ptolemy as a hostage. Plutarch (*Pyrrh.* 4.4–5.1) tells us that Pyrrhus, during his stay at Ptolemy's court, considered that Berenice, among the various women of Ptolemy I, had access to the greatest power and was first among them in terms of virtue and thoughtfulness, and so he paid particular attention to her.[77] According to Plutarch, Pyrrhus tried generally to ingratiate himself with Ptolemy. Plutarch pictures a competition among many prominent men for the hand of Antigone and asserts that his selection as groom gave Pyrrhus even more prestige, leading to Ptolemy's furnishing of money and troops to enable him to take his kingdom back. Plutarch's account, clearly from a source favorable to Pyrrhus, is difficult to assess in terms of what it tells us about Berenice's position. The marriage did seem to make Pyrrhus more honored and Ptolemy did give him the aid that would enable him to regain his kingdom (Plut. *Pyrrh.* 4.4–5.1). Thus, in the judgment of this savvy royal opportunist—a judgment apparently validated by his successful acquisition of troops and financial aid— Berenice had begun to take some sort of precedence over Eurydice. Since Plutarch portrays Pyrrhus as well-informed, Pyrrhus' conclusion that Berenice was the one who could be most useful to him seems telling. The description of the competition for Antigone, however, seems somewhat exaggerated and makes one wonder if Berenice's daughter was simply the best Pyrrhus could do at the time.[78] All things considered, it does look as though, at the very time Arsinoë left Egypt, her mother's prestige was beginning to outstrip that of Eurydice and had certainly equaled it.

This perhaps originally slight advantage increased in the course of the 290s. Earlier, Berenice's son had been too young to be a serious competitor against Ceraunus, but by the end of that decade, he had reached adulthood. Cassander, Eurydice's most powerful brother, was dead whereas Berenice now had two powerful sons-in-law. As the next decade began, those at court may have seen signs that Ptolemy I would choose the future Ptolemy II as his successor,[79] but he postponed this decision as long as he could and did not make things official until 285, when he made Ptolemy II his co-king. (Coregency functioned primarily as a means to insure a smooth succession—though it could have administrative benefits—and Ptolemy I seems to have waited until his age made him feel that a transition in rule was comparatively imminent).[80] It is unlikely that either Ceraunus or his mother, Eurydice, or his brother Meleager left Egypt until the announcement of Ptolemy Soter's preference was imminent;[81] until there was no hope left, it would have been foolish to leave. There is no indication that Ptolemy I divorced Eurydice or forced her to leave Egypt.[82] Appian (*Syr.* 62), an historian from Alexandria who wrote during the second century CE, says that Ceraunus left Egypt out of fear, because of his father's decision. Fear tended to be the driving force in succession struggles. Since fear can transform fearful people into violent people, sorting out who did what first tends to be difficult (see Introduction). As we have seen, Meleager apparently left with Ceraunus, and Pausanias (1.7.1) claims that Ptolemy II eliminated two other sons of Eurydice (Argaeus and an unnamed son) for plotting against him. Demetrius of Phalerum, the most prominent of Soter's *philoi* and a supporter of Ceraunus' candidacy for the throne died under possibly suspicious circumstances.[83]

How much did Berenice's advocacy of her son have to do with the fact that his father finally made him coregent with him and thus, effectively, his heir? Mothers and siblings functioned as succession advocates for sons, but their advocacy was hardly the only reason for a father's preference, though Ptolemy's preference for Berenice and her growing clout within court circles was surely a factor. Ptolemy Soter could have become dissatisfied with Ceraunus or grown more impressed with Berenice's son. Some older men seem to favor their younger children over their elder.[84] While the extant tradition about Ptolemy Ceraunus is unusually hostile, his subsequent violence against those who had reason to trust him seems fairly certain and distinctive, even by Macedonian standards. As his epithet, however acquired, suggests, Ceraunus was given to sudden and risk-taking action. Ptolemy I was a cautious man and the son he chose to succeed him seems to have resembled him in that regard as his older son did not.

Berenice's Chariot Victory

The breeding and racing of horses provided both a path to power and a way to demonstrate its possession (Isoc. 16.33).[85] Horse racing was literally the sport of kings in Hellenic antiquity, primarily because of its expense. Granted that equestrian victories were the most prestigious of all competitions, statues, commissioned poems, and coins commemorated victors.[86] Posidippus' poetry stresses Ptolemaic equestrian success in terms that put it in the long history of Greek aristocratic values.[87]

Olympic victories particularly appealed to those with Panhellenic political ambitions.[88] Argead Macedonian kings had won Olympic victories[89] and Ptolemies I through Ptolemy XII took part in Panhellenic competition, as did some of their *philoi*,[90] but a newly discovered manuscript containing some previously unknown poems by Posidippus[91] demonstrates that female Ptolemies shared in these Panhellenic victories. Berenice's chariot team won at Olympia,[92] probably the year after Ptolemy made her son his co-king.[93] Berenice, who had, so to speak, come from behind to win the dynastic stakes, celebrated one victory with another. Other Ptolemaic women including Arsinoë would replicate her success. Although women, at least married women, could not personally attend the games,[94] and no Macedonian woman had ever competed,[95] Berenice's triumph was not quite unprecedented: a Spartan royal woman, Cynisca,[96] had won the chariot competition in 396 and 392,[97] the first woman to do so.[98] Posidippus (AB 87), however, boasts that Berenice's victory has effectively wiped out that of the Spartan woman, one royal woman defeating another.[99] This first female Ptolemaic victory requires some attention, partly because it clearly became a model, for her own dynasty and daughter and for other female elites in the Hellenistic period.[100]

Olympic victories not only attested to individual accomplishments; they increased the fame of the victor's *genos* (clan, family) and demonstrated that the individual was worthy of it. Commemorations stressed the continuity of victory in a family, sometimes to the near exclusion of the individual victor.[101] Surviving epigrams about female victors emphasize the connection between royal women and their male kin. Cynisca's epigram begins, "My ancestors and brothers were kings of Sparta."[102] These female victories carried serious cultural weight.[103] Indeed, Posidippus (AB 88) has Ptolemy II boast of his own victory in the chariot races and his father's, but has him single out his mother's victory for praise because it was so unusual for a woman: "We are the first and only trio of kings to win . . . my parents and I. I named after Ptolemy and born the son of Berenice. . . . and of my father's glory I boast not, but that my mother, / a woman, won in her chariot—that is great."[104] We do not know that Berenice bred her victorious horses, but it seems likely that she and later Ptolemaic women did, as Cynisca had (Paus. 3.8.2). After all, women, particularly aristocratic women, and breeding must have seemed a natural combination; indeed in ancient Greece and today horsiness and old blood lines were and are associated in a way that inevitably implies a parallel and connection between one kind of breeding and another.[105]

The Consequences for Arsinoë of Her Brother's Coregency

The change in her brother's situation affected Arsinoë II, even though she was by this point the mother of three sons and had been gone from Egypt for fifteen years. It increased her prestige and that of her sons, the eldest of whom, not insignificantly, was also named Ptolemy. Her mother's subsequent Olympic victory further elevated and publicized the reputation of Berenice and Berenice's children.

At the same time that Berenice and her children were basking in their success, the fact that first (in 292) Seleucus I, ruler of most of Alexander's Asian empire, and then Ptolemy I (285) had made a chosen son coregent and so determined the succession, precipitated a succession crisis (283/82) at the court of Lysimachus, one that pitted Arsinoë and her sons against Lysimachus' son Agathocles; his wife, Lysandra, daughter of Eurydice; and their children.

This crisis will be discussed in the next chapter, but we should also note that the Egyptian succession decision had caused Ptolemy Ceraunus to flee to the court of Lysimachus, later to the court of Seleucus, and finally to Macedonia. All of his wanderings would affect Arsinoë's remaining career and, ultimately, force her back to Egypt, to her brother's court. Ptolemy's postponement of a decision about his successor until his old age colored the lives of all his children and, as we shall see, tended to generate a kind of "take no prisoners" attitude in all, most certainly including Arsinoë herself.

During the reign of Ptolemy II, particularly during and after his marriage to his sister Arsinoë, an understanding of monarchy and the royal dynasty began to develop that was more inclusive of royal women than practiced elsewhere in the Hellenistic world. There are some signs that the process began before the marriage of Ptolemy II and Arsinoë II. Posidippus' epigram AB 88, the poem that celebrates the victories of

Ptolemy I, Ptolemy II, and Berenice I, speaks of the three together, as "rulers" (*basileis*). Similarly, common Ptolemaic practice refers to a king and his wife together as *basileis*.[106] Young Arsinoë, as she departed for her marriage, may already have assumed that she was and would be part of rule, though hardly a dominant part. Events like her brother's coregency and her mother's Olympic victory would have reinforced a view that could have formed early in her life.

CHAPTER TWO

Arsinoë as the Wife of Lysimachus

CA. 300—281

AROUND THE TURN of the third century, Arsinoë married Lysimachus, ruler of Thrace. When she arrived at Lysimachia (Lysimachus' capital—the site, on the Gallipoli peninsula, is today part of European Turkey—and the primary locus of her husband's court), she was probably in her mid-teens while her groom was old enough to be her grandfather, about sixty.[1] In the Hellenic world, women were often a half generation younger than their husbands, but the age gap between Arsinoë and Lysimachus was unusually large. Ancient and modern writers have, in the light of the considerable discrepancy in their ages, tended to shape narratives about the pair that play to enduring stereotypes about "May–December" marriages: gold-digging sex kittens and doddering, indulgent old fools lie just out of sight behind many accounts of this period. A somewhat more upscale version of this same stereotype comes out of Greek myth and tragedy: the story of Phaedra, the young wife who falls in love with her much younger stepson. The Phaedra plot, as we shall see, does not simply lurk behind historical narratives; it actually directly enters some. Reality is likely to have been quite different.

This was a marriage born not of erotic passion but high politics: the alliance between Ptolemy I and Lysimachus, part of the post-Ipsus rearrangement of relationships among the remaining Successors of Alexander (see chapter 1). The Lysimachus-Arsinoë marriage was the first of three that linked the dynasties of Ptolemy and Lysimachus. Indeed, throughout the period of Arsinoë's marriage to Lysimachus, events at the court of one of these former companions of Alexander could affect the court of the other. Succession politics in Alexandria tended to rico-chet to Lysimachia and back again. We should forget those modern ste-reotypes of trophy wives of silver-haired CEOs and instead think of the marriage as more like a merger of Verizon and AT&T.

The conventional image of the two participants in the marriage may have born little resemblance to the historical personalities. Arsinoë, far from being the seductive Lolita so many seem to picture, could have been a very controlled, even repressed young woman, thanks to the tense situation in which she had grown up. We have no good idea of how she looked, particularly at this early stage (see chapter 6). Lysimachus, on the other hand, might well have been a dashing if aging figure; it would be unwise to underestimate the glamour attached, in the post-Alexander world, to the surviving companions of the conqueror. Justin's narrative includes two pas-sages that convey some sense of the appeal of the former companions of Alexander. The first is a description of the Diadochi at the time of Alexander's death (13.1.10–15):

> But Alexander's friends were justified in having their eyes set
> on the throne since their qualities and the respect they enjoyed
> were such that one might have taken each of them for a king, all
> of them possessing handsome features, a fine physique and great
> powers of body and mind alike—so much so that a stranger
> would have supposed that they had been selected not from one
> people only but from all the world. For never before that time
> did Macedonia, or indeed any other nation, produce so rich a
> crop of brilliant men, men who had been picked out with such
> care, first by Philip and then by Alexander, that they seemed
> chosen less as comrades in arms than as successors to the throne.
> Little wonder then that the world was conquered by officers of
> this mettle, when the Macedonian army was under the direction
> of so many men who were kings rather than generals. Such
> men would never have met their match had they not clashed
> amongst themselves, and the province of Macedonia would have
> produced many Alexanders if Fortune had not armed them to
> destroy each other by making them equals in merit.[2]

Twenty years later, Lysimachus would die in battle against Seleucus, an-other of Alexander's former companions. By this point, each was quite an old man, but the glamour lingered, as Justin (17.1.11–12) makes clear:

"At such an age both were still young in spirit and both had an insatiable craving for power. The two between them had the world in their hands, but they felt themselves confined and restricted, measuring the terms of their lives not by the passage of years but by the extent of their empires."[3] Moreover, Lysimachus would prove merciless in dealing with family members who offended him in some way.[4] He may not have been a "nice" man—not a character trait commonly found among members, male and female, of the Macedonian elite—but "doddering" hardly suits him either.

Lysimachus

We know little of Lysimachus' life, primarily because his dynasty died out and propaganda and histories affected by that propaganda were written by supporters of his enemies, by those who benefitted from his fall.[5] Apparently he was, like so many of the Macedonian elite of the generation of Alexander, brave to the point of foolhardiness and tough to the point of ruthlessness. His father, Agathocles, may have been a Thessalian who, like other non-Macedonians, joined the court of Philip II as a royal *hetairos* (companion).[6] Lysimachus and his brothers grew up in Pella and held important military and diplomatic posts.[7] He became one of Alexander's royal bodyguards (Arr. 6.28.4) and was, like Arsinoë's father, part of the group that tried (unsuccessfully) to prevent Alexander from killing Cleitus in a fit of drunken rage (Curt. 8.1.46). Lysimachus was wounded in India (Arr. 5.24.5), commanded vessels on the trip down the Indus (Arr. *Ind.* 18.3), and was crowned at Susa along with the other royal bodyguards (Arr. 7.5.6). He apparently had a taste for philosophy but is best known for his role in royal lion hunts:[8] in one, Alexander had to tell him to step back when Lysimachus tried to protect the king (who did not think he needed protection) from a lion and in another Lysimachus killed a lion but received grave wounds while doing so. Lysimachus, in later propaganda, would make much of his lion-hunting activity; like Alexander before him he would take on a lionlike image himself. Lysimachus emphasized his close personal relationship with Alexander.[9] Along with Ptolemy and Perdiccas, he was summoned to Alexander's deathbed.

For some time after the death of Alexander, Lysimachus' career remained relatively modest. In Babylon, the general divvying up of

Alexander's empire gave him Thrace (Curt. 10.10.4; Diod. 18.3.2; Dexippus *FGrH* 100 F 8).[10] When the initial round of the wars of the Successors ended in 321 with old Antipater on top, many of the generals, Lysimachus among them, married daughters of Antipater. For many years, Lysimachus kept busy dealing with Thracian rulers, consolidating power, and played little role in the major confrontations of the era, though he was often allied with Cassander, ruler of Macedonia. He did, like the others, found an eponymous city (Lysimachia, in 309)[11] and, again like the others, assumed royal title in 306/5 (Plut. *Demetr* 18.3; App. *Syr.* 1.54, 55). His invasion of Asia Minor in 302 contributed to the decisive defeat and death of Antigonus at Ipsus in 301. After Ipsus, Lysimachus played a more prominent role in the struggles of the Successors since he and Seleucus were the main people responsible for victory against Antigonus.[12] The result of this victory was his acquisition of much of Anatolia, territory that brought him considerably greater wealth, some of it used to extend his European territory. This was the context for his marriage alliance with Ptolemy. At the time of the marriage alliance, Lysimachus did not yet control Macedonia (this did not happen until ca. 285), but his role in the defeat of Antigonus had given him the power base that would ultimately enable him to acquire it.

As we have seen in the case of Ptolemy, the Successors imitated Philip II and Alexander in their polygamous marriage policy. While it is possible that Lysimachus was a serial monogamist,[13] it is much more likely that, as Plutarch claimed (*Demetr. and Ant.* 4.1), he was married to more than one wife at the same time. Around 321, he married Nicaea, daughter of Antipater (the widow or divorcee of Perdiccas), a prestigious marriage suggesting his closeness to Antipater.[14] This marriage probably produced a son (Agathocles) and two daughters (Eurydice and Arsinoë I).[15]

Just before Ipsus, in about 302, Lysimachus married Amastris, the twice married (Craterus, Dionysius of Heraclea) regent/ruler of Heraclea Pontica. Amastris was a member of the former royal family of the Persian Empire and marriage to her strengthened Lysimachus' base in the former Persian territory he controlled. This marriage also gave him a port on the Black Sea.[16] Lysimachus later moved Amastris from Heraclea to Sardis, obviously giving her some prominence, but his marriage to Arsinoë disrupted his relationship with Amastris, though how thoroughly remains unclear. Granted, Lysimachus' continuing ties to her and her court, rather than divorcing Lysimachus, Amastris apparently separated from him as a consequence of the arrival of Arsinoë,[17] probably because she would no longer have been his most prestigious wife. Considering that we hear of no similar development in terms of Nicaea, it seems likely that she was already dead. The episode of Amastris' separation is part of a developing lack of enthusiasm for royal polygamy on the part of royal women (as Arsinoë's own career demonstrates) and a consequent coyness or indirectness about continuing polygamy.[18]

On the other hand, Lysimachus had yet another wife, an Odrysian whose name is unknown, the mother of his son Alexander (Paus. 1.10.4; App. *Syr.* 64) who was an adult in 281.[19] Quite possibly Lysimachus married her about the same time he married Arsinoë.[20] This wife, clearly of lesser status because of her "barbarian" origins, may have remained at court after Arsinoë's arrival or perhaps did not arrive until after Arsinoë. Arsinoë II would have been the most prestigious of Lysimachus' wives, from the time of her arrival and on, assuming that Nicaea, the mother of Lysimachus' apparent heir, was no longer alive. Amastris, a Persian and the mother of no children by Lysimachus, however important she was in terms of his Asian possessions, could not have had higher status at a Macedonian court.

Virtually nothing about Arsinoë II's life prior to the later 280s can be dated, apart from the fact that she produced three sons by Lysimachus: Ptolemy (born ca. 298), Lysimachus (born ca. 296), and Philip (born ca. 293).[21] Lysimachus had at least two older sons (Agathocles and Alexander) by other wives, so probably none of Arsinoë's sons were, initially, considered likely successors to the throne, simply because they had older, adult or nearly adult, half brothers and their father was already so old. In the 290s, it must have seemed implausible that Lysimachus would live so long that the oldest of Arsinoë's sons would be more or less adult at the time of his father's death. Arsinoë I, Lysimachus' daughter, must still have been in residence at her father's court since she did not marry Ptolemy II until at least 275, possibly later (see chapter 4). Unless she was an unusually elderly bride, Arsinoë I was quite young when the other Arsinoë arrived. Indeed, her stepmother may have brought her up, making subsequent events (see chapter 4) particularly ironic or possibly personally painful. Presumably, Arsinoë II spent the 290s quietly, a young mother of young boys, probably without, at first, serious expectations about the possibility of kingship for her sons. Her upbringing, however, had certainly taught her how necessary it was to "watch your back" at court, and events would prove that she did.

Hellenistic courts traveled and Lysimachus' certainly did because of the Asian territories he had come to control in addition to Thrace. In Anatolia were ancient and famous cities, but Lysimachia (presumably Lysimachus' base, particularly because of its location) was new, newer even than Alexandria; we know virtually nothing about what it was like, but it was much smaller than Alexandria and, granted that Lysimachus' fortunes were modest until Ipsus, likely much more modest in appearance. We could picture Arsinoë somewhat bored in this remote city, waiting for news from Alexandria of the improving fortunes of her family there, but it is difficult to know if that is a remotely accurate picture, particularly since we cannot calculate how much of her time was spent in Asia Minor, in places like cosmopolitan Ephesus. Assuming that Nicaea was long dead, Arsinoë, however limited the expectations of her sons, may have led a pleasant and less stressful life than that of her mother in Alexandria.

Though she did not appear to be the mother of Lysimachus' heir, Arsinoë enjoyed considerable prestige and wealth; that, at least, is what several pieces of information likely relating to the roughly fifteen-year period between the beginning of her marriage and the succession controversy involving Agathocles suggest. Strabo (14.1.21) and Stephanus Byzantinus (*s.v. "Ephesos"*) report that when Lysimachus refounded Ephesus in the later 290s, he renamed it after his wife, Arsinoëa.[22] Lysimachus, of course, had a daughter with the same name as wife and he did rename Smyrna Eurydicea in honor of his other daughter (Strab. 14.1.37),[23] so it is possible but unlikely that our ancient sources confused their Arsinoës.[24] Years later, Arsinoë took up residence at "Arsinoëa-Ephesus" when her husband went off to confront Seleucus.[25] Indeed, Arsinoëa-Ephesus may have been a royal residence.[26] Coins from that city may show, on the obverse, Arsinoë or Arsinoë as Artemis; the image bears some resemblance to later Ptolemaic coin images, though quite possibly simply because the images are all so generic.[27] In Aetolia, a village was refounded as a city named after Arsinoë, probably as a consequence of Aetolian dealings with Lysimachus.[28] An inscription, Delos' decree for Demaratus (*SIG*³ 381), speaks of the *eunoia* (goodwill) of the people of Delos to *basileus* Lysimachus and *basilissa* Arsinoë. This decree was originally dated 295–94, but may date to ca. 285.[29] This inscription, whatever its date, speaks to the formal and public role that Arsinoë played in Lysimachus' monarchy.[30] Thus, Lysimachus incorporated his wife Arsinoë into the publication and legitimization of his dynasty, along with the other women of his clan.[31]

Did Arsinoë have any control over the city named after her or, for that matter, any cities? Did she, in short, have any kind of institutionalized power inside Lysimachus' realm? The answer is yes. Memnon (*FGrH* 434 F5.4–5) asserts that Lysimachus gave Arsinoë the city of Heraclea, presumably after the murder of Amastris ca. 284, since Amastris had previously governed it, and he also reveals that Arsinoë chose someone to govern the city.[32] Memnon implausibly claimed that her interest in the cities of Heraclea, Tios, and Amastris, was inspired by Lysimachus' praise for them. According to the hostile Memnon (see Appendix), she ignored assorted privileges previously enjoyed by the citizens of Heraclea and appointed a governor who ruled tyrannically until the defeat of Lysimachus at Corupedium. The story of Philetaerus (Paus. 1.8.1; Str. 13.4.1 C 623) indicates that Arsinoë attempted to have some control over Pergamum as well. There is no other clear evidence for her control of other cities, although her later position in Cassandria—Justin (24.3.3) terms it "her city"—and similar situations for other royal women of the era might well suggest that she did control others.[33] Granted that several different sources testify to what they understood as her interference in previously independent cities, we must conclude that Arsinoë herself did exercise some political control over several cities and that it was resented. This level of

FIGURE 2.1. Foundations of the Rotunda of Arsinoe II, from the south.
Photo: Bonna D. Wescoat.

control, however, may have been acquired after her son had become his father's probable heir.

Arsinoë controlled great wealth. She paid for the largest round building in the Greek world, the rotunda, as an offering to the Great Gods at Samothrace (*OGIS15* = *IG* XII 227). Earlier Macedonian rulers had patronized the sanctuary on Samothrace, and both Lysimachus and her brother and later husband, Ptolemy II, made offerings there as well (Figs. 2.1 and 2.2). Unfortunately, the inscription on the frieze recording her dedication is damaged and the name of her husband cannot be read. The wording of the inscription ("*Basilissa* Arsinoë, daughter of *basileus* Ptolemy, wife of *basileus* X, to the great gods")[34] stresses the royal status of Arsinoë herself, her father, and her husband.[35] Most likely, she dedicated the building while married to Lysimachus. After her disastrous marriage to Ptolemy Ceraunus (see chapter 3), she took refuge on Samothrace probably because her previous patronage made it an obvious place of refuge.[36] Familial and public piety had long been a particular

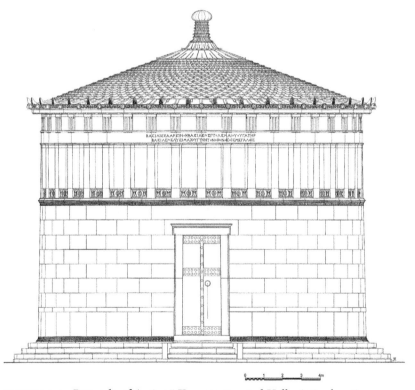

FIGURE 2.2. Rotunda of Arsinoë II, reconstructed Hellenistic elevation. Drawing John Kurtich, Samothrace excavations.

specialty of Greek women, and elite women often functioned as patrons and priestesses.[37] Architectural dedications by women were rare in the Greek world, although there is another at Samothrace.[38] Female patronage and a public role for women did, however, become more common in the Hellenistic period, perhaps on the model of royal women.[39] To what degree such patronage publicized the woman and to what degree it was intended to advertise her male kin (who may have funded or helped to fund the enterprise) is difficult to say. The question itself depends on a distinction that the ancient world may not have made.

Our scattered sources preserve a tradition about Lysimachus as a tyrant that has affected the tradition about Arsinoë. Lysimachus certainly could be ruthless, though not necessarily more so than other rulers of the period.[40] Hostility toward Lysimachus appears to be the main impetus for some unpleasant tales about Arsinoë (apart from those related to the succession struggle), rather than actions of her own.[41] These anecdotes, though generally portraying Arsinoë in a negative way, also suggest that she was Lysimachus' most prominent wife. Although these stories probably have no literal truth, they imply that she had a considerable public presence in his realms, that she was part of the public face of his monarchy.[42] Plutarch (*Demetr.* 25.6), while discussing rivalry between Demetrius Poliorcetes and Lysimachus and Lysimachus' mockery of Demetrius' notorious affair with the courtesan Lamia, reports that Demetrius responded by commenting that his prostitute *(porne)* had more *sophrosune* (moderation, here clearly sexual moderation) than Lysimachus' Penelope, thus questioning the chastity of Lysimachus' wife. Athenaeus (14.616c), in a discussion of jokes at symposia, cites Myrtilus for the story that professional joke tellers often made fun of Lysimachus and that Tlesephorus, one of his own officers, at a drinking party, mocked Arsinoë's supposed tendency to vomit and that Lysimachus, in punishment, had him caged till he died.[43] From these dubious anecdotes one can deduce some unsurprising things—in the Hellenic world, particularly in the freer context of a drinking party, the sexual habits of a man's wife could always constitute a vulnerability; jokes in bad taste apparently have some weird universal appeal—but they also assume that royal women were public in a way that always made them susceptible to innuendo of any sort. Royal women were a bit too much like Lamia and her ilk, since both kinds of women were so much more public than ordinary women.[44]

Did Arsinoë possess more than her demonstrable prestige and wealth; did she have power and influence? Influence is difficult to demonstrate for any person because, by its very nature, it works behind the scenes, and for women, it often involves the notion of their being "the power behind the throne."[45] Public statements that either assert or imply influence (like the Delian decree mentioned above) are tricky, since those who make such statements are not necessarily speaking about literal truth but rather dealing in innocuous ideals and diplomatic pleasantries.[46] She may already have had some influence on her husband's policy, but there is no proof that this was so until late in his reign, when we know that he allowed her freedom to act in some of the cities of his empire.

Outside Lysimachus' realm, the struggle for the succession continued to divide the court in Alexandria, and Ptolemy I continued to create marriage alliances using his daughters and stepdaughter. Not for the last time, plans made in Alexandria affected Lysimachus' court (see chapter 1). As we have seen, soon after Arsinoë had left her father's court for Lysimachus' (ca. 300–298), Pyrrhus concluded that Berenice had the greatest power among Ptolemy's wives and accordingly married Berenice's daughter (and Arsinoë's half sister) Antigone. Arsinoë's part of the Ptolemaic dynasty was moving up, and this, in turn, could only increase her prestige at her husband's court.

As I have noted already, the Successors arranged a number of marriage alliances after Ipsus, and for Ptolemy that included planning the marriages of four daughters (one actually a stepdaughter): Arsinoë herself to Lysimachus; Antigone to Pyrrhus; Lysandra to Agathocles, son of Lysimachus (Plut. *Demetr* 31.3);[47] and Ptolemais to Demetrius Poliorcetes (Plut. *Demetr* 32.3). The first two marriages happened right away, but the second two were delayed. Ptolemais' marriage need not concern us further, but the situation and marriages of her sister Lysandra are important and puzzling. Unless Ptolemy had two daughters named Lysandra, it would appear that, prior to her marriage to Lysimachus' son Agathocles, Lysandra first married the youngest of Cassander's sons, Alexander V (Euseb. *Chron.* 1. 232). Cassander probably arranged this marriage and that of his second youngest son, Antipater, to Lysimachus' daughter Eurydice in 398;[48] he died the next year and the death of his oldest son, Philip, shortly followed. Cassander's two remaining sons, the teenaged grooms, then apparently coruled while struggling for power against each other. Antipater, believing that his mother, Thessalonice, favored his younger brother, murdered her. After this matricide, both brothers sought help from some of the Successors. Pyrrhus aided Alexander (in return for territory), and Antipater therefore sought refuge from his father-in-law Lysimachus who initially tried to reconcile the brothers. In the end, Demetrius Poliorcetes killed Alexander and briefly ruled Macedonia himself, and Lysimachus killed his son-in-law Antipater, primarily to placate Demetrius (Just. 16.2.4; Euseb. *Chron.* 1.232).

One consequence of this less than edifying series of events, apart from chaos in Macedonia for some time to come, was the presence in Lysimachus' court of the two young widows of Cassander's thuggish sons. Lysimachus' sudden betrayal of Antipater is unsurprising; self-interest and perhaps a dislike for matricides were reason enough. But more interesting is the fact that Lysimachus imprisoned his own daughter on the grounds that she had sided with her husband, against her father (Just. 16.2.4; Euseb. *Chron.* 1.232). This episode demonstrates that royal women were, at least from the point of view of their fathers or male kin, only temporary members of the families into which they'd been married. More relevant to the story of Arsinoë, however, is Lysimachus' willingness to imprison one of his children, one of his children by Nicaea at that.

The other young widowed daughter-in-law of Cassander, Lysandra, married Lysimachus' son Agathocles, according to Pausanias (1.9.7), after he returned from his war with the Getae, that is, about 293.[49] Apparently the marriage planned in 300 was for some reason canceled but then reinstated after the murder of Lysandra's first husband, Alexander.[50] Possibly the widowed Lysandra went back to Alexandria in the intervening period or perhaps she fled immediately to Lysimachus' court, but her father, Ptolemy, was still alive when she married Agathocles, and doubtless Ptolemy and Lysimachus arranged the match.[51]

What this means is that by 293 (or possibly earlier), another round of the struggle between the line of Berenice and the line of Eurydice was developing at the court of Lysimachus rather than in Alexandria, this time involving their daughters. Each woman hoped, as had each one's mother, to have her children succeed to the throne and each feared the other and for the safety of her children. If Arsinoë and Lysandra knew each other as children, as seems likely, they would have known each other as enemies, probably early on channeling the rivalry of their mothers and brothers. All of Ptolemy I's children, both sons and daughters, seem to have been scarred by the dynastic infighting in which they had grown up, something worth bearing in mind as we consider subsequent events.

By the 280s, Lysimachus' son Agathocles was in his thirties.[52] He had children by Lysandra, though we do not know if any were male. Agathocles had played a part of some sort in Lysimachus' inglorious Getic campaign.[53] In 286–85, however, Agathocles covered himself with glory: he thoroughly defeated Demetrius Poliorcetes who was trying to wrest Lydia and Caria from Lysimachus' control (Plut. *Demetr.* 46–8; Just. 17.1.4). This impressive victory against a well-known general brought him popularity in the Greek cities of Anatolia and a large number of *philoi* (friends), men committed to his succession to the throne.

The events of 285 may have precipitated the vicious struggle for succession to Lysimachus. In that year, Lysimachus acquired Macedonia but developments in Egypt mattered more in terms of the struggle for the throne. Ptolemy I now chose Ptolemy II, Arsinoë's full brother to corule with him. The children of Eurydice had lost the succession battle in Egypt.[54] Eurydice, though perhaps never divorced, may have left Egypt at this point but certainly her son Ptolemy Ceraunus, the rejected heir, now did so. Apparently he soon arrived in the court of Lysimachus,[55] where his full sister Lysandra was married to the apparent heir, but his half sister, the full sibling of the man who had won the succession battle, was the wife of Lysimachus himself. Ceraunus' arrival may, in itself, have helped to precipitate events, but the reason for his arrival was itself a precipitant.

A pattern had by this time developed among the Diadochi to make their chosen heirs co-kings, thus smoothing the succession in dynasties still new (see Introduction). Antigonus had made Demetrius Poliorcetes co-king in 306. In 293 or 292, Seleucus had made his son and heir Antiochus coregent with him. Now, in 285 Ptolemy had done the same. Thus, Lysimachus' old companions and age equals, the rulers of the two other apparently stable Hellenistic kingdoms (Demetrius not being, at the time, in that category), had all but guaranteed the succession, inventing coregency (for which there was no Argead precedent) in an attempt to generate continuity and smooth succession. Lysimachus, despite Agathocles' recent success, had not done the same.[56] Agathocles was a proven commander, widely known in Lysimachus' Asian realm, and his father was in his seventies. Justin (17.1.4) does claim that Lysimachus had somehow (his language is vague) arranged Agathocles' succession to the kingship, but there is no other evidence of this decision and Justin's narrative does not inspire much confidence.[57] In any event, Justin does not say that Lysimachus had made Agathocles coruler. Agathocles had doubtless long been expected to succeed his father, just as had Ceraunus, but expectation is not formal status as coregent. Other signs hint that Lysimachus allowed Agathocles only a limited public role.[58] Agathocles' brother-in-law, the newly exiled Ptolemy Ceraunus, may have encouraged the growth of tension between Agathocles and Arsinoë and her sons: doubtless bitter against the children of Berenice, perhaps wanting some payback, he could have deepened the suspicions and fears of his sister and brother-in-law.

Apart from Lysimachus' probable failure to make Agathocles his official successor (and certainly his failure to make Agathocles coregnant with him), there was another precipitant for conflict: Arsinoë's son, Ptolemy, was about fifteen in 283, perilously close to adulthood. Arsinoë was probably promoting her son as heir. An inscription from Thebes for a statue of Arsinoë that her son dedicated, not for himself but for his father, seems to confirm this, if it predates the death of Agathocles.[59] Another statue of Arsinoë once on Delos may have formed part of the same campaign for recognition, though its date is also uncertain.[60] If this indirect self-promotion happened before the fall of Agathocles rather than after it, it could have been part of Arsinoë's reaction (and so her son's) to the presence of her half brother Ceraunus at her husband's court. She may have worried that his arrival meant even poorer chances for her sons if Agathocles succeeded.

The driving factor in the crisis, in other words, probably for all parties, was fear, as was characteristic of succession battles (see Introduction). Appian (*Syr.* 62) says fear is why Ptolemy Ceraunus left Egypt after Soter had chosen his younger half brother as heir. Fear would soon drive Alexander, son of Lysimachus, from his father's court after the death of Agathocles (App. *Syr.* 64). Fear was what Arsinoë felt for her sons if Agathocles inherited (Paus. 1.10.3) and later, when she contemplated marriage to Ceraunus, she did so out of fear for them once more (Just. 24.2.7). Sons and wives who lost succession struggles could, at best, hope for exile and had reason to fear for their lives. Neither side in this struggle had many options. Arsinoë was not a villain or a heroine, but fixed on her own survival and the rule of her sons, goals shared by her rivals.[61]

The evidence (Memnon *FGrH* 434 F. 5.6; Paus. 1.10.3; Just.17.1.4–5; Lucian *Ikaromenip.* 15; Strab.13.4.1) for the events leading to the death of Agathocles ca. 283/82 is poor and contradictory,[62] because as is typical in succession strife, few other than the participants themselves knew what motivated them or who actually did what, granted that most deaths were not public events. Memnon, for instance, may well preserve hostile gossip from Heraclea (where the majority favored the party of Agathocles) about the goings-on at Lysimachus' court, but one doubts that he had any real evidence or even understanding of the court dynamic.[63] In some sources, Arsinoë convinces her husband to kill his son or even perpetrates the deed herself. In others, Lysimachus instigates it, using Arsinoë merely as his instrument. In yet others, Agathocles causes his own death by plotting against his father. Motivation, when mentioned, also varies: one source has Arsinoë inspired either by fear for her sons or anger that Agathocles had spurned her sexual advances,[64] another claims that Lysimachus acted out of hatred for Agathocles, and still another pictures Lysimachus as the trusting dupe of his wife's murderous aggression.

Though some sources blame Arsinoë either directly or indirectly, referring to the traditional women's weapons, poison and sexual favors, it is evident that Lysimachus either caused or countenanced the death of Agathocles.[65] Strabo's conclusion (13.4.1), that Lysimachus, encompassed by troubles in his household, was compelled to kill Agathocles,[66] convinces. Why did Lysimachus feel compelled to kill his son? The most obvious answer is that, rightly or wrongly, he believed that his son was conspiring against him. Any number of factors could have inspired or contributed to this conviction: his reluctance to pass on or share power and thus suspicion of his obvious successor; Agathocles' actual desire to eliminate his father and take over immediately,[67] perhaps a consequence of Lysimachus' prolonged refusal to choose a coregent;[68] growing dislike of Agathocles and affection for young Ptolemy,[69] who had the advantage of being too young to threaten an aging father;[70] and Arsinoë's advocacy for her young son/sons.

As Strabo's description hints, tensions had reached such a height at Lysimachus' court that he felt he had to choose one of his sons, and he made his choice, either by ordering Agathocles' death himself or by failing to punish Arsinoë and her son for doing so. Even if Lysimachus was indeed a ruthless and tyrannical father and ruler and was indifferent to the fate of Agathocles, it could not have been a decision taken lightly.

Lysimachus was no fool and had spent years gradually building up his extensive realm; it is unlikely that he was unaware of the support that Agathocles had established within the ruling elite of his father's empire, particularly in Anatolia. This then was a decision of last resort; we will never know what finally led Lysimachus to do it and how large a role Arsinoë had in it.

The aftermath of the elimination of Agathocles proved, ultimately, to be the death of Lysimachus, the collapse of his kingdom, and gradual disappearance of his dynasty from international Mediterranean politics. Lysandra, with her children and brothers and also Alexander, Lysimachus' son by the Odrysian woman, fled to Seleucus, begging him to make war on Lysimachus (Pausanias 1.10.4–5).[71] Equally important, our sources indicate that a large faction in Asia Minor apparently previously committed to the succession of Agathocles, including important royal *philoi* and military officials and possibly some of the general population, now abandoned Lysimachus' dynasty, switched sides to Seleucus, and encouraged him to attack (Paus. 1.10.4–5; Memnon *FGrH* 434 F. 5.7; Just.17.1.5–12).[72] The story of Philetaerus, commander of Pergamum and its treasury, exemplifies the phenomenon. Strabo (13.4.1B 624) says that Philetaerus was loyal to Lysimachus but had difficulties with Arsinoë, who had made charges against him, so he revolted and continued to govern the citadel under Seleucid rule. Pausanias (1.10.4–5) somewhat similarly reports that Philetaerus, taking Agathocles' death badly and worried about how he would be treated by Arsinoë (implying that they were already enemies),[73] seized Pergamum and offered it and himself to Seleucus. The references to Arsinoë's differences with Philetaerus should not be taken as simply hostile propaganda. They suggest that Arsinoë too was engaged in the network of *philia* (friendship) relationships and that this failed *philia* caused terrible problems.

Demonstrably, Lysimachus had lost the support of the faction that had entrenched itself with the man they expected to succeed him. Though the sources mention fondness for Agathocles as the motivation of those who switched allegiances, other factors may have mattered more. Lysimachus' hold on the Anatolian territory he acquired after Ipsus may never have been strong; many cities there retained pro-Antigonid sentiments and resented Lysimachus' harsh fiscal policies.[74] People may have lacked confidence that Lysimachus' dynasty could survive. Awareness of Seleucus' arrival with his army on the coast of Asia Minor could also have led to change in allegiance.[75]

Seleucus, having been invited, invaded Asia Minor and had apparently gained control of Sardis before Lysimachus, hearing of these events, himself invaded Asia and confronted Seleucus, on the plain of Corupedium, to the west of Sardis. Lysimachus was defeated and died in battle at Corupedium (Memnon FGrH 434 F 5.7) in February 281.[76] His son Alexander, although he had fled with Lysandra after Agathocles' death supposedly fearing for his own life (App. *Syr.* 64; Paus. 1.10.4), managed to persuade Lysandra (who apparently had Achilleslike plans for the corpse of her enemy) to yield up his father's body; he later buried it in the Chersonese (Paus. 1.10.5). Appian (*Syr.* 64) claims that Lysimachus' faithful dog guarded the body of his fallen master until it was buried by, according to some sources, Alexander, according to others by someone named Thorax. Plutarch (*Mor.* 970c) and Aelian (NA 6.25) even claim that the dog hurled himself onto his master's funeral pyre. As this more or less shaggy dog story might suggest, our sources treat the battle between the two elderly former companions of Alexander as a heroic and even legendary struggle, particularly because the death of Seleucus followed so soon after that of Lysimachus.[77] This is most obvious in Justin (17.1.9–2.5), who emphasizes the age of the two rivals and yet their youthful spirit and desire for power.

The agency of the various personalities involved in the series of events just narrated was limited. Lysimachus' retention of the Argead practice of royal polygamy coupled with his refusal to have an official heir who coreigned with him appears, however, to be the critical factor in these events. Essentially he opted for tradition and resisted sharing power, whether because he did not want to accept the realities of his age or because he lacked confidence in Agathocles. Individuals like Arsinoë and Agathocles acted and reacted, as we have seen, in a climate of fear, justifiable fear so far as one can tell, and determining who acted first is virtually impossible. Ancient and modern historians tend to assume that the person who benefitted was automatically the author of all action, but this need not be the case, certainly not entirely.

Arsinoë worked for her son's succession and Agathocles for his own, but Lysimachus was the decision maker. He felt somehow compelled to kill his own son. It will not work, no matter how scheming one conceives Arsinoë to have been, to blame all that happened on her.[78] In a sense, she was simply doing her job as her sons' succession advocate, a job that in the past had often involved murders, the work of both men and women. Had she not acted (assuming she did), her sons could have ended up dead much sooner than they did. Arsinoë's actions, even if they included precipitating the murder of Agathocles—something we do not know for certain—were not a "foray into politics"[79] but rather part of a fairly common pattern for royal women, one that sometimes led to murder.

The departure of *philoi* who supported Agathocles was important, but once one ignores the moralizing narratives' tragic coloring, it is clear that while the succession crisis endangered Lysimachus' rule, his defeat, not to mention his death in battle, was the decisive factor in the collapse of the dynasty. Military success was vital in the era of the Diadochi. Granted lack of information about the battle itself, it is impossible to tell whether defections by former supporters of Agathocles made the size of Lysimachus' forces smaller, and thus that his political problems contributed to his military failure.[80] The best way to understand these events is not to cast Arsinoë as either heroine or villain but rather to conclude that this was a case where this particular form of monarchy was hoist on its own petard. Indeed, I will suggest (see chapter 3) that the story of the end of Lysimachus' empire proved to be a cautionary tale, both for the survivors and for other Hellenistic courts.

Polyaenus (8.57) gives us our only information about Arsinoë at the time of her husband's defeat and death. According to him, she had followed her husband to Asia Minor but had not gone with his army to the battlefield; she was in Ephesus/Arsinoëa when the grim news came. Polyaenus reports that, thanks to the news, the city of Ephesus was in uproar, with the pro-Seleucid faction tearing down the walls and opening the gates. In order to escape, Arsinoë supposedly dressed one of her maids in royal garments, put her in a litter with an armed escort, and sent her through one door while she, alone and disguised by dirt and rags, left by another. One of the opposing faction did indeed stab to death pseudo-Arsinoë (whether the murder of the supposed queen was proof of Lysimachus' unpopularity, Arsinoë's, or of the simple desire of the citizens to be on the winning side, we cannot tell),[81] but the real Arsinoë rushed to waiting ships and sailed off. In modern times, her willingness to consign the maid to certain death would seem inhumane, but in Polyaenus there is no criticism whatsoever and instead implicit admiration for Arsinoë's cleverness.[82] This tale of disguised escape could be a literary construct; certainly it is not the only such story,[83] but the elaborate robes of royal women, wives, and courtesans, and the ups and downs of Hellenistic kingship may have made such a situation more commonplace than we realize. The maid cross-dressing as a royal woman may be fiction, but Arsinoë got out of Ephesus somehow, most likely not dressed to look like the wife of Lysimachus. It is plausible that Arsinoë escaped by sea in vessels loyal to Lysimachus, part of his fleet.

Intriguingly, Polyaenus does not mention the sons of Lysimachus and Arsinoë; he may simply have omitted them from his tale (their presence would complicate the story of her disguised escape; she could dress as a maid, but what could two young boys and an adolescent do to conceal themselves yet accompany their mother), but they may not have been with her.[84] If they were not, it signifies that Lysimachus had not brought his roughly seventeen-year-old heir Ptolemy with him to battle. He may have considered the risk too great. If so, then one wonders why he chose to have Arsinoë accompany him to Asia. Did Lysimachus think he could still win? The fact that she did not follow him to the battlefield suggests that he wanted to allow for the possibility of his defeat, yet her presence in Asia, surely also his decision, is puzzling and suggests that he thought he had a good chance of prevailing. A widowed royal mother's duty was certainly to work for the succession of her sons; that duty Arsinoë clearly embraced. Lysimachus could not, at this point, if defeated, have counted on anyone other than Arsinoë to work for his sons. We could conclude that Polyaenus' story is mere fiction, but whether or not the tale about the costume change is true, Polyaenus apparently came on a source that told him that Arsinoë had been in Anatolia with Lysimachus and that she escaped from Ephesus. Lysimachus hedged his bets and put Arsinoë (and possibly his remaining sons) in a dangerous situation, but one from which they could escape, as they certainly could not have, had they accompanied him to the site of the battle.

CHAPTER THREE

Arsinoë and Ptolemy Ceraunus

281—279—76

WE NOW TURN to a dramatic and bloody period in Arsinoë's life, the time between the death of Lysimachus at Corupedium (and her flight from Ephesus) in February 281 and her departure from Samothrace for a return to Egypt, possibly in 279, perhaps as late as 277/76.[1] Arsinoë herself; her half brother Ptolemy Ceraunus, her father's rejected heir; and her oldest son, Ptolemy, son of Lysimachus played the major roles in this bizarre series of events. This episode, however brief, proves central to understanding Arsinoë's life because it is the only time one can be certain she made her own decisions. Before and after this, her male kin acted as official decision makers, so Arsinoë could only attempt to influence their decisions. This short and tragic period illuminates her priorities, not only during these events themselves, but during her entire life; this is not to presume that Arsinoë—or anyone else, for that matter—always acted for the same reasons. Subsequent circumstance and experience probably did, to some degree, affect her later goals and priorities.

The Evidence

The wars of Successors did not end with the death of Lysimachus. A few months after Seleucus' victory against Lysimachus, Seleucus crossed the Hellespont (fall 281) in order to seize the European remnant of Lysimachus' realm. Ptolemy Ceraunus accompanied him and his army. In Thrace, near Lysimachia, Ceraunus, though previously the beneficiary of Seleucus' patronage, suddenly stabbed Seleucus to death (App. *Syr.* 62–63: Just. 17.2.4–5; Strab. 13.4.1 624b),[2] the action that Pausanias (10.19.7) says gave him his epithet of "Ceraunus," meaning "thunderbolt." (His epithet not only describes his actions but also alludes to Zeus, the wielder of the thunderbolt and also to Alexander, sometimes pictured with a thunderbolt.)[3] Seleucus, after he began his attempt to claim Lysimachus' former European possessions, had nothing more to offer from Ceraunus' point of view.[4] Apparently he saw a chance, if he eliminated Seleucus, to be king in Thrace and Macedonia, and took it. After the murder, Ceraunus jumped on a horse and galloped into Lysimachia, where he put on a diadem and somehow acquired an impressive bodyguard (his suspiciously rapid success in doing so implies that he had some wealth, a well-thought out plan, and collaborators).[5] He and his escort then went out to meet the army which, despite the fact that its members had served under Seleucus, acclaimed him king (Memnon *FGrH 434* F8.3). Again, Ceraunus may have made some efforts beforehand to smooth his way with the army, possibly aided by members of Agathocles' former faction.[6]

Antigonus Gonatas, on news of events at Lysimachia, attacked by land and sea (hoping to regain Macedonia for the Antigonids), but Ceraunus, employing Lysimachus' fleet, drove him away (Memnon *FGrH 434* F 8.4–6; Just. 24.1.8). Ceraunus moved quickly to patch things up with Seleucus' son Antiochus and with Ptolemy II. Ceraunus wrote to his half brother, hoping to reconcile with him, claiming that he was no longer upset about his brother's "seizure" of their father's kingdom and would no longer seek it, and that he also had made peace with Pyrrhus (Just. 17.2.9).[7] Having dealt with immediate external threats, Ceraunus then turned (winter 281/80) to the internal situation and the problem of Arsinoë and her sons.

Justin's lurid, sometimes bombastic account constitutes virtually all the evidence for what happened to Arsinoë and her sons after the fall of Lysimachus and Arsinoë's return to Macedonia. Worse yet, Justin deals with these events twice, but his two versions contradict each other.[8] In the first (17.2.6–8), Ceraunus' motives are not initially murderous. Since Ceraunus wants to make use of the memory of his father and of Lysimachus by portraying himself as Lysimachus' avenger, he tries to conciliate Lysimachus' sons. For that reason he asks his half sister Arsinoë to marry him, promising to adopt her sons. He does this so that once he is married, the boys will not work against him because of their mother and because he would be their stepfather.

Justin's longer and more complete second version (24.2.1–3.10) pictures a more villainous Ceraunus, one with murderous intent from the start. It also focuses on the city of Cassandria as the other does not. Ceraunus plots to kill Arsinoë's sons and deprive Arsinoë of control of Cassandria. He wants to marry her since there is no other way to get to her sons. Arsinoë, knowing her brother's character, initially refuses him. In any effort to win her over, Ceraunus promises that he will no longer war with her sons, will rule conjointly with them, and swear an oath to this effect in front of the gods and a witness of her choosing. Arsinoë vacillates about what to do and delays, fearing even to send a witness to the oath but also that she will provoke him if she does not. She is more frightened for her children than for herself. Concluding that the marriage will protect her sons, she sends one of her *philoi*, Dion, as her witness. Ceraunus swears in front of an altar that he will proclaim her queen, will not hold her in contempt by taking another wife, and will not recognize any children other than hers as his sons. Arsinoë then gives up her fear and agrees to marry him, despite the protests of her son Ptolemy that some sort of deception was going on. The wedding happens with public ceremony. Arsinoë, now relieved from anxiety, invites him to "her own city Cassandria" and organizes a festival for his arrival. Ceraunus, once inside the citadel, orders it seized and the boys killed. Arsinoë is driven from the city.

Arsinoë's Situation

After her departure from Ephesus, Arsinoë had settled in Cassandria. If her sons had not accompanied her to Asia and on her flight, they must have joined her there. Cassandria was a major city and citadel. Significantly, she and her sons chose Macedonia as their base rather than Thrace, though Lysimachus had ruled there for more than forty years. Her choice indicates that Macedonia, the most recently acquired part of Lysimachus' lands, had proved the most loyal to the dynasty of Lysimachus; Cassandria, by the time Ceraunus turned up if not earlier, had somehow become her city. Judging by the reference to Dion—her agent for hearing Ceraunus' oath—as "one of her friends" (Just. 24.27), she and her sons were not alone but had a group of *philoi* with them.

Since Ceraunus was apparently unable to enter Cassandria without the marriage, the city must have been defended, whether by mercenaries Arsinoë had hired or forces still loyal to her sons and Lysimachus (possibly forces originally with her in Ephesus), or both.[9] In the late fourth and third century, a number of royal women appeared in front of armies and exercised administrative control over mercenaries, often in the context of defense of citadels. It is tempting to associate the storming of the city with the "storming" of the woman who controlled it. Women had long played a role in sieges, presumably because anything they did for the city also defended the *oikos* (house, household).[10] Ceraunus' promise (Just. 24.2.4) that he would no longer go to war with the sons of Lysimachus must signify that he previously had;[11] possibly he had already attempted to take the city. Arsinoë and her sons may have been under siege or threatened with it; other cities they controlled may have been as well (Trogus *Prol.* 24).

Political chaos had periodically struck Macedonia since Cassander's death in 297; when Lysimachus took control in 285, the country had experienced a brief reprieve, but now disorder resurfaced. There is no evidence that Arsinoë's son Ptolemy was ever proclaimed king.[12] As we have seen, the troops who went over to Ceraunus were not choosy about whom they recognized as king; a murderous nature was hardly a disqualification, granted the past record of Macedonian kings. Moreover, Ceraunus' defeat of Antigonus Gonatas argued in his favor, both pragmatically and in terms of the cultural power of military victory. At this point, for Macedonians (let alone the heterogeneous army that had accompanied Seleucus), any port in a storm would do.[13]

Still, Arsinoë and her sons apparently commanded troops, possessed supporters, and controlled Cassandria and some other cities. Her sons had at least as good a claim on rule of Macedonia as anyone else and her eldest was probably about eighteen, a new minted adult. One way or another, Arsinoë retained some portion of power in Macedonia but was not secure in whatever territory she did control. Ceraunus, with the title and his victory, was in a much stronger position than she and her sons, but Cassandria and the boys themselves were important bargaining chips. If, however, they were effectively already besieged in Cassandria, there may never have been a safe way out of the city for both Arsinoë and her boys.

Until 281, Ptolemy Ceraunus had played a relatively minor part in Arsinoë's personal life, if a major one in the struggle of his branch of the Ptolemies against hers. Ceraunus must have been a kind of dynastic bogey man for Berenice and her children. Like Arsinoë and Ptolemy II, Ceraunus had grown up in the tense atmosphere of Soter's court with its rival royal mothers. His, however, was the most embittering experience. In his early years, Ceraunus expected to succeed his father and so did everyone else. Then, as he grew older, his mother's status began to decline and Berenice's rose. He and his mother must have started to worry about his future. Soter's treatment of him may also have begun to signal his preference for the future Ptolemy II. The final blow was Soter's choice in 385 to make the other brother coregent. At this point Ceraunus left Egypt, whether of his own choice or by compulsion. Appian (*Syr.* 62) says he left out of fear, implying that Ceraunus did not wait to find out what would happen if he stayed.

Ptolemy Ceraunus, as we have seen, traveled first to the court of Lysimachus where his full sister Lysandra was married to Agathocles, probably hoping for some kind of preferment and help to overturn his brother's rule in Egypt. He had no better place to go. The court in which he took up residence became just as tense as the one he had left. Lysandra and Agathocles, his presumed sponsors, were about to lose power and thus any ability to help him. The dynastic enemy was equally familiar: Arsinoë, daughter of Berenice. For Ceraunus as for Lysandra, it was déjà vu. Odds are Soter's two sets of children hated each other, the result of their strife-ridden childhoods. Indeed, Ceraunus' subsequent actions confirm that deduction. Conceivably Ceraunus had encouraged antagonism between the two camps, though there is no evidence that he did. Ceraunus had nothing to do with the death of Agathocles, as only Memnon (*FGrH* 434 F 5.7) mistakenly claimed (see chapter 2). After the execution of Agathocles, Ceraunus, Lysandra, and her children fled to Seleucus. His sister would hardly have accompanied him if he had just killed Agathocles, and Seleucus, who justified his campaign against Lysimachus as vengeance for the death of Agathocles, would certainly not have sheltered Agathocles' murderer.

Thus, Ceraunus' murder of Seleucus was probably the first of Ceraunus' sudden violent acts, not the second. He clearly violated *philia* (friendship) by killing Seleucus but did not shed kindred blood by doing so. Other

Macedonians had succeeded despite similar acts of violent betrayal.[14] The man Arsinoë hesitated to marry had demonstrated that he was a ruthless opportunist (like so many in the Macedonian elite), but also that he was a fairly competent general and politician (again, like many of the others).

Ptolemy Ceraunus' Motivation
in Proposing Marriage

Ceraunus' proposal happened in the context of his general program to consolidate his rule of Macedonia. He wanted Cassandria but more than that, he wanted to co-opt the legacy of Lysimachus by controlling his remaining sons and his widow, in effect neutralizing her by preventing his rivals from marrying her.[15] Royal women, widows or not, had an ability to stand in for and symbolize their dead male kin.[16] Arsinoë could personify continuity with the past regime.[17] Whether Arsinoë had any real control of areas outside Cassandria or not, she had symbolic capital, some remaining *philoi*, and another sort of capital—wealth—still at her disposal. Both sorts of capital could help establish legitimacy in a country in such disarray.

Although the usual succession dynamic was doubtless in play, generating fear in both sides, granted the short period of time between the wedding and the murders, Ceraunus probably planned the murders from the start, just as he had probably planned the elimination of Seleucus. This was a trick marriage all along; Justin's second version deserves far more credence than the first.[18] Some dynastic struggles, like Ceraunus' earlier losing effort, ended not in death but exile, but the Argeads had regularly eliminated other claimants to the throne soon after their accession, murdering them as often as exiling them, and some of these victims were even younger than Arsinoë's sons. Ceraunus had no reason to want another man's children as his heirs, even if they were half nephews. Though we know of no sons of his,[19] he was comparatively young; there was certainly time for sons to be born.

Reaction of Arsinoë's Son

If Arsinoë's two younger sons—still children—had any views on her remarriage, we do not know them. The real question is the view of Ptolemy, son of Lysimachus, about eighteen at the time of the projected marriage. Justin (24.2.10) claims that, despite Ceraunus' promises, the son of Lysimachus objected. He may simply have feared a trap or resented public acknowledgment by his mother that Ceraunus was king and therefore that he would have to wait. Young Ptolemy would surely have considered Ceraunus an enemy for some time, if not because of the history of intrigue in Alexandria, then surely because of the succession struggle at Lysimachus' court, when Ceraunus presumably favored Agathocles.[20] Since Ptolemy, son of Lysimachus, was not, apparently, around to be murdered with his brothers and we know of a subsequent career, he must either have departed before Ceraunus' entry into Cassandria and possibly before his mother's remarriage or refused to take part in the ceremony: in any event he was not available for slaughter.

Though Lysimachus had not involved his son Ptolemy in the battle against Seleucus, Justin's reference (24.2.4) to war between Arsinoë's sons and Ceraunus means that he, at least nominally, had been leading whatever military defense, perhaps just in Cassandria, perhaps in other places as well, that had been mounted. Granted subsequent events, young Ptolemy appears to have been a good judge of character and situation, but one should be careful not to exaggerate. His subsequent failure to overthrow Ceraunus demonstrates that his apparent belief that he and his family could succeed or survive in Macedonia without the marriage to Ceraunus was incorrect; he did not have a strong enough military base. His objections must mean that he considered the marriage unnecessary, but events indicate that he was wrong about that, though right about not trusting Ceraunus.

Arsinoë's Motivation

Ordinarily, widows, even Macedonian royal widows, returned to their birth families and their fathers or brothers arranged a new marriage, often very quickly. Some royal widows engaged in their own marriage arrangements, though not with great success, but in all the other cases known, their fathers and brothers were dead.[21] Arsinoë had living brothers, not only fickle Ceraunus but her full brother Ptolemy II, the powerful ruler of Egypt. When she fled Ephesus, she could have sought safety in Alexandria. Even if her sons were still in Macedonia at the time of Lysimachus' death, a number of months passed between Corupedium and the bloodbath in Cassandria. She had ample time to retrieve her sons and sail to Egypt, but she did not. Ptolemy II tended to find positions for his male kin, so she must have known that this was an alternative for herself and her sons. While Ceraunus had tried to make peace with Ptolemy II, nothing suggests that Ptolemy II had a role in his sister's marriage; this was not a marriage alliance between the two sons of Soter; the marriage was Arsinoë's decision, the alliance was between her and her half brother.

Only one possible reason explains why Arsinoë risked staying in Macedonia and marrying Ceraunus (her hesitation confirms that she knew the latter was a risk): she still hoped to secure rule and kingship for her sons. This was not solely a selfless goal: she wanted to rule for them and she desired the status that came from being the mother of the king and the power that often accrued to a royal widow with still young sons. Her decision resembles the one Olympias, mother of Alexander the Great, made in 317 when, years after the death of her son, she returned to Macedonia with her young grandson, hoping to make his position on the throne secure; she too hesitated because she knew the danger inherent in her effort but in the end rolled the dice and lost her life (and ultimately that of her grandson). Arsinoë lost her gamble too, though she did manage to live. Since it is impossible to know who supported whom or at least who said they would, we cannot really tell exactly what she expected to happen when she landed in Macedonia after her flight from Ephesus. Likely she hoped that her son Ptolemy would be able to build enough military support to defend against whichever of the generals turned up to capitalize on the fall of Lysimachus. The important thing is that she and her sons stayed.

Why did Arsinoë decide to marry Ceraunus? Whatever her view of Ceraunus' past character (Just.24.2.3, 6), Justin represents her as more fearful for her children than herself (24.2.7). This could simply be a projection into the past of future events, but it is true that Ceraunus had more reason to want them dead than he did her. Justin provides several reasons for her decision: she believed that she could protect her sons by marrying Ceraunus (24.2.7), that he would adopt her sons and recognize no others as his, that he would proclaim her "regina" (queen), and would not take another wife in an affront to her. These promises gave her hope and freed her from fear (24.2.9–10). After the marriage happened, Ptolemy put a diadem on Arsinoë's head in front of the army assembly and he did hail her as "regina." Having received this title,

Arsinoë was joyful because she thought that she had retrieved what she had lost with the death of Lysimachus (24.3.2–3).

In essence, Justin portrays her motivation as a combination of a desire to secure the succession for her sons and for her own position, a reasonable interpretation, one supported by the motivation and actions of other royal women. While her marriage signified that her son Ptolemy would have to wait to be king, she thought she had insured that he would be. Her actions imply that she considered their situation untenable without the marriage, not that she was indifferent to her sons' future.[22] What Justin has to say about the title promised to Arsinoë herself is probably not correct. *Regina* is a Latin word so the presumption has been that Ptolemy promised her that she would be *basilissa* and later proclaimed her such. His promise wrongly assumes that she was not, at the time of her remarriage, a *basilissa*: we do not know that widows lost the title and Ptolemaic royal daughters had the title, whether or not they married.[23] Even if it was not practice in Macedonia for widows and king's daughters to have the title, Arsinoë had only to return to her homeland where, with no risk, she could have it. What Arsinoë apparently wanted was the actuality of being both a king's wife (not widow) and the mother of his heirs. The diadem and proclamation in front of the army, otherwise unattested for Macedonia but known in other dynasties, is interesting and could be true.[24] The story of Ceraunus' public "crowning" of Arsinoë with a diadem—the first time a diadem is mentioned in terms of a Hellenistic royal woman—is more likely true, though the significance of the female diadem remains as ambiguous as the title *basilissa*.[25]

Perhaps the most interesting of the promises Ceraunus made was that he would not take another wife, insulting her by doing it. Philip II and Alexander the Great and most of the Successors had done exactly that. No one knew better than the children of Soter the pain and trouble royal polygamy could cause. Arsinoë had moved from one contested succession in the court of her birth into another in the court of her husband. The promise that there would be no more wives and no other recognized sons had great appeal, and Ceraunus must have known it would. He had been a witness to the struggle in Lysimachia as well as the one in Alexandria. This promise could have been based on personal knowledge of his half sister, although at the end of the fourth century and early third, kings had begun to move away from polygamy, often in the direction of some sort of endogamy (see chapter 4).

Up until now, my discussion of motivation for the marriage has ignored the fact that this was a marriage of half siblings. First-cousin marriages were quite common in the Graeco-Macedonian world and uncle/niece marriages were well known and not considered incestuous (e.g., the marriage of Antigonus Gonatas to Phila, his sister's daughter). Apparently Athenians and some other Greek peoples did permit the marriage of half siblings, if the shared parent were the father, not the mother. Possibly the Spartans took the opposite point of view and allowed only the marriage of siblings with the same mother. Half-sibling marriages seem to have been rare and may have generated some popular discomfort.[26] We know of two possible half- sibling Macedonian marriages, but even these are hardly certainties.[27] The marriage of Ceraunus and Arsinoë was unusual at the time, but seems more so because her next marriage would be to her full sibling and sibling marriage would then become the ideal and often the reality for the Ptolemaic dynasty. We will discuss the possible role of Egyptian precedent in the marriage of Arsinoë and Ptolemy II later (see chapter 4). For the moment, it is enough to say that even if either Arsinoë or Ceraunus believed that the Egyptians, at least the royal dynasties, practiced brother-sister marriage, it is unlikely that the "Egyptian model" had anything to do with her marriage to Ceraunus. On the other hand, a half-sibling marriage among the Seleucids may have taken place the late 280s, likely in the period when Ceraunus was at court. If it really was a half-sibling marriage, this precedent could have inspired Ceraunus.[28]

In one sense, judging by the narrative of Justin, both parties in this marriage conducted themselves as though the fact that they were half siblings was irrelevant to the decision to marry. Ceraunus wanted both Arsinoë's territory and her sons under his control. It mattered more that they were Lysimachus' sons than that they were his half nephews. Even if one concludes that—if, of course, he did not plan to murder Arsinoë's sons from the start—he hoped to conciliate Ptolemy II by this marriage, such a goal was no different than his desire to make peace with Pyrrhus or Antiochus.

Similarly, Arsinoë's concerns, so far as we can tell, were for the succession of her sons and for her own status as a royal wife. Nothing suggests that Ptolemy's sibling status affected her concerns about the marriage; she was worried about what he would do, not who he was. She had to deal with him because of the base he had established in Macedonia; his blood relationship to her was irrelevant. Justin's diction consistently singles out the fact that the parties involved were brother and sister (17.2.7, 24.2.1, 2, 3, 6, 10, 24.3.2), but he stresses the relationship—not because he disapproves, but rather to imply that Ceraunus' actions were especially horrific because they were done to a woman who was not only his wife but his sister. In this sense Justin might be said to share the sensibility of the two half siblings as he has described it; their relationship is of relevance only because it makes what happens worse, not because it is bad or even ill-omened, in and of itself. This is a point we will want to recall when we discuss reaction to Arsinoë's marriage to her full brother.

Despite the apparent matter-of-factness with which both participants and Justin treat the half-sibling marriage, there was probably an element, perhaps a very strong element, of the irrational and emotional in the construction of the marriage and particularly in its violent end. The marriage, had it been lasting and relatively happy, possessed the potential to heal the rift between the two branches of the Ptolemaic dynasty, a rift that had caused pain and suffering to these same people. Each one's life had been profoundly affected, for decades, by the fear and paranoia the dynastic struggle had generated. Moreover, their marriage could have been a kind of reversal, if not a literal one, of the polygamy that had caused all the trouble. Clearly, the opposite of polygamy is monogamy, not sibling marriage. Still, in the sense that their marriage would not only combine the two rival branches but, with Ceraunus' promise to make Arsinoë's sons his, unify her own smaller family by creating an artificial nuclear unit, it was the opposite of the life each had lived in various courts. These two cannot have known each other well as children, though they must have been close in age. Boys and girls might have had comparatively little contact after early childhood in any household, let alone a large court, and the rivalry of their mothers and the court factions that formed around that rivalry would have kept them apart. Still, they may both have suffered from nostalgia for Alexandria and what had been lost and this marriage appeared to ease that need. For Ceraunus, if he planned to kill the sons of Lysimachus from the start, then this peculiarly unifying marriage was a fantasy concocted to satisfy needs he knew his sister to have. Imagining this sort of happy ending, in terms of the specific promises he made, implies that he, in an odd way, shared the same fantasy, but unlike Arsinoë, recognized that it was one. It is not likely a coincidence that the same woman married a half brother and then a full brother. Despite the sad and inauspicious end of the Arsinoë-Ceraunus marriage, this marriage proved a suggestive precedent for the second.

We shall consider in the next chapter whether it was a precedent that first struck Ptolemy II or Arsinoë.

The wedding happened in the winter of 281/80, perhaps at Pella or Dion or, most likely, Aegae,[29] and the murders of Lysimachus' sons presumably happened soon after, perhaps within a matter of weeks.[30] Let me turn to the specifics of these events (Just. 24.3.1–10). After the ceremonies of the wedding and diadem, Arsinoë organizes an urban festival at Cassandria for him, and sends her two younger sons to meet him outside the city. Ceraunus greets them affectionately but, once inside, seizes the citadel and orders the deaths of the two boys. They race to their mother, who offers herself in their place, but the boys are slaughtered in her arms,[31] she is not allowed to bury them, and in torn clothes and disheveled hair, she is driven from the city, attended by two slaves. Arsinoë retreats to Samothrace, lamenting that she has not been allowed to die with her sons.

This gothic account does not inspire confidence in the modern reader. Nonetheless, the dramatic coloring in the narrative may not be all or even largely the work of Justin (or Trogus). It is not simply the kind of "tragic history" popular in the fourth and third century BCE. Arsinoë herself shaped these events, became a kind of "author" of them, as did Ceraunus. One could attribute these details to Justin's sensationalizing and slough them off as borrowings from tragic plots, but that would probably be wrong. Recent work has dealt with the staging of monarchy, the ways in which rulers employed images, rituals, costume, and processions to legitimize, stabilize, and empower themselves and their dynasties. Theaters were often used for assemblies as well as for dramatic performances, obscuring the distinction between political and theatrical events.

Philip II had transformed royal weddings into public events, festivals celebrating the gods and monarchy.[32] In the period after Philip, this trend became increasingly important, so much so that royal marriage functioned as legitimizing devices for dynasties.[33] Arsinoë's marriage to Ceraunus is the first of two "trick" marriages in third-century Macedonian history, marriages in which royal women handed over control of citadels in return for a marriage with public ceremony, only to lose the citadel and the marriage. The public royal marriage had become a symbol of royal legitimacy, but as these two incidents demonstrate, one that could easily be eliminated.[34]

Arsinoë first insisted on such a public wedding and then fabricated another public ceremony and festival (the temples, houses, and altars were decorated, sacrifices made, and her sons—ironically—garlanded) to welcome her new husband to Cassandria (Just. 24.3.4–5). Apparently she intended the second ceremony to force Ceraunus to act out his promised recognition of them as heirs, by greeting them outside the city gates. Ceraunus, however, was working with a different script, one in which vengeance played an important role, as his refusal to allow the burial of Arsinoë's sons indicates, as well as his disposition of Cassandria to his mother after Arsinoë's departure (see below). He staged these murders in the context of a festival, just as Philip II's assassin staged his regicide at a wedding festival. Arsinoë, in turn, had to play, not simply be, the grieving mother. Homer and tragedy provided plotlines. Arsinoë's departure from Cassandria resembles the end of *Oedipus Tyrannos*, when Oedipus flees Thebes, having lost all his royal power and trappings. Ceraunus' refusal to allow the mother to bury her sons recalls Creon's refusal to allow the burial of Polyneices.

The Macedonian elite consciously imitated the world of Homer in various ways—for instance, in their burial habits—and may actually have preserved (or re-created) customs found in Homer but not in the classical and early Hellenistic era farther south. Alexander's imitation of Achilles is a famous example.[35] Refusal to bury the enemy dead, however, was something that really happened. Cassander, for instance, refused burial to Olympias (Diod. 17.118.2). Such treatment of a corpse conveyed the notion that those so treated lacked legitimacy and possibly had committed treason. As in Homer, it could be an act of vengeance and an attempt to wipe out the memory and repute of the dead.[36] One often feels that many of the major figures in Macedonian history had Homer and Greek tragedy in their heads, available as life script when necessary.[37] The staginess of some scenes—the deaths of Adea Eurydice, Alexander the Great's niece (Diod. 19.11.5–9), or Olympias (Just. 14.6.9–12)—is palpable but that does not necessarily mean they didn't happen more or less as reported.

Ceraunus extracted vengeance for his disappointed youth and a kingdom lost; doubtless he would have preferred to extract it from Ptolemy Philadelphus himself but Arsinoë was the next best thing. He could not take vengeance on Berenice, but he could and did install his own long-suffering mother, Eurydice, in charge of Cassandria, the city that had belonged to Berenice's daughter, making a point by the identity of Arsinoë's replacement.[38] Ceraunus must have known that, ultimately, Arsinoë would to go back to Alexandria. He may have relished the thought that he was sending her back to her brother in this fashion. That may be why he didn't kill her too. (Possibly he thought that killing her might cause him more trouble with the Macedonian populace than it was worth.)[39]

Circumstance forced Arsinoë to be a tragic queen, so she played one, with appropriate costume. Hecuba, who lost her husband and her many sons to war and was driven from her city immediately springs to mind as a possible example.[40] Arsinoë's experience also recalls that of Andromache, who saw one son killed and another young son threatened with death by those taking vengeance. Andromache's reversal of fortune ("Andromache, in the old days oh so lucky / But sunk in misery now, if anyone is." Eur. *Andr.*) resembles that of Arsinoë. She, doubtless recalling that her remaining son waited, offstage so to speak, but ready for a return appearance, may have remembered that, after all the pain, Andromache experienced yet another reversal of fortune, ending her days in a new kingdom, mother to a new dynasty. In fact, Arsinoë would experience another and more positive reversal too, with the result that she ended her days much as Andromache supposedly did. Reversals of fortune, a commonplace of tragic plots, were a constant actuality in the era of the Successors, something that may help to explain the fondness of the Macedonian elite for tragedy.

Even Arsinoë's refuge in Samothrace had a scripted aspect. Earlier Macedonian rulers had patronized the sanctuary on Samothrace, and in fact, both Lysimachus and Ptolemy II made offerings there. As we have seen (see chapter 2), Arsinoë, almost certainly while she was married to Lysimachus, paid for the rotunda as an offering to the Great Gods at Samothrace. The Samothracians had given Lysimachus divine honors, apparently because of his assistance at a critical time.[41] One should probably picture Arsinoë arriving at Samothrace as a suppliant, a mother whose sons lay unburied, like the women in Euripides' *Suppliant Women*. Others also sought asylum at the shrine. Arsinoë, already a great patron of the shrine, was almost certainly an initiate,[42] and of course, her brother was a rich and powerful king. Moreover, at this time, Samothrace, conveniently, was probably independent of Macedonia proper.[43] Arsinoë had found an ideal safe haven, one from which she could continue to observe Macedonian affairs, including the actions of her surviving son, Ptolemy son of Lysimachus.

Granted that she and her son had argued at the time of her proposed marriage, that he had apparently left her court, and that his point of view was vindicated (though not entirely) by Ceraunus' murder of the younger sons of Lysimachus, mother and son may have become estranged. We do not know that they were ever in personal contact again, though that is hardly telling in the light of the sparse evidence.

Even if they were estranged, Arsinoë might well have continued her advocacy for her son and his career. While she could have sojourned in Samothrace only briefly, merely long enough to arrange for her return to Egypt (perhaps as early as 280/79),[44] she more likely delayed her departure for several years. Had she left Macedonia soon after the deaths of her younger sons, it would mean, in effect, that she had given up on any hope that her son could be king of Macedonia. The son of Lysimachus and an Illyrian named Monunius fought a war against Ceraunus (Trogus *Prol.* 24), a war that probably began in spring of 280, just a few months after the murder of Ptolemy's brothers, and lasted at least until the Gallic invasion in early 279.[45] If, however, the Ptolemy mentioned by some sources as active in Macedonia after the death of Ceraunus (Diod. 22.4; Porphyry *FGrH* 260 F 3.10–11) is the son of Lysimachus, Arsinoë's son continued to attempt to gain the throne of Macedonia until Antigonus Gonatas established himself in 277/76, when the son of Lysimachus' efforts had clearly failed. His mother may have waited at Samothrace until that point. Despite their apparent disagreement over her marriage, she likely hoped that her son could succeed (the goal that had brought her back to Macedonia), and so would have stayed as long as that remained a possibility.[46] Indeed, she might have seen it as a betrayal of the memory of her younger sons to give up hope. If so, she lingered on till 277/76 (see chapter 4 on the subsequent career of Ptolemy, son of Lysimachus).

Justin relishes the fact that Ceraunus' dastardly deeds did not long go unpunished. An invading Gaulic army defeated and slaughtered Ceraunus, a sign of divine vengeance for his crimes (Just. 24.3.10). The death of Lysimachus and the subsequent disarray in Macedonia had helped to trigger the invasion.[47] Justin portrays Ceraunus as a foolhardy and arrogant tyrant who takes unnecessary risks, underestimates the gravity of the threat, refuses diplomatic solutions, only to fall in battle, a massacre, and have his head cut off and paraded around by the victors on a lance (24.4.1–5.11). Ceraunus had previously shown himself a competent general, but he does not seem to have had sufficient forces or experience with their method of fighting to do well against the Gauls. Antigonus Gonatas, by defeating the Gauls in a battle at Lysimachia, managed to be recognized as king of the Macedonians, at long last establishing a firm base for the Antigonid dynasty. Victories against Gauls came to be a standard part of Hellenistic royal propaganda and Gonatas' propaganda may have exaggerated his former rival's mistakes, the more to glorify his own victory.[48]

The tragic episode of the murder of Arsinoë's sons hardly demonstrates that she possessed tremendous political acumen, particularly granted that her oldest son (even if motivated partly by anger that his mother did not apparently believe that he would be able to be recognized as king on his own) did not trust in the marriage to Ceraunus. She was not a political genius and her miscalculation was, in this case, disastrous.[49] That said, one must also recall that, had she refused Ceraunus' offer, she would have had only two other options. She and her sons could, perhaps, have fled to Alexandria (assuming that they could have escaped from Macedonia or that Ceraunus would have allowed them to leave) where she could hope that her brother would do something for them, but this would have meant that she conceded, for practical purposes the loss of any chance for kingship for any of them. Alternatively, she and her sons and their apparently small force could have continued to try to hold Cassandria under what was demonstrably a much larger force led by an experienced general. That option could certainly have ended in all their deaths, had she pursued it. Arsinoë consistently chose to risk her own life and those of her sons in hope of securing for them their father's throne. Rather than retreating to Alexandria, she played some part in the succession struggle with Agathocles; after her husband's defeat and death, rather than departing for her brother's court, she took the risky course of returning to Macedonia to pursue the possibility of rule for her sons, and when confronting the fact of Ceraunus' recognition as king, she chose to take the risk of marrying him in hopes of keeping the throne open to her sons, once more refusing to retreat to Alexandria. Arsinoë repeatedly chose peril in pursuit of political power for her sons (and herself); Alexandria proved the rejected option, the road not taken. Only when Arsinoë had no other options left did she take ship for the city of her birth, and even then, if I am right, only after a considerable passage of time. Had Arsinoë any expectation at all of her future marriage and the unusual position it would bring her, she might have acted differently.

CHAPTER FOUR

Arsinoë's Return to Egypt and Marriage to Ptolemy II

279–275

NO ONE WOULD have predicted a glorious future for Arsinoë upon her return to Egypt. She had treated going home as the least-attractive alternative open to her until no other remained. Perhaps she finally chose to return to Egypt herself, perhaps her brother summoned her. Some negotiation may have preceded the decision.[1] Everyone, including Arsinoë, probably expected that she would end her days in royal obscurity, like so many other royal women (for instance, Agathocles' widow Lysandra) whose factions had lost out.

It must have seemed quite literally true to her that you can never go home again. Alexandria would have been nearly unrecognizable. Many of the great Ptolemaic foundations were not even begun at the time of her departure; now they were completed or well on their way to completion. The contrast between Alexandria and Lysimachia on her return would have seemed far more dramatic than it would have when she was a new bride. Her family, as it had existed during her girlhood, was gone: her father was dead. When Arsinoë had left home, her brother was a small boy, but now he was a powerful king, the father of several children. If Arsinoë arrived after 279, as suggested, then her mother Berenice was already dead[2] and probably deified,[3] though Philotera, her only full sister, was likely still alive (see chapter 5). Arsinoë's return may not have felt like a homecoming because "home" had altered in so many respects; what had been familiar was now alien.

The death of Lysimachus in battle, the slaughter of her two younger boys, a possible estrangement from her surviving son, his failure to regain his father's throne, and the degradation and pain Ceraunus had inflicted on her would doubtless have preoccupied Arsinoë herself, even though by now she knew that Ceraunus, in turn, had died a humiliating death. It would have been natural for her to have second guessed her decisions, blamed herself, blamed her son. She could have been bitter. Surely the contrast between her expectations at the time she had first left home and her apparent prospects upon her return must have seemed sharp.

Instead of living out these gloomy prospects, Arsinoë II experienced yet another dramatic reversal of fortune, one that once more raised her to a position of influence. The dating problems that bedevil this last period of Arsinoë's life obscure how quickly this change came about, in what context, and to some degree, why. She returned to Egypt; her brother exiled his first wife (unfortunately also named Arsinoë and hereafter always referred to as Arsinoë I); he later married his sister. This much we know. Depending on which dates one chooses for this series of events, Arsinoë I could have fallen from favor even before the Arsinoë II's return to Egypt; a gap of a number of years could have occurred between Arsinoë II's return and the fall of Arsinoë I and Arsinoë II's final marriage, or alternatively, Arsinoë II's marriage could have followed soon after her return and the disgrace of Arsinoë I. In some calculations, her last marriage was nearly twice as long as it is in the estimation of others. Arsinoë II, we should recall, could have returned to Egypt as early as 279 or as late as 276/75.[4]

Ptolemy II

Ptolemy II (who coruled with Ptolemy I from 285 till 283/82 and ruled on his own from then till 246) implemented aspects of Ptolemaic monarchy initially conceived by his father and invented many others.[5] Despite this, scholars have often portrayed him as indolent, luxury loving, and passive, the first unwarlike Macedonian king.[6] He did have a remarkable number of mistresses, even for a king (see chapter 6), and he did initiate the first brother-sister marriage of the dynasty (something people used to see as proof of his sensuous and lax ways). This second Ptolemy made his dynasty a byword for luxury and extravagance, possibly a personal preference, but also a metaphor for the power and stability of his family's rule. He did not, so far as we know, personally lead his troops in battle, but he was involved in a number of wars or military actions, employed many troops (Theoc. *Id.* 14.59), and the Alexandrian poet Theocritus pictured both him and his father as spearmen (Theoc. *Id.* 17.56–57, 103).[7] Ptolemy II experienced neither tremendous success nor great military failure in his various wars, but he kept Egypt safe from invasion. In fact, Ptolemaic holdings grew more extensive during his long reign. We do not know why Ptolemy II did not participate in warfare directly, but physical illness was not likely a factor.[8] In terms of policy, he and the rest of his clan tended to support "Greek freedom" outside of Egypt, in the cities of the Greek mainland, primarily as a way of opposing the Antigonids, who constituted the main challenge to Ptolemaic naval ambitions. While only court poets could picture a warlike Ptolemy II, his long-term foreign policy was cautiously imperialistic; he was not willing to risk Egyptian resources in any fundamental way, but he consistently and successfully attempted to extend his realms and to recover lost territory.

Ptolemy II proved most inventive and successful in terms of religion and the development of dynastic cult: he created the first dynastic divine pair, the *theoi soteres* (the savior gods), his own parents, and he would build on that initial invention, portraying the dynasty as a series of linked pairs. He was also the first Ptolemy to engage in massive temple building, a critical element in Egyptian kingship that demonstrated that ruler was maintaining good order and the favor of the gods.[9]

Ptolemy II completed his father's plans for the Library and Museum. We consider his reign, in good part because of his cultural patronage, the golden age of Hellenistic literature. Many poems from his reign reflect, directly and indirectly, events of his reign and visions of his power. For instance, Callimachus may have composed his first hymn in celebration of Ptolemy I's choice of Ptolemy II as coruler, coinciding with the festival of *basileia* (kingship) and may even, very discreetly, refer to his struggle and victory over Ceraunus.[10]

Arsinoë I

Arsinoë I, daughter of Lysimachus (Paus. 1.7.3; Schol Theoc. 17.128), married Ptolemy II around the time he began to coreign with his father, so between 285 and 282.[11] Lysimachus and Ptolemy Soter, old comrades and longtime allies, arranged this marriage. A poet, possibly Posidippus, may have written an *epithalmium* (marriage hymn) in honor of the bride, although the Arsinoë so honored could have been Arsinoë II.[12] If Arsinoë I married in her mid to late teens, more or less the norm, then she would have been born around the turn of the third century or soon after.

No ancient source names Arsinoë I's mother and Lysimachus (see chapter 2) married a number of women. Granted that Arsinoë I's marriage was a major alliance, we can probably discount minor wives and mistresses as Arsinoë I's mother.[13] Nicaea, daughter of Antipater, seems most likely to have been Arsinoë I's mother; she might have died in childbirth having her.[14] Granted the odds that Nicaea was dead by the time Arsinoë II married Lysimachus, this could easily mean that Arsinoë II brought up Arsinoë I. If so, granted Arsinoë II's role, whether direct or indirect, in the death of Agathocles, likely Arsinoë I's full brother, the two women, even if earlier friendly, are unlikely to have remained so.

With the death of her father Lysimachus in 281, Arsinoë I no longer had any close male kin, no family to defend her interests or about whose views her husband might worry.[15] Still, she was the only woman, wife or mistress, we are certain had children by Ptolemy II;[16] they had three: Ptolemy, Lysimachus, and Berenice (Schol. Theoc. 17.128). Nonetheless, Ptolemy II concluded that his wife was conspiring against him, along with two of her *philoi*, Amyntas and Chrysippus, the Rhodian doctor; he had the two men executed and dispatched Arsinoë I to internal exile at Coptos, in the Theban region (Schol Theoc. 17.128). The date of the alleged plot of Arsinoë I is unknown, but Arsinoë I's fall from grace almost certainly happened after Lysimachus' death made her vulnerable.[17]

Could Arsinoë I actually have been plotting against Ptolemy II, presumably in order to put her son on the throne? She might have been, particularly if she had begun to fear that her husband was about to repudiate her.[18] Fear was the operating dynamic in succession intrigue. The future Ptolemy III would, however, have been very young throughout the period in which these events could have transpired, even assuming that he was born soon after his parents' marriage.[19] Granted his youth, he was not a particularly likely candidate to supplant his father immediately. Later in the dynasty, when the prestige of royal women, mostly royal sisters, had increased, a mother and young son might consider corule, but there was as yet no precedent, and Arsinoë I was not a Ptolemy.[20] At most, such a plot would have constituted an act of desperation, one conceived by a woman who realized that her future had suddenly turned grim. More likely Ptolemy II simply chose this charge as a way to get Arsinoë I out of court. True, he eliminated her two *philoi* on the grounds that they were part of her conspiracy, but this need mean nothing more than that the king wanted to remove her important supporters at the same time.

Our only source on Arsinoë I's exile attributes the decision to the king and makes no mention of his sister.[21] Despite this, granted the picture constructed in the sources about Arsinoë II's supposed scheming at the court of Lysimachus,[22] many have assumed that Arsinoë II engineered the exile of Arsinoë I. Arsinoë II benefited by her brother's rejection of his first wife and, based on past actions, was capable of plotting against her, but there is no evidence that she did. In life, people often benefit from actions initiated by others. Whereas we know that Arsinoë II was present at the time of Agathocles' death and several ancient sources claimed that she had some sort of role in his fall, we do not even know that she had returned to Egypt at the time Arsinoë I shuffled off the dynastic stage, and no ancient source accuses Arsinoë II of complicity in her predecessor's fall. Granted the hostile treatment of her on the earlier occasion, the absence of charges that Arsinoë II schemed to bring about the elimination of Arsinoë I is significant. There is no good evidence that Arsinoë II had anything to do with the rejection of Arsinoë I. At most, if she were already on the scene, Arsinoë II could only have influenced Ptolemy II's decision, but it was his to make.

Moreover, despite all the chronological uncertainties, it seems probable that some period of time separated the departure of Arsinoë I and the marriage of Arsinoë II,[23] that Ptolemy II spent a length of time as an unmarried monarch,[24] and that Arsinoë I's downfall may well have occurred before Arsinoë II returned to Egypt.[25] I have already suggested that Arsinoë II probably did not reappear in Egypt until at least 276. Even if one assumes a much earlier return, years could still have passed between Arsinoë II's return and the downfall of Arsinoë I, and more years yet could have passed between Arsinoë's exile and Ptolemy II's marriage to his sister.

What was the motivation for Ptolemy II's decision to exile Arsinoë I? He may really have believed, rightly or wrongly, she was plotting against him. Even if Arsinoë II had not yet arrived, others at court could have encouraged this belief in hope of advantage to themselves. Ptolemy II may have wanted to be free of his wife so that he could marry again; brutally put, she had given him the children he needed but no longer had useful political connections. Alternatively, perhaps he had already decided to marry Arsinoë II and so needed to see the back of Arsinoë I. All things considered, Ptolemy II's rejection of Arsinoë I, like his marriage to Arsinoë II, seems part of a considered policy focused on the nature and future of Ptolemaic monarchy rather than some personal whim, but it may have been a policy worked out over several years, not one arrived at overnight.

Two points remain. First, Ptolemy II did not kill Arsinoë I; he simply sentenced her to internal exile. Macedonian court intrigue more consistently involved violence toward males rather than females, but the charge that she was working against her husband could have justified execution or, at the very least, foreign exile; other royal women were executed[26] or, like Eurydice mother of Ceraunus, went into foreign exile. Ptolemy II almost certainly spared Arsinoë I because of her children.[27] By not eliminating Arsinoë I, Ptolemy II kept his options for a successor open. It would have been hard to work with an heir whose mother he had killed. We know that Arsinoë II adopted his children by Arsinoë I. Many assume that the adoption of his children was posthumous, but no evidence confirms this.[28] It seems more likely that an agreement to that effect was made at the time of her marriage (though perhaps not formalized until after her death); in effect, it is the mirror image of the promise Arsinoë herself extracted from Ceraunus. Second, Arsinoë I's status is unclear. An inscription from Coptos, the location of her exile, has been read as evidence that Arsinoë I remained there, kept her title, and maintained an extensive household there, but it could refer to Arsinoë II, not Arsinoë I.[29] Still, in the absence of evidence to the contrary, we should assume that Arsinoë I lived out her days in the Coptos, perhaps more "retired" than "repudiated."[30]

The Marriage of Ptolemy II and Arsinoë II

Ptolemy II astonished the world by marrying his full sister. The marriage had many consequences and ramifications.[31] The historical context of this royal decision is therefore critical, and yet we do not know its context in any absolute sense. Inscriptional evidence demonstrates that the brother and sister were married by 273/72.[32] If the suggested "late" return of Arsinoë II is accepted, then the period of the marriage is further limited to 276–273/72, most likely happening ca. 275.[33] The later one dates their marriage, the closer becomes its relationship to the creation of cult of the *theoi adelphoi* (the sibling gods; see chapter 5).

Ptolemy II's marriage to Arsinoë II was the first full sibling marriage of the Ptolemaic dynasty,[34] but within another generation close-kin marriage (usually sibling marriage) came to characterize dynastic ideal and later practice.[35] Generations of scholars have labored over the reasons for their marriage.[36] Of course, the reasons for this first marriage were not necessarily identical to those for the subsequent brother-sister marriages.[37]

Before we can turn to the specific motivation and context of this marriage, we must reflect on Greek and Egyptian practices and attitudes toward the marriage of siblings. Since the Ptolemies ruled people of Hellenic culture and people of Egyptian culture, and maintained a dual or double monarchy, we must consider this problem in terms of both cultures, keeping in mind that sibling marriage, cross culturally and worldwide, has been uncommon, except among narrow elites like royal families. In both Egyptian and Hellenic cultures, it proves easier to determine previous practice than to assess attitudes toward such marriages.

Ordinary Egyptians in the pharaonic and Ptolemaic period did not marry their full siblings,[38] although no evidence suggests a specific Egyptian prohibition or moral horror about such marriages.[39] Some members of pharaonic dynasties, certainly by the eighteenth dynasty if not earlier, married their siblings, occasionally their full siblings.[40] DNA evidence may now confirm this.[41] Pharaohs often embodied various gods and these brother-sister marriages, reminiscent of the marriage of Isis and Osiris, emphasized the distinctive and divine natures of rulers.[42] Marrying a royal sister also avoided entangling alliances with elite families, keeping them from becoming plausible claimants to the throne, and generally intensified royal authority, particularly in periods of "formation or restoration."[43] Royal sibling marriage, however, was not the pharaonic norm, nor essential to being a king.

Nothing indicates that Egyptians reacted negatively to the first Ptolemaic sibling marriage and Ptolemy II used and reinvented Egyptian tradition to build acceptance of the marriage. While the cult of Osiris had long played an important role in Egyptian religious life and pharaonic kingship, the cult of his sister-wife, Isis, did not become prominent until the Ptolemaic era. Many Ptolemaic royal women were associated in cult with Isis, particularly Arsinoë II.[44] Thus divine brother-sister marriage and royal brother-sister marriage in the Ptolemaic period appear to be connected, though whether and in what direction the relationship is causative or not remains problematic. Ptolemy II's Egyptian subjects likely found the marriage more acceptable than did Greeks because of the Osiris/Isis parallel and the pharaonic tradition co-opted by the Ptolemies that understood the kings (and royal wives) as embodiments of various deities. If Ptolemaic-era Egyptians knew, as the politically powerful priestly class probably did, that some of the old pharaohs had married sisters, this too would have made them see the sibling marriage more favorably.

In the Greek world, full-sibling marriage was unknown among mortals and, as we have seen, half-sibling marriages were rare (virtually all known examples involved members of royal or elite families). Arsinoë's marriage to Ceraunus remains the only certain Macedonian example. The second-century CE author Pausanias (1.7.1) asserts that the marriage of the full siblings Ptolemy II and Arsinoë II was something never customary with the Macedonians.[45] Greeks (unlike the Romans) had no single term that described the marriage or sexual relationship of people understood to be too closely related.[46] Still, it is not simply that the practice was unknown, but that the marriage of full siblings repelled many Greeks, if not so much as did the marriage of fathers and daughters or mothers and sons; when a Greek writer offers an example of inappropriate sexual relations, it tends to deal with parent-child intercourse (e.g., Pl. *Rep.* 571).[47] Diction used to describe sibling relationships suggests an understanding of them as unlawful or somehow unholy.[48] Greek morality stressed restraint, the famous *sophrosune*, and so understood sexual relationships considered inappropriate as wrong, among other reasons, because they were excessive.[49] On the other hand, Zeus and Hera were sibling spouses.

Although views of brother-sister marriage expressed in the Greek world were generally negative in a way that lacks parallel in Egyptian evidence, we should be careful to recognize that reaction was not as negative as in the modern Western world nor as absolute (thus the occasional half-sibling marriage), and even objections that seem based in morality, related to a different moral code than any familiar to us today. We will, for instance, encounter dirty jokes about sibling marriage. Whatever anyone might say about marriages or relationships generally considered incestuous now, no one would likely understand them as excessive nor would anyone who disapproved make dirty jokes about them. In short, Greek views tended to the negative about sibling marriage but their disapproval was different than that of modern Westerners.

Many have insisted that the marriage of Ptolemy II and his sister Arsinoë II was hugely unpopular with Greeks, including Greeks in Egypt. In fact, little evidence (two passages in Plutarch and one in Athenaeus) supports this view and most of it comes from centuries later, when such marriages happened among ordinary Egyptians, but the Ptolemaic dynasty was long gone.[50] The first Plutarch passage (736e–f) is part of a conversation set in Athens on the theme of well-timed remarks and the handiness of being able to make them. The conversants immediately think of an example of their theme: the rhapsode (performer of epic poetry) who attended Ptolemy II's wedding to his sister and began his recitation with a quotation from the *Iliad* (18.356), "Then Zeus called to Hera, his sister and wife." Plutarch editorializes that Ptolemy's action was considered *athemis* (unlawful, contrary to divine law) and *allokotos* (unusual, strange in a bad way).[51] Thus the passage takes a critical view of the marriage, but that view is not Plutarch's main point, but rather the cleverness of the rhapsode. Moreover, the contemporary rhapsode is not the one who is critical but Plutarch himself who, like Pausanias, lived in the second century CE.

Both the second Plutarch passage and that of Athenaeus deal with the views of Sotades, a poet who was active in the reign of Ptolemy II Philadelphus. The Plutarch passage (11a) happens in the context of a discussion of the virtues of keeping one's mouth shut. Plutarch refers to Sotades' joke about the marriage—that Ptolemy Philadelphus had done something "unholy" in spurring that mare—commenting that Sotades suffered in a prison a long time for making other men laugh by his untimely chatter. The point of Plutarch's story is not the horror of incest but the foolishness of talking first and thinking second. The Athenaeus passage describes Sotades as a specialist in sodomy jokes. Athenaeus (621a) speaks of Sotades' "tactless frankness," notes that he attacked other princes, not just Ptolemy II, provides several examples of Sotades' witticisms, including his notorious comment on the royal sibling marriage that Ptolemy had "put his prick into an unholy hole,"[52] and Athenaeus editorializes that Sotades got what he deserved (death).[53] Sotades' famous remark may not be directly connected to his death,[54] may not have been seriously intended (particularly if he uttered it in the context of a drinking party),[55] and certainly does not demonstrate that he spoke for some general group.[56] Both Plutarch and Athenaeus clearly disapprove of his remarks.

If Sotades did not speak for Greek popular opinion, then what was the reaction of the Hellenic audience? It was colored by an important misperception. Curiously, Graeco-Roman writers believed, incorrectly, as we have discovered, that sibling marriage was a traditional, general Egyptian practice,[57] but nothing indicates recognition by these authors that the practice in Egypt, to the degree it previously existed, was limited to ruling families. Thus classical authors tended to understand the marriage of Ptolemy II and Arsinoë II as following Egyptian tradition but not Egyptian royal tradition.[58] Ptolemy II himself (likely via Manetho and others), perhaps hoping to explain or justify his marriage by ascribing it to Egyptian tradition or law, may be the source of this interesting misunderstanding.[59] Possibly the king actually decreed permission for sibling marriages.[60] Perhaps because of this misunderstanding and for a number of other reasons as well, in the very late Ptolemaic and in the Roman period, full sibling marriage did, for a century or two, become common in Egypt.[61]

Thus, available evidence implies that Ptolemy Philadelphus' Hellenic audience in Egypt would have been more uncomfortable with his second marriage than his Egyptian subjects,[62] but the absence of objections other than those of Sotades, the Greek belief that the marriage imitated Egyptian custom, the tremendous success of the subsequent cult of Arsinoë II, the many subsequent close kin marriages of the Ptolemies,[63] and the fact that their marriage habits were actually occasionally imitated by the Seleucids, all suggest that Greeks and Macedonians in Egypt and elsewhere were not terribly disturbed by the marriage and that whatever disapproval was initially felt softened over time. In a world where some Greek communities accepted half-sibling marriage (however rare it was in practice), it is difficult to argue that deep resentment greeted the full sibling marriage of atypical royals whose entire way of life was remote from that of ordinary Greeks,[64] nearly as remote as Zeus and Hera themselves, whose marriage no one criticized.

What then was the motivation for the marriage? Needless to say, neither participant published some sort of public declaration or explanation. We can only judge by the actions, past and present, of the bridal pair. Let us begin with Ptolemy II. The general purpose of ancient marriage was to produce children, but the production of heirs was not likely the purpose of this marriage, certainly not Ptolemy II's. The king already had children, including several sons, and while Arsinoë probably could still bear children, she was likely toward the end of that period of her life—perhaps about forty—and therefore less fertile.[65] Ptolemy did not marry her in order to produce more sons because he must have known that it was unlikely she would be able to do so. Indeed, in order to avoid the kind of succession strife seen in his father's reign, he may never have intended to have children by Arsinoë II.[66] We know that Arsinoë adopted Ptolemy II's children,[67] quite possibly at the time of her marriage as I have suggested.

Ancient writers, as we have seen, typically asserted that rulers married out of sexual passion *(eros)* despite the fact that virtually all marriages were arranged and those of rulers arranged for political purposes. Pausanias claims (1.7.1) that Ptolemy II fell in love with his sister Arsinoë and married her. In this case, granted the apparent oddity of marrying your full sister, people may have been even more inclined than usual to attribute royal marriage to erotic impulse. Ptolemy II, with his innumerable mistresses, certainly indulged his erotic impulses.[68] Earlier generations of scholars quaintly assumed that Philadelphus could not have married his sister for erotic reasons because she was older than he.[69] Indeed, despite the sexualizing interpretation of Arsinoë's plotting against Agathocles as a kind of new Phaedra (see chapter 2), scholars have tended to neuter her in terms of her life in Egypt, to assume that if she really was a political figure, then she could not have been a sexual one as well, though her brother was both.[70] Oddly, despite the tendency of scholars in the early twentieth century to stereotype Ptolemy II as a self-indulgent womanizer, none considered the possibility that the king actually found the notion of marrying his sister titillating. Those who think that the experience of growing up together tends to prevent erotic interest cannot claim such a situation for this sibling pair. In a large royal household, for children of different genders even with the same mother, closeness may not have been a significant factor.[71] Arsinoë was eight years older and had long been absent. Since we know so little of the personalities of either of the royal pair, we can neither rule out the possibility of an erotic bond between them nor assert that it existed. More to the point, if Ptolemy II wanted to sleep with his sister, he did not need to marry her to do it.

Could other personal factors have motivated the unusual marriage? Suggestions that Ptolemy II married Arsinoë II because he was weak and needed a big sister to run the kingdom[72] seem unconvincing now:

Ptolemy II did a perfectly credible job as king before his sister returned and long after her death.[73] Apart from political reasons (see below) Ptolemy II and Arsinoë II could have chosen to marry partly because each felt safer married to the other. Typically, royal siblings, full siblings that is, acted with their mothers as succession units. Even if Ptolemy II and Arsinoë had not known each other well before her departure from Egypt, in a court and world full of intrigue, a spouse who was a fellow veteran of some of the same or similar battles may have seemed a confidence-inspiring choice. But speculation about personal reasons that might have contributed to their decision to marry remains just that.

Political calculation primarily inspired this marriage, like other royal marriages. Most royal marriages during this era, however, functioned as a foreign alliance between two ruling males. In Argead Macedonia, kings had sometimes married the daughters of foreign rulers, but often chose women from elite families within their kingdom. Ptolemy II's marriage to Arsinoë II was closer to the latter kind of marriage. An event in his reign could have inspired, or helped to inspire Ptolemy II's distinctive marriage, though dating uncertainties make it impossible to be single out anything specific.[74] Marrying a royal sister suggests greater interest in domestic rather than foreign policy. In this sense, brother-sister marriage is an isolationist marriage policy.[75] Ptolemy II used the marriage to unify his dynasty, to focus attention on himself and his sister, the children of Ptolemy I and Berenice, and on their children, excluding more extraneous members of the dynasty.[76] The title *(basilissa)* and posthumous deification he awarded to his unmarried sister Philotera suggests a similar concern.[77] Ptolemy II could simply have associated his sister Arsinoë II in rule without marrying her, as he did by involving her in the cult of the *theoi adelphoi*, but instead combined this cult with the more attention-grabbing option of marrying his sister. This was an act of policy, probably a thoroughly calculated and ultimately a successful choice.

One reason Ptolemy II chose to marry his sister had to do with the viability of previous polygamous royal marriage practices. Kings continued to make multiple marriages into the third century, but they were less common, perhaps in part because in the late fourth and early third some royal women chose marriage partners for themselves. Arsinoë, as we have seen, had demanded that Ceraunus promise that he would not treat her with indignity by taking another wife or by recognizing children other than her sons as his (Just. 24.2.9). Her familiarity with the situation of her mother and brother and her own experience at the court of Lysimachus obviously shaped the terms she exacted from Ptolemy Ceraunus. Both Lysimachus' and Ptolemy I's court had seen bruising battles for the succession. Ptolemy II and his sister found those events cautionary tales.[78] Extreme endogamy solved the problems of polygamy.[79]

If, however, the desire to avoid the pitfalls of polygamy was the only reason Ptolemy II opted for marriage to Arsinoë II, his successors might simply have been monogamous. Instead, subsequent Ptolemies, with the exception of Ptolemy III, made close-kin marriages, most often to their sisters.[80] Brother-sister marriage became fundamental to the image of Ptolemaic monarchy and thus supported the security, stability, and success of the dynasty.[81] Here Ptolemy II and Arsinoë II, though innovators, could build on the policies of their father.

Ptolemy I had already set the precedent for making his dynasty turn endlessly inward by naming two sons after himself and none, by a major wife, after his own father, Lagos (see chapter 1). Because of his decision, we speak of Seleucids, Antigonids, and Attalids—all names indicating a line of descent from one ancestor—but only for the Ptolemies do we employ a single male name (only occasionally are they called the Lagids). In all monarchies, one tends to think (and is meant to think), "The king is dead, long live the king," that the king never dies but simply is differently embodied. The Ptolemies made this explicit, possibly in connection to the pharaonic notion that the king is continually reborn.[82] The custom of naming multiple sons by the same father "Ptolemy" has caused confusion but testifies to the determination of rulers of the dynasty to ensure that a man named Ptolemy held the throne.[83] If the king was always Ptolemy, who was his consort? Sibling marriage enabled the current pair to appear to reincarnate earlier pairs.[84] This distinctive naming practice encouraged the institutionalization of close-kin marriages, mostly to the sisters of kings. Full sisters are as close as one can come to female versions of kings, mirror images but for gender.[85]

Ptolemy II was the primary craftsman of the Ptolemaic dynastic image and brother-sister marriage played an important part in the self-presentation of the dynasty. The tendency of Ptolemaic monarchy to turn in on itself increased in his reign. Ptolemy II created the first paired dynastic images: a cult of his parents as *theoi soteres* (savior gods) and later of himself and Arsinoë as *theoi adelphoi* (sibling gods; see chapter 5), the two pairs visibly linked in coins on which both couples appeared

(Fig. 4.1) Ultimately, the Ptolemies in official cult would picture themselves as a long series of linked pairs.[86] Ptolemy II created the cult of the royal couple.[87] He did not do this overnight, however: the cult of the *theoi adelphoi* more likely came several years after the marriage itself and the single cult of Arsinoë as *thea philadelphus* (sibling loving goddess) happened no sooner than 270. Thus the image making, or at least important parts of it, followed rather than preceded the marriage.[88]

When Ptolemy II and Arsinoë II decided to marry, they took a risk; doubtless discussions within the court had gone on for some time before the decision was made. We should picture the king, his *philoi*, and Arsinoë II and her *philoi* taking part in the discussions. Perhaps the decision was more imaginable in the comparatively removed and somewhat self-congratulatory circles of court (see chapter 5),[89] but since we cannot demonstrate serious and certainly lasting difficulties caused by the marriage, even in the Greek world outside of Egypt, it might be more significant that the court—a royal image-making machine of sorts—was where the advantages of the marriage could be imagined and then developed.

Cult, Greek and Egyptian, and religion related to Ptolemy II's decision. For Egyptians, the brother-sister marriage resonated by resembling and mirroring that of Osiris and Isis. For Greeks, the obvious referents were Zeus and Hera. A godlike marriage could play well to both his Greek and his Egyptian audience.[90] The marriage was meant to unify, not divide or prioritize one part of the population over the

FIGURE 4.1. Gold octadrachm showing Ptolemy II and Arsinoë II (obverse) and Ptolemy I and Berenice II (reverse). © The Trustees of the British Museum / Art Resource, NY.

other. Egyptian and Greek influence interacted even early on in the construction of Ptolemaic self-presentation.[91] Ptolemy's courtiers, doubtless following on royal policy, tried to make the connection clear in the Greek world. As we have seen, supposedly the rhapsode made the obvious allusion to Zeus and Hera. Theocritus, who worked under Ptolemy's patronage, both glorified and justified the marriage (*Id*. 17.128–30) by comparing it to that of the divine Greek pair, stressing its distinctive nature.[92] Three other Alexandrian poets celebrated the marriage of Arsinoë and Ptolemy II, at least one of them also referring to the Zeus/Hera parallel.[93] Callicrates, the Ptolemaic admiral, erected statues of the royal siblings at Olympia, just opposite the temples of Zeus and Hera,[94] creating a kind of "visual dialogue between the two sibling couples."[95] In Pindar's *Hymn to Zeus*, Zeus' marriage to his sister constituted the final stage in the consolidation of his power; clearly this version of the myth would appeal.[96]

The epithet "Philadelphus" (sibling loving), ultimately applied to both Arsinoë II and Ptolemy II and later commemorated in cult for Arsinoë, emphasized and idealized the marriage that paired siblings, sentimentalizing the relationship and putting in the context of what one might call "family values." The epithet may first have been employed about Arsinoë after her marriage.[97] It may not have been uncommon that an informal epithet first spread in common usage and then was transformed into a cult title.[98] While these image-making activities helped to justify the marriage, they do also tell us how the Ptolemies wanted their marriage to be understood as divine.[99] The establishment of the cult of the *theoi adelphoi* (see chapter 5) speaks to the continuing efforts of Ptolemy II to use his distinctive marriage to shape the dynastic image, as do the subsequent individual cults of Arsinoë (see chapters 5 and 6).

The distinctiveness of the marriage, not simply its similarity to the gods, may also have appealed to Ptolemy. Doing something others did not do seemed appropriate for royalty,[100] a symbol and a demonstration of royal power. Ptolemy II invented the two hallmarks of Ptolemaic self presentation: *truphe* (wealth, luxury, excess), signaling wealth (and the ability to confer its benefits on others) and power,[101] and sibling marriage, meant to be read as excessive, the opposite of sophrosune.[102] Ptolemy II and Arsinoë II, rather than playing their marriage down, highlighted it, glorified it, and glamorized it; it was not an embarrassing secret that the couple concealed from a supposedly hostile Greek public but rather something they publicized (see chapters 5 and 6).[103] Greeks liked to talk about moderation but did not necessarily practice it and often proved intrigued by the excessive. Going back as far as Homer, the culture exhibited a fascination with the large scale and excessive in action, especially in heroes. Kings, very much part of heroic tradition, did not necessarily want to look or be moderate. Ptolemaic image making appealed until the Romans eliminated the dynasty and Roman authors then reused it to demonstrate that the Ptolemies were decadent and incompetent.[104] Excess and excessive marriage remained the "dynastic signature" of the Ptolemies until the end, and it was Ptolemy II and Arsinoë II who initiated this dynastic theme.[105]

Let us turn to Arsinoë. Up to this point, I have spoken only of Ptolemy II's motives for marrying Arsinoë II. In the Hellenic world, women did not choose their husbands; their fathers, brothers, or other male kin made the decision. Male control of decision making about marriage generally applied to royal women too, though widowed royal women sometimes chose their own husbands, as we have seen. Granted, however, that full-sibling marriage was unprecedented and some found it objectionable, it is unlikely that Ptolemy II would have forced his sister to marry him against her will. Some sort of consent to the marriage on her part must be assumed.

We have already considered a number of motives for committing to this unconventional marriage that she may well have shared with her brother. In the light of her age, childbirth would have been a risk; she likely did not marry to bear more children and, like her brother, *eros* probably did not inspire her consent, though perhaps affection and desire for security did, as it may have Ptolemy II. Consolidating the dynasty made her and her lineage more important; she would hardly have objected. During the rest of her life, she played a role in the monarchic image that was unprecedented (see chapter 5): she acted in concert with her brother in terms of ritual and public display; served as a literary and religious patron; as part of the cults he generated, she like he was elevated to divinity, Greek and Egyptian. Moreover, she likely embraced political policies similar to her brother's. While not all of these aspects of her role may have been worked out at the time of her final marriage, surely enough had been planned to make it appealing to a woman who otherwise would have foreseen an obscure future for herself.

Was the marriage her idea? Arsinoë had already married a half brother, a marriage that could have given her the idea for her marriage to Ptolemy II.[106] She must have debated the merits of sibling marriage on the earlier occasion. Justin's narrative (17.2.6, 9) implies that, apart from hoping to safeguard the throne for her sons by marrying Ceraunus, she may also have seen the projected marriage as a way to unify the family and end the enmity between the children of Eurydice and of Berenice. The denouement was tragic, but did not necessarily compromise the potential power of the image that Ceraunus, however falsely, had conjured up. Both her second and third marriages aimed at dynastic consolidation.[107] Ptolemy II himself, however, well aware of her marriage to Ceraunus and less traumatized by it, could have come up with the idea. The siblings could have conceived of it together, or some of their *philoi* (foreseeing future benefit to themselves) could have.

Greek women, especially elite women, did not usually remain unmarried for long.[108] Arsinoë, a twice-married royal woman pushing forty, was hardly, however, typical. One doubts that her brother would have felt compelled to arrange another marriage for her and certainly nothing necessitated that he be the groom. Arsinoë herself had more reason to desire remarriage. True, she was a *basilissa* whether or not married to her brother, but widows of kings who had lost their kingdoms had little value. The combination of being the king's wife as well as his sister held out potential for great influence and even power. Her third marriage gave her tremendous prominence, likely considerable influence, and certainly wealth. The king was still the king before and after the marriage, but Arsinoë's situation changed dramatically. Ptolemy II, long term, benefitted in a number of ways from this marriage, but Arsinoë benefitted more dramatically and more immediately. All these factors likely helped to make Arsinoë want to marry Ptolemy II and could have inspired her to come up with the notion to begin with.

Finally, granted that she had consistently embraced danger in order to secure a position for her sons as kings, Arsinoë may well have embarked on this risky and controversial marriage because she hoped it would benefit her remaining son, Ptolemy son of Lysimachus. Indeed, in the light of her past priorities, perhaps ambition for her son was the primary reason she agreed to the marriage. Surely, she would have expected some sort of preferment for her son within Ptolemaic realms. He and she may have dreamed that Ptolemy II would assist his nephew to overthrow their common enemy Antigonus Gonatas and enable the son of Lysimachus to rule Macedonia, as his father had done. No evidence dating from Arsinoë's marriage to Ptolemy II provides information about her son's status during that period, but information survives that confirms he did receive office within the dynasty's sphere of influence after his mother's death and that offers up the possibility (though not, in my view, the reality) that, soon after Arsinoë's demise, he played a very grand role indeed in his uncle's kingdom (see chapter 6).

Arsinoë apparently saw the potential advantage in marrying her brother, a potential he and she developed over the remaining years of her life and he extended after her death. She married her brother because of her prospects and perhaps because she had nothing better to do. Her last marriage did not put her in physical danger but once more involved her in taking a gamble on a plan of action that had great potential benefit and risk.

CHAPTER FIVE

Arsinoë II as Wife of Ptolemy II

CA. 275–270 (268)

ARSINOË II, DURING her marriage to Ptolemy II, played a prominent, indeed an unprecedented, role in the public face of Ptolemaic monarchy at home and abroad.[1] This public, highly visible Arsinoë contrasts with the nearly invisible private life of Arsinoë while married to her brother.

Life at Court

Arsinoë spent her life in Hellenistic courts.[2] Hellenistic rulers performed their kingship,[3] using the palace as their stage set. The façade of palaces resembled the permanent backdrop of theaters (and, not coincidentally, those of temples); ironically, the theater backdrops had themselves been modeled on palaces.[4] Events in the lives of the royal family became public occurrences, often linked to religious events, and royalty dressed the part as though they were actors playing kings. Costly processions and festivals built loyalty and enthusiasm for a dynasty. This royal theatricality could be taken on the road to gain friends and consolidate influence through the personal presence of members of the dynasty, appearances by their representatives (usually royal *philoi*), or assorted avatars (statues or expensive dedications or even successful racehorses). The kings and their kin (for the Ptolemies, especially their female kin)[5] staged monarchy and displayed their authority by demonstrating their ability to command wealth and to create memorable, often divinized images of their power.[6] A king like Ptolemy II could, by exhibiting his power, in effect, extend it.[7] Moreover, as we have already noticed, the lives of royalty sometimes resembled events from tragic drama.

Arsinoë had tried to use royal ceremony to secure the position of her sons and herself in Macedonia, only to have Ceraunus upstage her. Earlier, she orchestrated her escape from Ephesus, complete with a dramatic costume change. Back in the land of her birth and the wife of a king who epitomized the theatrical elements of Hellenistic monarchy, Arsinoë participated in the staging of Ptolemaic power and wealth. All Hellenistic dynasties hoped to display their wealth, but for the Ptolemies *truphe* became the most distinctive visible hallmark of the dynasty, and women, with their layers of fabric and jewelry, made *truphe* visible.

The primary Ptolemaic royal stage, Alexandria, had evolved into something far more impressive than the raw new city Arsinoë had left behind.[8] The Ptolemaic *basileia* was now much grander,[9] not so much a palace or even a palace complex, but rather an entire royal sector, taking up at least a quarter of the entire city (Strab. 17.793–4).[10] In addition to administrative areas and the famous Library and Museum, there was the royal residence itself, with Greek style peristyles but Egyptian elements as well.[11] The complex included banqueting rooms of various sizes, an audience hall, living quarters, guard rooms, some temples, and all set in a gardenlike park with waterways and private access to the harbor.[12] Ptolemy II even maintained some sort of zoo.[13] The palace sector offered a variety of recreational opportunities to its royal inhabitants.[14] It was, at least at times, open to the public (see below), a venue for Lagid display through both festivals and audiences.[15]

This vast and complicated collection of structures contained a varied human population: the royal family; many servants, largely slaves; the royal *philoi* who served the king as counselors as well as eating and drinking with him; a royal guard; assorted intellectuals and artists; visiting dignitaries.[16] The Ptolemies probably supported the largest court population of all the Hellenistic dynasties.[17] Life at court varied from dynasty to dynasty; more rules, offices, and formality grew up over time.[18] At court, kings made decisions with the aid of *philoi*. At the same time, the exchange between the king and his *philoi* of benefits and praise, much of it mirrored in court literature and art, made the king seem more accessible than he literally was.[19]

The Presentation of Ptolemaic Monarchy

The Ptolemaic kings presented themselves both as *basileis* and pharaohs; this dual presentation extended to the women of the dynasty and certainly to Arsinoë. Just as the monarchy was two-headed, Greek and Egyptian, so too was the style of much that Ptolemy II built, including the temple he would construct after his sister's death for her cult. One style might dominate a given building, but it would also contain elements of the other.[20] Recent archaeological excavation has demonstrated that Egyptian-style Ptolemaic images were present in Alexandria, even in the palace area. Colossal Egyptian-style statues of a Ptolemaic pair—perhaps Arsinoë II and her husband—may have greeted those arriving at the harbor of Alexandria.[21] Yet Greek style statues of the pair appeared in many places, including those erected by their admiral Callicrates in Greek sanctuaries. Images of the royal pair appeared again and again in both styles.[22]

Arsinoë's presentation in some Egyptian contexts differed dramatically from her presentation in more Hellenic contexts. (Egyptian royal women, as we have seen, had a more institutionalized and articulated role in Egyptian monarchy than had royal women in that of ancient Macedonia and among the Successors.) Arsinoë acquired an Egyptian throne name, "King of Upper and Lower Egypt," a title usually considered exclusively that of a king. Other Egyptian evidence endows her with kinglike attributes.[23] Since all or most of this evidence may date to the period after her death, it will be discussed at greater length in the next chapter. If, however, we assume that some of the Egyptian evidence derives from her lifetime, it would mean that, for his Egyptian audience, Ptolemy II chose to project an image of Arsinoë as important and powerful, a partaker in the rule of the kingdom. Manetho, who worked under Ptolemaic patronage, may even have contributed to this image by including in his history the assertion that in the second dynasty of the Old Kingdom the decision was made that women could rule in Egypt.[24]

Images are not the same as reality—showing Arsinoë as kinglike does not make her so—but this image making is certainly quite different from Ptolemaic Hellenic images of her. Greeks of that era, perhaps more than Macedonians, would have been uncomfortable with suggestions of female rule or corule, and Greek art lacked the highly elaborated royal iconography of the Egyptian tradition, which could refer to Arsinoë's rule and yet nuance the reference. Thus the public presentation of

Arsinoë's role in the kingdom differed considerably in the two faces of Ptolemaic monarchy, but whether either presentation reflects political reality remains problematic.

The Grand Procession of Ptolemy II, an outrageous extravaganza, provides a vivid example of the carefully constructed royal public presentation (Ath.5.196a–203b).[25] The day long procession was an event of astonishing scale and a polymorphous nature: there was some focus on Ptolemaic ancestors, stress on Dionysus as a god of wine, all sorts of symbolic tableaus (statues and figures representing places and concepts), high-tech automatons that did things like pouring libations of wine or milk, endless displays of gold and silver plate, particularly drinking vessels, platoons of gorgeously costumed (gold and purple often playing a prominent role) groups, wild animals, hunting gear and dogs, displays of splendid larger-than-life-size armor, and finally a military procession (infantry and cavalry) of about eighty thousand men. Ptolemy II targeted both the population of Alexandria and the international Greek world when he constructed the procession and festival to be spectacles celebrating his monarchy.[26] Like most other Greek examples, the festival that the procession celebrated included competitions primarily though not exclusively geared to a Hellenic audience and to Hellenic culture.[27] Apparently the procession traveled through the main roads of Alexandria and then crossed the central area where the king and his guests sat.[28] The festival served as an ekphrasis of Ptolemaic monarchy: it showcased the king's military power, perhaps more than anything else,[29] his wealth (and thus ability to give it away), his role as promoter of culture and learning, his connection to Dionysus (and the wine industry), and his personal courage in hunting and war.[30]

The occasion was a celebration of the dynastic festival Ptolemy II invented, the Ptolemaea; this festival happened first in 279, or 275/74 or 271.[31] Athenaeus reports (5.197d) that the first part of the procession was named in honor of the "parents or ancestors of the rulers"[32] and that the display included statues of Alexander and Ptolemy I (Ath. 5.201d). Granted the dynastic concerns of the procession, it might seem odd that there Athenaeus makes no direct reference to Arsinoë II or to Ptolemy II's first wife. The festival described is most likely the first dynastic festival, and if it happened in 279, the absence of Arsinoë II is easily explained: she had not yet returned to Egypt and had not yet married her brother. Since Athenaeus mentions no wife, this date would also imply that, by the time of the festival, Ptolemy II had already sent Arsinoë I to Coptos and had not yet remarried.[33] Though Arsinoë II apparently missed the show, it does provide a wonderful example of that image of excess that the Ptolemies had begun to cultivate, one in which she would play a large part.

Alexandria now had a number of buildings purpose-built for public entertainment, all part of Ptolemaic display. By the time of the first Ptolemaea, there were locations for equestrian, gymnastic, and musical contests. The Lageium served as both a hippodrome for horse racing and a stadium for athletic competition. By the second half of the 270s the Great Theater had appeared.[34] There was also a sumptuous banqueting tent constructed for Ptolemy II as part of his great procession, a construct that could contain a hundred banqueting couches.[35]

Arsinoë at Court

While many aspects of Macedonian elite culture differed only slightly from that of Greek culture generally, the role of women in monarchy was necessarily Macedonian because monarchy had persisted there but not in most of the rest of the Greek peninsula. Though these days we usually speak of Ptolemaic monarchy as double—Greek and Egyptian— in many respects there was a third aspect, the Macedonian. This is true despite the fact that comparatively few *philoi* or administrators were Macedonian.[36] Ptolemy I Soter himself emphasized his Macedonian identity and Posidippus' celebratory poems stress the Macedonian (and Argive) origin of the Ptolemies.[37] Arsinoë, though a Ptolemy by birth, had been the wife of two different rulers of Macedonia and lived, for twenty years or more, in courts on the mainland as well as Asia Minor. As we consider her role in her brother's reign, we should recall her personal experience of Macedonia and its culture.

It is difficult to assess, as it is for Hellenistic royal women generally, how much Arsinoë appeared in public and was accessible to the public. We do not know, for instance, if she personally attended royal audiences or received petitions in person.[38] Whatever her living circumstances, her daily life cannot have been entirely secluded and limited to the world of women, because she, like other royal women, had male *philoi* at court,[39] probably including the admirals Callicrates and Patroclus (see below). Some *philoi* may have followed her to Lysimachia, to Cassandria (Just. 24.2.7), and then back to Alexandria, some she may have acquired along the way, including *philoi* shared with her husband.[40]

She accompanied her brother-husband on a trip to the Egyptian borders, and she would probably have appeared, heavily robed and costumed, at various public rituals (most certainly those connected to the cult of her parents, the *theoi soteres*, and that of her sister Philotera, as well as that of the *theoi adelphoi*), as she had in Macedonia. Royal women generally served as symbols of continuity. This was particularly true in the Ptolemaic dynasty, especially once brother-sister marriage had become the ideal and often the reality. Arsinoë became critical to the projection of the image of the dynasty,[41] though her importance actually increased after her death.

Arsinoë proved popular with Alexandrians and Egyptians generally;[42] it is worth reflecting on the origin of her popularity. She must have been a familiar public figure believed by her subjects to have accomplished benefits for them. Immigrants filled Alexandria. Displaced from their native cities, they gradually became part of a new, conglomerate Hellenic culture.[43] Arsinoë was herself a displaced person, someone who had changed places and roles multiple times, but was yet again in need of a new identity.[44] True, she was not an immigrant, like so many of her fellow citizens, but her experience of dislocation not only replicated that of many of the inhabitants of Alexandria and Ptolemaic Egypt but contributed to the development of her popular appeal. We do not know exactly how much the people of Alexandria (and the rest of Egypt) knew of Arsinoë's past, but they would have heard of her marriage to Lysimachus and the murders of her sons. Surely they knew that she had suffered multiple losses in her personal life. The same stories and rumors about the intrigue surrounding the death of Agathocles preserved in our sources had probably reached her homeland, spreading outward from the court (royal *philoi* and artists frequently traveled from one court to another) to the general populace. Hellenistic royals, the celebrities of the day, like their modern counterparts, provided fodder for endless gossip. Glimpses of royal life that made royalty seem just like everyone else intrigued.[45] People would have speculated about Arsinoë and, most likely, romanticized her, just as court poets would do. Perhaps the populace found it easy to identify with a royal woman whose life involved dramatic reversals, highs and lows.[46]

In order to determine whether Arsinoë exercised influence in areas other than in the traditional feminine ones, we must look at her role in international relations and warfare. We will need to reflect on how her situation in these areas resembled and differed from earlier royal women.

Posidippus (AB 78) reveals that Arsinoë won all three harness victories at Olympia in a single year, perhaps in 272.[47] We have already discussed her mother's Olympic victories and how the Ptolemies understood such renown as familial and were particularly proud of their female victors. One attractive aspect of equestrian competition was that it kept the hoi polloi out and that there was a greater chance of success, because the number of competitors was comparatively small and the super wealthy could afford to put forward multiple entries, as Arsinoë apparently did.[48] Her victorious horses, like the many statues of her, functioned as international avatars for Arsinoë, publicizing her wealth and power as well as that of the dynasty.

Military Affairs

In the ancient Greek world, foreign policy and war were hard to separate. Warfare and military success had always been central to Macedonian monarchy; the post-Argead Hellenistic rulers first claimed the right to rule based on their victories. Greek women did not generally participate in military affairs; the appeal of the myth of the Amazons was that it was just that. Toward the end of the Argead period, however, some royal women began to assert or accept a military role.[49] One woman, Cynnane, actually went into combat. Her daughter, Adea Eurydice, regularly addressed Macedonian armies and dressed as a Macedonian soldier when the forces supporting her and her husband (Philip Arrhidaeus the mentally limited half brother of Alexander the Great, co-king with Alexander's son after Alexander's death) confronted an army championing Olympias, mother of Alexander the Great, and young Alexander IV. Duris called it the first war between women (*ap.* Ath. 13.560f). Olympias' role in the army was symbolic but powerful; the opposing army changed sides when it saw her. The royal woman buried in the antechamber of Tomb II at Vergina was buried with weapons and armor.[50] Olympias not only traveled with an army but ran a siege and had administrative control of troops. Arsinoë, as we have seen, may have exercised this same kind of symbolic and administrative leadership of military forces in Cassandria.

Similar Egyptian examples connect royal women who were members of ruling dynasties to military matters. Ahhotep I, a king's daughter and probably the mother of Ahmose I, the founder of the eighteenth dynasty, held a position of responsibility in terms of the army. A stele from Ahmose I's reign speaks of Ahhotep as "one who cares for Egypt. She has looked after her soldiers; she has guarded her; she has brought back her fugitives, and collected together her deserters; she has pacified Upper Egypt, and expelled her rebels." The burial of another royal Ahhotep (II) contained a number of military items, including a military decoration. Hatshepsut, the female king of the eighteenth dynasty, accompanied her army on campaign in Nubia and may have appeared with it.[51]

The symbolic military role of some Egyptian royal women differs from the Macedonian because of the richer royal iconography in Egypt. Images, for instance, from the New Kingdom depict royal women as military leaders, with the attributes of a warrior; in a few cases, women appear as female sphinxes or smiting enemies, images usually limited to kings. Two women appear behind their husbands while the king smites enemies.[52] Granted Ptolemaic imitation of other pharaonic practices relating to royal women (see chapter 6), these precedents may have been known to Egyptian priests of the third century and to the Ptolemies. In any event, all known Macedonian/Hellenistic and pharaonic precedents for actual female military activity (as opposed to a symbolic military role) transpired in a circumstance involving the absence (temporary or permanent) of adult males of the dynasty: women took on military roles because men were not available to do so.

What is unprecedented about Arsinoë's admittedly modest actual military role is that it developed while she was married, when her husband the king was living, present, active, and competent; indeed her role was joined to that of her husband, reflecting the growing institutional role of the sister-wife.[53] Arsinoë II and Ptolemy II traveled to the frontier (Heroonpolis/Pithom on the Isthmus of Suez) on a visit to inspect defenses against foreign attack (threatened, presumably, because of the failures of Ptolemy II's campaign in Syria), as well as irrigation repairs, and the statues of the gods returned from Persian control.[54] Some aspects of her military persona survived her death, as we shall see. Later Ptolemaic royal women appeared in overtly military circumstance,[55] but this seemingly modest incident remains important, particularly since so much of Ptolemaic military policy was in essence defensive. Keeping the homeland safe was always the priority. (Indeed, there was no attack on Egyptian territory until 170.)[56] The very matter-of-fact nature of her appearance speaks for itself; it is to be assumed that the sister/wife has a role here.

A more mysterious militarized Arsinoë appears in a poem of Posidippus, a dedication of linen by a young woman to Arsinoë in which she addresses the queen. The young woman dreams of Arsinoë and in the dream Arsinoë appears armed, "the sharp / spear in your hand, the hollow shield on your arm" (AB 36).[57] The dream image of Arsinoë of the poem may relate to one of her cults or to a statue of her,[58] possibly a cult statue.[59] The poem may imagine an Athenalike Arsinoë[60] or an Aphroditelike one (some Aphrodite cults portrayed the goddess armed).[61] The armed image may well refer to her support for the Ptolemaic policy of "Greek freedom" that led to the Chremonidean War.[62] The war, fought between ca. 268–61, pitted a number of Greek city-states—notably Athens and Sparta—supported by Ptolemy II, against the power of the Macedonian king, Antigonus Gonatas.[63]

In the past, royal women had sometimes symbolized the dynasty, perhaps because they could not have such individualized careers as royal men. Similarly, royal men in Egypt appeared only in cults that paired them with their sister/wives whereas women sometimes had stand alone cults. Arsinoë's visit and this armed image suggest that she had become a symbol of Egyptian power and the protection, particularly naval protection,[64] her dynasty afforded.

Foreign Policy

Before we turn to Arsinoë's role in foreign policy, it helps to reflect on Macedonian and Egyptian precedents. Macedonian royal women had begun to play a role in foreign affairs by the days of Philip II (Alexander the Great's father) when sometime in the 360s his widowed mother called on an Athenian *philos* of her dead husband to aid her sons in retaining their claim on the throne and he did (Aeschin. 2.26–29). Royal women took a part in the *philia* (friendship) networks that played so important a role in Greek international relationships. The daughters and sisters of kings could also act as intermediaries between the families of their birth and marriage. In the period after Alexander's death, his mother and full sister in effect formed alliances with some of the Successors. The religious patronage of royal women should be understood as part of this pattern of engagement in foreign affairs. Indeed, we often see their *philoi* acting on their behalf in international shrines (see below).[65] In pharaonic Egypt, the king of the Mitanni considered Tiy, Amenhotep III's widow, so knowledgeable he advised her son to consult her about previous relations between the two countries and another royal widow corresponded with a foreign king attempting to arrange her own marriage alliance.[66]

Royal women in the past had maintained specific foreign and domestic policies. In Egypt, female kings had formally acknowledged foreign policy and activity—Hatshepsut's expedition to Punt (a region to the south of Egypt in Africa) would be an example. In Macedonia, several royal women pursued consistent policies. An Athenian orator (Hyp. *Eux.* 20) associated Olympias with her son in a way that implies a shared policy. After Alexander's death, Olympias tried to ally herself with those of Alexander's former officers who could offer the most support for her grandson. Adea Eurydice, Alexander's niece and the wife of the mentally limited king Philip Arrhidaeus, may have formed an alliance with Cassander.[67] Arsinoë herself, while still in Macedonia, consistently tried to preserve the throne of Macedonia for her sons. Still, though these women followed coherent policies, there was no formal acknowledgment, certainly not in Athens, a city hostile to public actions by women, that they did so.

It is with Arsinoë II that this changes: for the first time, at least in the Greek world, a public document recognized the policy of a woman and did so with apparent approval.[68] The Athenians probably passed the decree proposed by Chremonides (an anti-Macedonian Athenian politician) in 268/67.[69] The decree (marking the beginning of the Chremonidean War) happened after Arsinoë's death, though possibly only by a few weeks.[70] The decree proclaims that "King Ptolemy, following the policies of his ancestors and sister, demonstrates his concern for the common freedom of the Greeks." Greek cities and Hellenistic kings had long manipulated the diplomatic catchphrase "freedom of the Greeks" to serve various ends; the first two Ptolemies did indeed generally support Athens and other cities against Macedonian encroachment.[71] Many Greek inscriptions speak of someone acting in keeping with the traditions of his ancestors but hardly with those of his mother or sister.[72] The Athenian document's matter-of-fact reference to Arsinoë's policy and its assumption that it is appropriate to speak of her brother the king as acting in accord with it are new. On the one hand, the wording of the decree lacks precedent, but on the other, it treats the notion of Arsinoë as having a public policy as normative and unremarkable. One cannot be conventional when one is inventing the convention, yet that is what the decree seems to do.[73]

What does the decree demonstrate or at least suggest about Arsinoë's power and influence?[74] It speaks to the ways in which her power was embedded in that of the dynasty, by assuming that royal women played a part in family action, success, and renown, just as the poems of Posidippus assume the same in terms of matters equestrian.

Moreover, the well-informed Athenians[75] thought that it would be appropriate to mention her policy.[76] The decree was not a mere diplomatic courtesy[77] that accidentally precipitated the subsequent development of actual power for Ptolemaic royal women.[78] The fact that Arsinoë was recently dead and that Chremonides (and his supporters) doubtless believed that Ptolemy II would appreciate the phrase does not compromise its significance. Like the visit to Heroonpolis, the decree demonstrates a new understanding of the role of Ptolemaic royal women in monarchy, one profoundly affected by the fact that the royal woman in question was herself the daughter, not just the wife, of a Ptolemy. More specifically, the decree of Chremonides, again like the trip to Heroonpolis, shows Ptolemy II and Arsinoë (even after her death) working—or at least thinking—in concert. It indirectly creates a paired image of royal power, if only a retrospective one (see chapter 6).

More specifically, the decree establishes the importance of the image of Arsinoë in war propaganda, an importance confirmed by other evidence. During the war, a number of port cities used by the Ptolemaic fleet were named after Arsinoë, as either new foundations or refoundations.[79] Arsinoë's cult in Sparta also related to the war effort of the Greek allies.[80] All this suggests continuing Ptolemaic policy to associate Arsinoë with the war and the policy that led to Ptolemaic involvement. Arsinoë alone did not generate the Ptolemaic role in the war, but the king and his Greek allies made her a prominent part of the imagery they generated about the war.

Although Ptolemy II could have chosen to associate Arsinoë with the war solely for convenience's sake, simply furthering the picture of the harmonious royal couple, Greek liberty and opposition to Antigonus Gonatas, its primary enemy, were very likely things that Arsinoë herself had supported.[81] This is, after all, what the document says. Her personal experiences, as well as Ptolemaic tradition, make this extremely likely. Since Arsinoë had, while still in Macedonia, tried to see her son on the Macedonian throne, naturally one wonders if this ambition—surely one that would have endured—affected her views about Greek affairs. Did she want to contain Macedonian power by advocating "Greek freedom" for reasons more personal than those of her brother, to put her son back on his father's throne?[82] Though she died before the Chremonidean War began, planning for the war or at least discussion of its possibility may have gone on for a long time, and she could have been an active proponent of Ptolemaic involvement.[83]

Assessing Arsinoë's role in the formulation of foreign policy is part of a more general problem. The decision-making process of the second Ptolemy or that of other kings remains obscure, but we do know that royal *philoi* played an important role in Hellenistic courts and presumably part of that role was policy and the implementation of policy. So when we speak, for instance, of the planning for Philadelphus' Grand Procession, we do not literally mean that the king turned himself into some sort of event planner. Obviously, he delegated the whole project to someone and probably exercised only a supervisory role. Quite possibly the person responsible had advocated the project to begin with. Where alternative policies were under consideration, some *philoi* probably advocated one approach, others the opposite. A royal wife or sister was also bound to the king by *philia*. I see no reason to doubt that Arsinoë would have made her views on Greek affairs known to her husband; arguably it was her duty. After all, she had spent years on the Greek peninsula and had personal knowledge of its affairs and personalities.[84]

Archaeological remains at Samothrace suggest how Arsinoë's influence might have functioned. Arsinoë (see chapter 2) had dedicated the rotunda to the Great Gods at Samothrace, and subsequently her brother Ptolemy II dedicated a great propylon at the same sanctuary, one with so many similarities to Arsinoë's rotunda that both buildings likely had the same architect, probably a Macedonian. These marked similarities may mean that the architect chosen by Arsinoë was then selected by her brother, on her recommendation.[85] Arsinoë could also have influenced her brother's interest in the cult itself. This example could be suggestive for other aspects of their dealings, particularly since their dual patronage had political aspects, much like the cult of Arsinoë Aphrodite Euploia. The Great Gods of Samothrace were, like that goddess, protectors of seafarers.

Arsinoë's advocacy of some sort of Greek alliance does not mean that her brother committed to such an alliance only because of her views,[86] though her advocacy likely contributed to his decision, along with the advice of others. Ptolemy II had no motive to yield all his power to his sister and had reasons of his own for hoping to limit Antigonus Gonatas.[87]

Cults

Cults—private, civic, dynastic—began to develop around Macedonian kings and other prominent Greeks in the late fifth and early fourth century. Philip II and Alexander flirted with some sort of divinization in their lifetimes and certainly received cult worship after their deaths. Some of the Successors were given civic or private cults even before they actually took the royal title. Cults for royal women developed in the late fourth century as well,[88] but discussions of the growth of cults for Arsinoë and Ptolemaic women have tended to ignore these earlier cults, implying, perhaps inadvertently, that features of Arsinoë's cults were unique or unprecedented when, in fact, some were and some were not.[89] My aim is to provide the Macedonian context for the various divinizations of Arsinoë and, at the same time, single out what was distinctive about Arsinoë's cults from what was not.

Alexander may have intended to deify his mother Olympias after her death (Curt. 9.6.26, 10.5.30), but Alexander's runaway treasurer Harpalus actually initiated a posthumous private cult for the *hetaira* (courtesan) Pythionice.[90] Theopompus (*ap.* Ath. 595a-c), the fourth-century BCE historian, reports that Harpalus erected a temple, sacred precinct, and altar for her under the name Pythionice Aphrodite. Harpalus, a precursor of the Hellenistic kings, maintained a quasi-royal court and blurred the distinction between royal women and *hetairai*.[91] He first associated a mortal woman with the goddess Aphrodite in cult.

Some of the subsequent women associated with Aphrodite were also courtesans, albeit courtesans of kings, or men soon to be kings, but some were wives. A *philos* of Demetrius Poliorcetes founded a private cult of Phila Aphrodite (in honor of Demetrius Poliorcetes' wife Phila) in Attica (Ath. 255c) around 307, about the same time and in the same polis the Athenians created civic cults for Demetrius; his father, Antigonus; and Phila (Ath. 254a).[92] The Athenians put up temples to two of Demetrius' *hetairai*, as Lamia Aphrodite and Leaenea Aphrodite (Ath. 253a) and the Thebans also established a temple of Aphrodite Lamia (Ath. 253b).[93]

Thus about a year before Demetrius and his father began to employ a royal title and Phila became the first woman attested with the title *basilissa*,[94] the men had a civic cult, Phila both a civic and a private cult, and soon after Demetrius' *hetairai* had civic cults as well. Similar private and civic cults for other women (many of which were lifetime cults that associated these women with Aphrodite), quickly sprang up.[95] Cults that assimilated a mortal to a deity were almost exclusively female; assimilations gave them a "divine personality," and in effect explained them.[96]

The cults the Athenians (and later other cities) instituted to Demetrius and Antigonus and other leaders were a way for them to recognize the power of these larger-than-life Macedonian generals, integrate them into the existing structure of the polis, and conceptualize the kind of power they held over them, power, as the cult title of the father and son (*soteres*) suggests, of salvation.[97] A similar explanation works for the civic cult to Phila: woman had not exercised political power in Greek cities before the advent of the Macedonians, but now they did and this reality too needed to be integrated into civic life. Though divinization, in these cases, preceded any royal title, a rough connection, whether because both cult and title recognized similar qualities or because acquiring the first helped to justify the second, seems to exist.

Why the early and certainly persistent connection of the women associated with kings to Aphrodite? In most of these cases, the name of the woman and the goddess were simply juxtaposed; the significance of the practice remains uncertain.[98] Mere flattery, focused on a woman's beauty, might explain cults instituted by cities or royal *philoi* but does not work for cults like those of the Ptolemies generated by the rulers themselves. Moreover, such a view ignores the common Greek understanding of beauty as a manifestation of divine and mortal power.[99] Aphrodite was a model for all women and thus an obvious one for a royal woman.[100] Granted that royal *hetairai* were also identified with Aphrodite in cult, our explanation for assimilation to Aphrodite must involve sexuality. The main thing royal wives and royal courtesans had in common was that they all were sleeping with ruling men, access that guaranteed both sorts of women had influence and a public role.[101] Let us bear all these possibilities in mind as we turn to Ptolemaic female cults.

Cities or royal *philoi* had instituted cults for rulers and women associated with them, but ca. 279, Ptolemy II inaugurated the cult of the *theoi soteres*, in honor of his parents, Ptolemy I and Berenice I. This dual cult broke new ground in two ways: now a ruler himself generated a cult and the new cult paired a male and female member of a ruling dynasty. This is the first example of the duality that would characterize Ptolemaic monarchic ideology long into the future. Like later paired cults, this initial creation focused on the shared affection of husband and wife, particularly appropriate for a woman whose husband chose her for personal, not political reasons.[102] In Hellenistic kingdoms, cults for the kings, dynasties, and royal women were common, but there were no cults for sons who did not yet rule.[103]

In or by 272/71,[104] well before Arsinoë's death and long before his own, Ptolemy II once more innovated. He established a dynastic cult of Alexander and the *theoi adelphoi* (the sibling gods, Ptolemy II and Arsinoë II).[105] Although Ptolemaic scholarship has long fixated on whether any of Arsinoë's various cults happened in her lifetime, lifetime cult for royal women, as we have seen, had been around for a generation in 272. The innovation in terms of this cult was that those venerated were the ones creating and shaping the cult.[106] The cult epithet highlighted their blood relationship, explained, justified, and elevated not only the sibling marriage, but the married pair, whatever the cult's chronological relationship to the date of their marriage. Love became part of the basic imagery of the dynasty, perhaps connected to the ability of the pair to convey benefits.[107] While the cult of the *adelphoi* was associated with that of Alexander and the cults shared a priest, a sacred precinct in Alexandria for Ptolemy II and Arsinoë, without Alexander, also existed (Herod. 1.30).[108]

Ptolemy II gave his admiral Callicrates the great distinction of being the first priest of the cult of the *theoi adelphoi*, and Posidippus (AB 74) tells us that Callicrates dedicated statues of his winning chariot team and charioteer in honor of the *adelphoi*.[109] Callicrates honored the now divine pair in other ways. He established a sanctuary of Isis and Anubis at Canopus on behalf of Ptolemy and Arsinoë (SB I 429). On his native Samos, Callicrates' statue appeared with that of the *adelphoi* (*OGIS* 29.3–4 with II p. 539), probably during Arsinoë's lifetime.[110] Callicrates made a spectacular dedication to Zeus at Olympia in honor of the pair, statues of both on columns (*OGIS* 26, 27). These statues faced the temples of Zeus and Hera and were aligned with them.[111] The images celebrated the marriage of Ptolemy II and Arsinoë and attempted to build support for it in the wider Greek world at the same time they explained the marriage.[112] Callicrates' prominence in spreading the cult and acceptance of the marriage demonstrates how important the king considered the image of his queen to be to the stability of his kingdom and power.[113]

At some point in the 270s, probably after the institution of the *theoi adelphoi* and certainly before the death of Arsinoë II,[114] Philotera, the unmarried full sister of Ptolemy II and Arsinoë II, was deified, presumably by the decision of her brother.[115] She had both Greek and Egyptian cults.[116] An inscription (*OGIS* 35) on a statue base from Didyma (an Apollo sanctuary in what is now southwestern Turkey) terms her *basilissa* and tells us that the Milesians offered an honorific statue of her to Artemis.[117] This statue might have formed part of a group with images of her full brother and full sister.[118] Philotera's name was written within a cartouche (a practice usually limited to royalty).[119]

The case of Philotera and her cult is striking because her very unimportance highlights the high profile of royal women in the Ptolemaic dynasty. Though she never married—whether because of early death or more likely physical disability[120]—and so never played a part in any alliance, cities and regions were named after her,[121] if not as many as those named after Arsinoë II.[122] Indeed, Philotera's lack of attachments outside her family made her an excellent symbol of her family and its closeness.[123] In other royal dynasties, unmarried royal women did not receive the attention given to Philotera and subsequent unmarried Ptolemaic women.[124] While her cult elevated the dynasty by deifying one of its most obscure members, it did lessen the distinctiveness of Arsinoë's individual cult, despite its far greater popularity. Philotera's cult, if it preceded Arsinoë's, may represent, in essence, a stage in the process that ultimately produced Arsinoë's individual cult (see chapter 6).

Callicrates dedicated a temple to Arsinoë Aphrodite on Cape Zephyrium near Alexandria; though a Greek cult, it had some Egyptian aspects.[125] Since almost everything we know about the cult comes from poetic allusions (Posidippus AB 39.2, 116.6–7; 119.2; Callimachus (frg. 5 Pf), and Lock of Berenice frg. 110 Pf),[126] much about it remains problematic.[127] Posidippus (AB116 and 119) calls her Cypris-Arsinoë (an epithet associated with Aphrodite) and Arsinoë Euploia (good for sailing; AB 39), a cult epithet borrowed from Aphrodite, though Arsinoë's assimilation to the goddess is so complete Aphrodite herself is not mentioned by name (AB 39);[128] for Posidippus, Arsinoë was a goddess of the seas, a protector of sailors and travelers. This cult spread quickly to harbors around the Mediterranean to cities that were either Ptolemaic possessions or places where the fleet had influence, many of them eponymous foundations for Arsinoë.[129] The cult also celebrated married life or rather a young woman's entry into it. This aspect of the cult catered to women's experience, reinforcing ideas already present in poetry about the love match of Ptolemy I and Berenice I and in the image of the *theoi adelphoi* as a loving couple.[130] Both aspects of the cult at Zephyrium suit a role frequently played by Hellenistic queens, that of intercessor. Being a helpful, protective goddess was one way for the queen to intercede and make monarchy less remote.[131]

The Zephyrium cult and the cults of the *theoi adelphoi* and *thea philadelphus* (brother-loving goddess; see chapter 6) parallel each other, and the boundaries between them are not clearly defined; sometimes we cannot tell which cult is referred to.[132] Callicrates' Zephyrium cult differed from others that assimilated royal women to Aphrodite because it focused on Arsinoë as a goddess of marriage and as a marine deity, the latter aspect well suited to Ptolemaic experience and policy.[133] This is the first instance—yet another innovation—in which the assimilation of a royal woman to Aphrodite was tailored to fit a specific circumstance, a particular political and dynastic image.

Arsinoë's Zephyrium cult seems to have been a private one,[134] similar to that of Phila Aphrodite at Athens, also instituted by a royal *philos*, a generation before Callicrates' temple. *Philoi* of royal women frequently played an important role in their divinization.[135] Although these cults certainly honored and elevated royal women, they also provided a new identity and increased royal connection to the *philos* who established a cult.[136] Granted that private lifetime cults for royal women generated by *philoi* of the king or queen had been around for some time, Arsinoë's was probably established in her lifetime, as Phila's had been.[137]

Callicrates,[138] the founder of the cult, belonged to the king's inner circle of *philoi*. No extant document terms him Arsinoë's *philos* as well, but his actions imply that he was perhaps even more closely tied to her than to the king.[139] Earlier contact between Arsinoë and Callicrates could have happened during Lysimachus' reign, since Callicrates was a Samian and Lysimachus had controlled Samos before the Ptolemies took over ca. 280.[140] Arsinoë and Callicrates arrived in Egypt about the same time; conceivably Callicrates came as part of her entourage;[141] certainly they established their positions at court in the same time frame. Callicrates, Samian in origin but Ptolemaic in allegiance, tied together old Greece and Ptolemaic Egypt, just as the Ptolemies themselves hoped to do.[142]

To what degree the cult was Callicrates' idea and to what degree it was that of Ptolemy II and/or Arsinoë II is difficult to say;[143] it is best understood as a product of the interaction at court of all three. As we have seen, royal *philoi* dedicated statues at major sites in honor of their royal patrons[144] and instituted private cults. The admiral and the king doubtless intended the cult to play a part in the expansion of Ptolemaic maritime power throughout the Mediterranean; the divinized queen became both the symbol and the patron of the fleet.[145] The cult must have had personal appeal for Arsinoë: she herself had twice escaped from danger by sea, and the sea had brought her safely back to her birth-place. Her affection for the gods of Samothrace suggests an interest in gods who offered safety to seafarers.[146] Moreover, her experiences while married to Lysimachus and then to Ceraunus may have made her par-ticularly aware of the importance of sea power.[147] Arsinoë probably played a part in shaping this cult and in that of *thea philadelphus* as well, even if that cult was not formally established until after her death. Many aspects of both cults suggest a familiarity with women's religious experi-ence that supports this conclusion.[148]

While fairly widespread agreement exists that the cult of the *theoi adelphoi* and that of Arsinoë Aphrodite were first established during Arsinoë's lifetime, no consensus has developed about the question of whether the cult of Arsinoë as *thea philadelphus* was formulated in her lifetime or soon after her death. One reason for the absence of consen-sus is the continuing dispute about the date of her death (270 versus 268) because the later dating makes it somewhat more likely that the cult developed in her lifetime (though hardly inevitable; see chapter 6). Although the later dating of her death is attractive, since there is no consensus on this issue, and since the full development of the cult in its various aspects certainly had not happened by the time of her death, I will postpone discussion of this development to the next chapter. None-theless, I must once more emphasize that lifetime cults for women had become familiar institutions and that there is considerable likelihood that Arsinoë had a hand in shaping the cult that developed, whether or not it was officially inaugurated while she still lived.

Arsinoë's Wealth and Patronage

Arsinoë demonstrably functioned as a religious patron.[149] In addition to her patronage of the shrine of the Great Gods at Samothrace, she was, as a goddess, a patron (assuming that at least some of her cults were estab-lished in her lifetime). In addition, she sponsored an elaborate and crowd-pleasing festival, one that built loyalty and affection for her dynasty.[150]

Theocritus (*Id.* 15) wrote a witty mime that tells the story of the trip of two Alexandrian housewives, both formerly from Syracuse, to the palace, during the festival of the Adonia sponsored by Arsinoë, to see a display of royal tapestries depicting the loves and troubles of Adonis and his lover Aphrodite, and to hear a hymn sung by a woman who has won the festival competition.[151] Other Greek cities celebrated the Adonia, but Arsinoë hosted a distinctive version. At Athens the festival was exclusively female, private, and has usually been understood as in some sense countercultural. Arsinoë's festival was public, attracted both male and female spectators, and was hardly countercultural, granted her sponsorship and the palace location.[152] She may have introduced this distinctive version of the cult to Alexandria.[153] Her Adonia, though primarily directed at Greeks and though it cast her as a patron of Greek culture, also featured Egyptian over- or undertones.[154] Arsinoë's Adonia was at once domestic and public, like the palace.[155] While Arsinoë had been assimilated to various forms of Aphrodite, the Aphrodite of the Adonis story might seem an odd, unrespectable choice on the face of it, but dynastic propaganda had, in somewhat different ways, celebrated sexual love between couples and in that sense her Adonia fits.[156] Although it attracted a coed audience, the festival appears to have been calculated primarily to appeal to women, not only because of its content but because of the fabulous textiles on display; the pair of matrons, themselves experts at this characteristically female task, could appreciate these symbols of the wealth and beauty of court life and, of course, the patronage of the Ptolemies.[157] Theocritus' poem celebrates Arsinoë's piety and generosity as a patron.[158] Although Ptolemy II could have funded the celebration,[159] Theocritus mentions only Arsinoë. The event enabled the queen to provide entertainment and demonstrate the wealth and culture of her family while at the same time she made the court somewhat accessible to her subjects, though Arsinoë was too elevated, like Aphrodite herself, to appear in person. Like Arsinoë's other connections to Aphrodite, this one normalized the power of the queen within the Ptolemaic dynasty to her Greek subjects.[160]

Arsinoë likely patronized other cults as well. The cult of the Dioscuri (the deified brothers of Helen, patrons of sailors and seafarers like Arsinoë) is one possibility; Arsinoë may have founded the Alexandrian cult.[161] According to Callimachus, it was the Dioscuri who carried the dead Arsinoë to Olympus (frg. 228 Pf) and their cult was often associated with that of the Great Gods of Samothrace, favorites of both Arsinoë and Ptolemy II.[162] In Egyptian cult, she was a priestess of the ram god of Mendes.[163]

Did Arsinoë serve as a patron of the arts as well as a patron of cults?[164] She likely did. One of her Macedonian predecessors, the mother of Philip II, made a dedication in association with the Muses on behalf of women citizens (Plut. *Mor.* 14c).[165] Arsinoë herself dedicated the rotunda at Samothrace, presumably having chosen the architect (see above). As part of her patronage of the Adonia, she gave a prize to a woman who won the competition for singing (Theoc. *Id.* 15.95–99).[166] Arsinoë may have met and patronized Callimachus while still married to Lysimachus; that is, at least, one explanation for the poet's interest in (and apparently travel to) the mysteries at Samothrace.[167]

The role of patron of the arts was particularly important for Ptolemaic rulers, as suggested by the proximity of the Library and Museum to their living quarters.[168] We know, however, little about the dynamics of Ptolemaic cultural patronage, let alone the role of royal women in the practice.[169] Ptolemy II's literary patronage was well-established by the time of Arsinoë's return; it would hardly be surprising if she, in keeping with the perfect harmony the couple supposedly enjoyed, joined in.[170] As demonstrated in the celebration of the success of female Ptolemies in equestrian competition, there was definitely the presumption that women and men shared in and contributed together to family *kleos*.

Royal women and their marriages generally featured prominently in Alexandrian poetry,[171] though, in other dynasties, royal women also inspired poets, if fewer.[172] Alexandrian poetry is full of references to Arsinoë,[173] as well as other Ptolemaic royal women, Posidippus' work especially so.[174] Arsinoë, however, inspired more literary compositions than any other Ptolemaic woman, partly because her husband's reign was such a literary high point.[175] Much of our evidence about Arsinoë in the last phase of her career comes from court poetry. Of course, these allusions could all have been flattery dispensed by men who, directly or indirectly, worked under or for her brother. Still, court poetry mirrored the court and its values.[176]

The poets, by their allusions or direct references to Arsinoë, created an image of a queen both feminine and unthreatening.[177] Apollonius Rhodius, royal librarian and thus perhaps the most prominent of intellectuals of his generation, composed an epic, the *Argonautica*, reimagining the world of Homer in terms of his own day, reflecting a number of aspects of Ptolemaic monarchy.[178] Arsinoë was certainly not a model for Apollonius' Medea,[179] though other allusions to the queen are present in his work.[180] Many consider Apollonius' portrait of Alcinous and Arete, king and queen of the Phaeacians, an allusion to Ptolemy II and Arsinoë II, and their dealings with each other, partly because the Phaeacians rulers were sometimes understood to be a brother-sister couple,[181] but mainly because they so clearly represented an ideal, as they did in Homer, but an altered ideal, of royal power and ruling couples. We will discuss this image at the end of the chapter because I believe it suggests the way the royal pair wanted their roles to be understood.

A number of passages in Hellenistic poetry intimate that Arsinoë served as an artistic patron. Posidippus (AB 37) focuses on a poet's lyre dedicated to her at one of her cults.[182] Callimachus apparently called Arsinoë the tenth muse, probably alluding to her literary patronage.[183] Indeed, outside of Egypt she may have been associated in cult with the Muses.[184] Callimachus and Theocritus regularly used Helen as a kind of veiled allusion to Arsinoë, though of naturally the "good Helen" who didn't go to Troy with Paris.[185] Theocritus (22.216) makes not only the Dioscuri but Helen patrons of poetry, possibly alluding to his queen as a patron. Much of the Ptolemaic in Theocritus' work relates to Arsinoë, not her brother, perhaps an indication that she personally was his patron.[186] Indeed, Ptolemaic-era poetry praised royal wives more than the kings themselves and this was particularly true of Arsinoë II, possibly because she exercised such extensive patronage.[187] The poets played an important role in publicizing and shaping the image of royal courtesans as well as royal wives,[188] more evidence of how comparatively small the distinction between the two could be. Perhaps *hetairai* too could act as patrons, although Arsinoë seems far more prominent than they. Arsinoë probably had the kind of education that would have enabled her to appreciate the erudite and clever productions of poets active in Alexandria (see chapter 1). Indeed, in the Hellenistic period women generally gained greater visibility and education, taking on more public roles in some cases.[189] While there is no indisputable evidence, it is difficult to reject the notion that Arsinoë II as well as Ptolemy II patronized the artists of the court and that some, at least, of the flattering references found in court poetry were calculated to please the queen and her tastes.

Although we do not know the cause of Arsinoë's death or how long she was ill, appropriately enough it is an Alexandrian poet who provides the only meaningful evidence about the reaction of her subjects and husband, as well as the information that her funerary rites were Graeco-Macedonian, involving cremation (other evidence suggests that even her funerary rites were both Greek and Egyptian).[190] Callimachus' *Iamb* 16, an emotional but fragmentary poem about the death and apotheosis of Arsinoë II, pictures a populace in deep and universal mourning for her. The people lament "our queen gone," Ptolemy II makes sacrifices and arranges her pyre, and the news of her death spreads around the world among mortals and immortals. Arsinoë's dead and deified sister Philotera sees the smoke from Arsinoë's funerary pyre as she departs from Lemnos and thinks at first that Alexandria itself is on fire but another goddess tells her that while the city is not ablaze, she has heard, "dirges / in your city . . . not as if for commoners . . . / . . . They cry for your sister, born / of the same womb with you: it is she / who has died, and the cities of Egypt, / wherever you look, are cloaked in black."[191]

The date of Arsinoë's death remains hotly disputed because the Mendes stele dates her death to year 15 of Ptolemy II's reign, thus apparently to July 270[192] while the Pithom stele has Arsinoë alive during year 16 of her brother's reign and puts her death in his seventeenth year, thus to 268. Grzybek and Hazzard have argued that this discrepancy arose not from error but rather because the stelai employed two different methods to calculate Ptolemy II's regnal years: originally, as in the Mendes stele, he calculated from the beginning of his individual rule in January 282, but later he began to calculate from the beginning of his corule with his father, 285. Based on the revised dating system, she died in early July 268.[193] The later dating has gained some acceptance[194] but remains too uncertain to depend on for major conclusions about Arsinoë's career.

Throughout this chapter, it has proved difficult to distinguish Arsinoë's actions and role from those of her brother because the royal pair was so thoroughly integrated into a joint image of monarchy. Ptolemaic monarchy preserved many elements of its Macedonian and pharaonic roots, but a new form of kingship was developing, one still military, but less so (or at least less directly so) than either Macedonian or Egyptian prototypes. Royal women in both pharaonic and Macedonian monarchy had exercised symbolic military command, but now the difference between the role of royal males and females had been narrowed, the distinction blunted. Kingship, as played out in Apollonius Rhodius' epic, apparently reflecting Ptolemaic ideology,[195] was less heroic, more inclined to compromise and conciliation than in Homer (not to mention in Macedonia).[196] In such a monarchy, royal woman could potentially play a role a greater role.

Apollonius' portrait of Arete queen of the Phaeacians seems to allude to Arsinoë. Apollonius' Arete is more conventional than Homer's; she operates behind the scenes, through persuasion, rather than directly as she does in Homer, though her functional authority proves no less than in the *Odyssey*. In the *Odyssey*, Arete publicly defends Odysseus, while in the *Argonautica* she defends Medea by speaking privately to the king, her husband.[197] If Apollonius' Arete was indeed an ideal as well as a reflection of Arsinoë, then we have a monarchy in which the male ruler has most but not all of the public power, but in private takes the advice of his wife and accepts her advocacy of a favorite.[198] Arete persuades her husband to do what she wants while talking to him in bed; this is not equal decision making but it is joint decision making and that may be suggestive about the role Arsinoë played during her last marriage. Arete/Arsinoë personified Aphrodite's power of "erotic persuasion."[199] This was, apparently, how a queen was supposed to act.[200] Moreover, Apollonius' epic stressed the religious honors of royal women, much as Arsinoë's publicly acknowledged power, during her life and posthumously, did the same.

This process of seeing royal power as paired, with male and female aspects, began with Ptolemy II's decision to marry his full sister. By the time of her death or soon thereafter, it had fully developed, so that the king was partly defined by his sister-wife, by their pairing in public images.[201]

CHAPTER SIX

Arsinoë's Afterlife

BEING DEAD HAD surprisingly little immediate effect on Arsinoë's career. No matter when one dates her death and whether or not one considers her individual cult posthumous, Arsinoë continued to play a major role in Ptolemaic Egypt during the rest of her brother's reign and remained a critically important figure in the memory history of the dynasty and in the evolving role of royal women in Ptolemaic monarchy. Only after the demise of the Ptolemies did her image grow dim, gradually subsumed in that of the most famous Ptolemy of all, Cleopatra VII, and of her half sister, another Arsinoë (IV).

The Cult of Thea Philadelphus

The traditional view has been that Ptolemy II organized and promulgated an individual cult to Arsinoë as *thea philadelphus* (the brother-loving goddess) only after her death, when he established a priestess for her cult (a *canephore*, or basket bearer);[1] a temple (the Arsinoëum) in Alexandria and another in Memphis; the honor of being a temple-sharing god with the gods in Egyptian temples; a festival, the Arsinoëa; and other honors as well. I will discuss her cult as if it were posthumous, though it may not have been.[2]

This cult constituted another step in the divinization of the Ptolemaic dynasty, an evolution that had begun with Ptolemy II's establishment of the cult of the *theoi soteres*, continued with the decision to initiate the first royal sibling marriage, and had already involved Arsinoë in two life time cults (the *theoi adelphoi* and the cult of Arsinoë Aphrodite at Zephyrium). Arsinoë may have helped to shape the new cult even if it did not appear until after her death; she had played a part in this evolutionary process up until the time of her death. The speed with which the initial stages of the cult appeared after her death strongly suggests that the creation of the cult had been planned before it, thus leaving open the distinct possibility that she had helped to shape it.[3] The cult of Arsinoë Philadelphus appeared very quickly, at least in Alexandria, though the king may not have extended its reach to all of Egypt and Egyptian temples until as much as five years later.[4] Apparently, he did not provide regular funding for the cult until 263, when he decreed that a considerable portion of the religious tax *(apomoira)* would be used to support the cult of Arsinoë.[5] Ptolemy II crafted much of the enduring image of Ptolemaic monarchy, and by the end of his reign, his sister-wife had become a critical part of that image, in good part because of the establishment of this cult.

The double nature of the cult was essential to its enduring success: Arsinoë was both an Egyptian and a Greek goddess. Her dual cults exemplified the dual nature of Ptolemaic monarchy. According to the Mendes Stele, Ptolemy Philadelphus made Arsinoë a temple-sharing goddess in all Egyptian temples. In Memphis, she shared space with and became the consort of the chief god of the city Ptah and the high priest of Ptah became her priest as well. As an Egyptian goddess, she appeared in completely Egyptian form on temple reliefs and stelai. The Mendes stele shows the royal family, including Arsinoë, worshipping the Egyptian gods, also including Arsinoë.[6] A priestess of the ram of Mendes in her lifetime, Arsinoë was given Egyptian cult titles meaning "beloved of the ram," "brother-loving goddess," and simply "Arsinoë."[7] On Egyptian style reliefs, most famously at Philae, Ptolemy II himself appeared worshipping his new goddess, who is often accompanied by other Egyptian-goddesses. Ptolemy II also established temples for Arsinoë alone, as an Egyptian goddess. Two reliefs show Ptolemy adoring Arsinoë by herself, without other Egyptian deities.[8] Arsinoë's new cult had Egyptian precedents: a number of pharaonic rulers had individual cults that continued into the Ptolemaic period (we know of an Egyptian who was both priest of Ramesses II, the New Kingdom ruler, and of Arsinoë II),[9] and in pharaonic times a few royal women had individual cults as well (see Introduction).

Some hieroglyphic inscriptions (as well as some Greek) associate Arsinoë with Isis instead of Aphrodite,[10] perhaps because Isis was connected to kingship and was married to her brother Osiris. In pharaonic times, Isis blended with Hathor and was a throne goddess, primarily identified as the mother of the king (Horus incarnate) and not associated with the king's wife (see Introduction). The Ptolemies changed this, as the formation "Arsinoë Isis" suggests, and the assimilation grew increasingly important; on the Pithom stele Arsinoë is dressed fully as Isis and appears standing by her husband who is shown in Greek style.[11]

The Egyptian cult of *thea philadelphus* effectively functioned as the first stage of an Egyptian Ptolemaic dynastic cult.[12] Arsinoë's Egyptian cult gained widespread acceptance with the Egyptian priestly class. Important Egyptian priestly families committed to the cult and to the Ptolemies; her priesthood, for instance, can be traced in two families over nine generations.[13] Egyptian priestly families in Memphis named their daughters "Arsinoë" (or "Berenice"), though otherwise resisting Greek personal names. They were, after all, naming their daughters after an Egyptian goddess.[14] Arsinoë's cult functioned as the primary anchor linking the native priesthood to the dynasty, a linkage that was critical to the ability of Ptolemy II to conduct foreign policy.[15] The cult also created a new bond between Greek and Egyptian inhabitants of Egypt.[16] The number of cult sites in Egypt attests to its popularity.

Arsinoë became a Greek goddess too. Callimachus (frg. 228 Pf) has Arsinoë taken up to the heavens by Helen's brothers, the Dioscuri—another examples of the poetic tendency to associate Arsinoë with Helen (see chapter 5)—and he describes the temple and altar that were established for her in Alexandria. Ptolemy II built this intricate shrine, the Arsinoëum, for his sister-wife,[17] within the royal quarter of the city.[18] He placed a single unusually tall obelisk from Heliopolis in front of it (Pliny *H. N.* 36.67–9, 37.108),[19] a gesture aimed at creating a combined Greek-Egyptian "front door" to the cult.[20] Pliny (*H.N.* 34.148) reported that by the time both Ptolemy II and the architect Timochares had died, the temple was still unfinished; it may never have been completed.[21] According to Pliny, the cult statue was made of iron and the vaulted roof (an Egyptian architectural technique)[22] of lodestone was magnetic so that the statue of Arsinoë was meant appeared to "fly" suspended from the ceiling.[23] Pliny (*H.N.* 37.108) also mentions another statue of peridot (an olive-green gemstone) made in honor of her and consecrated in the sanctuary.[24] Arsinoë became a temple-sharing god in Greek cult as well as in Egyptian.[25] In addition to her assimilation to Aphrodite, Arsinoë was identified with other Greek goddesses.[26] Every Ptolemaic harbor town had a cult to the *thea philadelphus*.[27] This cult was not simply imposed but actually popular.[28]

In connection with Arsinoë's cult, there was a festival, the Arsinoëa.[29] These festivals (held both in the countryside and Alexandria) increased the cult's popularity. Contests likely played a part in the celebration. The Arsinoëa happened at the end of the Egyptian year, at the beginning of annual inundation.[30] In Alexandria, her *canephore* led a procession during the festival; in the streets where the image of Arsinoë passed, inhabitants apparently put up altars and brought victims for sacrifice, whether out of enthusiasm or the feeling that loyalty to the royal dynasty needed to be demonstrated.[31] *Oinochoai* (wine jugs) with an image of the queen probably played a role in these festivals; loyal subjects/worshippers may have given them to a priestess of her cult so that the priestess could pour a wine libation on the street altars.

On these jugs, the queen stands, her right arm outstretched holding a *phiale* (cup) from which she pours a libation onto an altar and in her left arm she carries a *dikera* (double cornucopia) bursting with cakes and grapes. In the background is a garlanded sacred pillar. In a sense, the queen pours a libation to herself[32] or some aspect of herself.[33] Many examples are inscribed. The *oinochoai* inscriptions link Arsinoë not to Aphrodite but to either Isis or Agathe Tyche (a personification of good fortune popular in the Hellenistic period).[34] The production of *oinochoai* may have begun while Arsinoë still lived.[35] The jugs not only confirm her popularity and/or that of her cult, but demonstrate how the queen's spirit was understood to protect the domestic world.[36] The many dedicatory *oinochoai* with figures of Ptolemaic queens—found in Egypt and elsewhere in the Mediterranean—confirm their continuing acceptance.

Although Arsinoë had separate Greek and Egyptian cults, in the Fayum (a region in Egypt heavily developed by the Ptolemies and settled by Greeks), in the newly created Arsinoite nome (an administrative division), she became the nome goddess for both Egyptians and Greeks.[37] As we have seen, cults to Arsinoë developed in the ports of the eastern Mediterranean, particularly in the Aegean and on the island of Cyprus;[38] and even as far away as the coast of the Black Sea.[39] Thus, in a great variety of ways, Arsinoë's cult honored her dynasty but also had wide appeal around the Mediterranean world as well as at home in Egypt.

Although Arsinoë's cult aimed at the entire population of Egypt, both Egyptian and Greek, its formal perpetuation depended on a small group, those who directly benefitted from Ptolemaic benefactions.[40]

Eponymous Foundations

Philip II had named cities after himself, and his son Alexander followed suit. After his death, the Successors imitated this custom but also created a new one. In addition to new foundations or refoundations named after them, the Successors began to name cities after the women of their families.[41] In a world of competing dynasties, particularly in areas where two dynasties struggled for power, eponymous foundations functioned as markers of success or failure.[42] In some cases, kings may have chosen the name and in others the cities made the choice, out of fear or desire for patronage.[43] There has been an assumption that cities were named after royal women because of their male kin, that the naming involved no action on the part of the women; this assumption may well be correct, but some ancient sources, correctly or not, do speak of royal women founding the cities named after them (e.g., Strab. 10.2.22; see chapter 2). Eponymous cities often maintained cults for the person after whom they were named; citizens sacrificed to them as city-founders.[44]

Ptolemy II named streets in Alexandria after Arsinoë, often combining her name with epithets borrowed from other well-known deities, epithets that stressed aspects of her various cults.[45] But most of Arsinoë's eponymity related to city names, many within Egypt, many without. As we have seen, while married to Lysimachus, some cities may already have been named after Arsinoë, but more were named after her subsequent marriage to Ptolemy II. In many cases, the link between the city and Arsinoë was intensified or exemplified by coinage that showed her on the obverse.[46] Naming or renaming a city after Arsinoë was a popular option.[47] Tying down the date of these foundations and refoundations proves difficult, but a number seem to have to do with the Chremonidean War, the places named or renamed being critical ports for the Ptolemaic navy.[48] These eponymous foundations were, therefore, more than generic honors to the dynasty or Arsinoë herself but rather connected to specific policy attributed to her.[49] When Ptolemaic power subsequently declined, many of the refoundations returned to their original names, but for the new cities, her name remained as did, often, her cult, and the name lasted in areas central to Ptolemaic power.[50] In effect, the memory of Arsinoë became embedded in the Mediterranean coastline, the names of cities and the popularity of her cult making her a real and enduring presence over a wide area. The eponymous cities embodied her power and that of the Ptolemaic navy.

Image

Many images have been attributed to Arsinoë; her portraiture merits but has not yet received a monograph.[51] The great majority of portraits of Arsinoë, however, appear to be posthumous, doubtless many associated with her cult.[52] In a book focused on her life, it will therefore be necessary to discuss her portraits only briefly.

Just as cult for Arsinoë was twofold, so was her physical image; Ptolemaic art generally had a "split personality,"[53] like Ptolemaic monarchy. Egyptian and Greek representations of Arsinoë came out of very different traditions and remained separate, yet not entirely so. Over time, the tradition of Greek art affected the Egyptian-style portraits of Arsinoë (and other Ptolemies). The colossal statue of Arsinoë in the Gregorian Museum at the Vatican (along with a matching one of Ptolemy II), inscribed with her name and epithet (Fig. 6.1), is almost certainly an early, possibly lifetime,[54] highly traditional Egyptian style representation of Arsinoë: she wears a tripartite wig and two uraei (stylized upright cobras symbolizing sovereignty) on her forehead; her tight sheath is the kind shown in Egyptian art for thousands of years and her impassive face is not individualized. Discovered on Pharos Island (just off the coast of Alexandria) were fragments of a large-scale triad (Ptolemy II, Arsinoë II, and probably Ammon), also dating to the reign of Ptolemy II, possibly from Arsinoë's lifetime.[55] The triad was done in an archaistic style, linked to that of the nineteenth dynasty in the New Kingdom period, rather than the more recent Late Period style of many Egyptian-style Ptolemaic monuments. A statuette (Fig. 6.2), on the other hand, inscribed for Arsinoë now in the Metropolitan Museum (usually dated to the second century BCE) represents the later, more Hellenized Egyptian style: her face is more individualized; she has corkscrew curls ("Greek hair"), but the statuette retains the traditional Egyptian rigid pose with one foot forward.[56]

FIGURE 6.1. Egyptian-style statue of Arsinoë from the Gregorian Museum, Vatican, with statues of an unknown princess (far left) and Ptolmey II (far right). Photo: Scala /Art Resource, NY.

Her Egyptian-style images were far more distinctive than her Greek images, in several respects.[57] In Egyptian-style portraits, Arsinoë usually has three distinctive attributes, but the inscribed titles often accompanying her images prove even more significant.

While images show many royal Egyptian women wearing the vulture crown and/or high plumes with the horns and disk of Hathor (see

FIGURE 6.2. Egyptian-style statuette of Arsinoë from the Metropolitan Museum. Image © The Metropolitan Museum of Art.

Introduction), in Egyptian art Arsinoë usually sports an idiosyncratic crown of her own, one not previously seen (fig. 6.3).[58] It resembles the red king's crown of Lower Egypt, minus that crown's spiral, but with a number of additions: two high plumes, ram horns, cow horns, and a solar disk.[59] It remains to be seen whether the crown Arsinoë wears in Egyptian art, like other crowns shown in Egyptian art, had any physical reality;[60] variation in the way the features of the crown are shown suggests that artists worked from a list of features sent out by the court, but not from a standard physical image.[61] The crown has often been considered a posthumous attribute (typically by those who believe Arsinoë's cult was posthumous), somehow associated with her Egyptian cult, but some think the crown dates to her lifetime.[62] Arsinoë was the first Ptolemaic queen with special iconography,[63] though a few images of Cleopatra II, III, and VII show them wearing Arsinoë's crown.[64]

The significance of the crown and its constituent parts has been much debated; attempts have been made to connect features of the

FIGURE 6.3. Temple relief, from chapel of Ptolemy II, San el-Hagar.
© British Museum.

crown to specific deities or religious experiences.[65] Attempting to limit
or define the meaning of symbols, especially one whose roots go so far
back in time, is hardly an exact science. The crown implies a subtle and
mysteriously nuanced attempt to associate Arsinoë with the powers of a
king,[66] though it hardly demonstrates, in itself, that she was coregent
with her brother.[67] Showing someone with the attributes of power does
not make them powerful or demonstrate that they are,[68] but such a de-
piction must mean something, granted its idiosyncratic nature. It was
constructed for a purpose, though the specific nature of the purpose
remains obscure.

Arsinoë has another unique attribute; she often carries or is associated with the *dikera*, whereas other Ptolemaic royal women carry only
the single cornucopia. This feature is found in both Egyptian and Greek
style images of Arsinoë II.[69] Athenaeus (11.497b–c) says that Ptolemy II
himself was responsible for the creation of the cornucopia as an attribute
or ornament of her images.[70] Since Athenaeus remarks that the craftsmen

who created the image intended it to be richer than the proverbial horn of Amalthea, the symbol relates to some kind of abundance conveyed by Arsinoë, but could signify more.[71]

In addition to her distinctive crown and cornucopia, in Egyptian art Arsinoë also usually wears a double uraeus on her forehead. The double uraeus had both masculine pharaonic precedents and female ones, apparently signifying different things at different times, for different categories of people. For the rulers of the twenty-fifth dynasty, the uraei probably signified rule of both Kush and Egypt.[72] The pharaonic female parallels were eighteenth- and nineteenth-dynasty queens, often but not always ones who helped an heir get to the throne or acted as regent or in support of the son.[73] Arsinoë's double uraeus might allude to the political power of some earlier royal women, but it more likely somehow connects to the cult of the *theoi adelphoi*.[74]

But the most unusual and problematic feature of Arsinoë's Egyptian representation was her title. The names of royal Egyptian women had appeared in cartouches since, at least Middle Kingdom times, and a number of other symbols of royal power once exclusively male had gradually been given to royal women as well, part of the dualistic understanding of power that is frequently found in Egyptian monarchy (see Introduction). Only a very few pharaonic royal women, however, women who actually reigned and were not simply consorts, were given other kingly attributes, notably throne names.[75] Arsinoë not only had her name in a cartouche like other royal women, but was the first Ptolemaic royal woman to have a throne name added to her cartouche. She was designated "King of Upper and Lower Egypt," a title ordinarily held by the pharaoh.[76] Even if this title was not given her until after her death as seems likely,[77] it identifies her as a ruler.

Arsinoë's kingly titles, even if posthumous, raise a number of issues, none of them easily resolved. Whatever her actual power at court, one wonders why Ptolemy II chose to assign Arsinoë Egyptian royal titles. While Manetho and the priests of the Ptolemaic era probably knew of the existence of previous female kings, these women were hardly the pharaonic norm.[78] Since his Graeco-Macedonian subjects would have had no knowledge of these titles and their significance, his decision must have been aimed at the Egyptian priestly class, but this does not tell us why Ptolemy II thought this class would find such exceptional titles attractive. Perhaps he understood them somehow to support her Egyptian cult.[79]

Another problem is the discrepancy between Egyptian and Greek material in this respect. No Greek evidence indicates anything like this Egyptian title for Arsinoë;[80] indeed it is hard to imagine how a Macedonian or Greek would have been able to conceive of an institutionalized (as opposed to situational) rule by a royal woman. We have seen how Apollonius transformed the role of Arete, queen of the Phaeacians, from Homer's coruler to that of a woman who gets her way via pillow talk (see chapter 5). It is not so much that Greek authors concealed this indication of Arsinoë's power,[81] but rather that they do not know about this kingly role of Arsinoë's. In this case, we confront a literal example of the need to "see double"; we need to deal with the difference in the two kinds of sources in a way that recognizes the values of both.[82] Did literate Egyptians understand Arsinoë as more powerful than did Graeco-Macedonian subjects, or do we need to think about the Greek and Egyptian sources as attempting to describe the same situation in terms and in the context of two different cultures? I am more inclined to the latter view.

Finally, why, whether or not he thought it would please the priestly caste, did Ptolemy II give his wife these titles, the mysterious crown, and why did he generally institutionalize female royal power (during Arsinoë's lifetime and after her death) to an unprecedented degree? What was "in it" for him? Surely these practices mean that Ptolemy II increasingly found it in his interest to include royal women in Ptolemaic monarchy.

Do the special crown and the pharaonic title demonstrate that Arsinoë II actually exercised royal power in Egypt? The answer, particularly if both crown and title were awarded after her death, must surely be "no." One can exercise power without titles or insignia and one can possess them and yet be unable, in practice, to exert power or influence. On the other hand, the crowns, the title, Arsinoë's prominence in her lifetime, her lifetime cults, all are suggestive of her power.[83] In effect, while his sister still lived—and even more after her death—Ptolemy II acted to institutionalize the power some Egyptian and Macedonian women had occasionally exercised.

Female portraiture in Greek art tradition is extraordinarily generic. Artists demonstrated little interest in replicating specific features of actual individuals, though there was concern to represent virtues rather than individuals.[84] It is notoriously hard to tell mortal women from goddesses, ordinary women from royal women.[85] This task is particularly

FIGURE 6.4. Head of a goddess or queen, possibly Arsinoë I. Accession Number 96.712. Catharine Page Perkins Fund © Museum of Fine Arts, Boston.

problematic when the woman in question has been divinized and some statuary depicts her as a goddess.[86] For identification of a portrait, much depends on the attributes with which a woman is shown, her dress, her pose, and above all, on any inscription accompanying the image.[87] Many attributions of portrait heads to Arsinoë are based on their supposed resemblance to her coin portraits;[88] that, as we shall see, is problematic methodology. Museums around the world display beautiful female portrait heads bearing tentative labels, often referencing contradictory identifications (for instance, fig. 6.4),[89] that say things like "perhaps intended to be a portrait of a Ptolemaic queen, perhaps Arsinoë II or III" (fig. 6.5),[90] or the more noncommittal "Ptolemaic Queen,"[91] or the even vaguer "Head of a goddess or queen." Many of these heads may originally have been found in sanctuaries dedicated to Arsinoë but most have provenances that go no further back than some nineteenth-century private collection or a vague, word-of-mouth find-spot (e.g., "Egypt").

FIGURE 6.5. Portrait, possibly Arsinoë, found at Halicarnassus. © British Museum.

Context (or its absence) is vital. Arsinoë's portrait often appeared with that of her brother; the sculptural pairing in marble or bronze relates to the cult of the *theoi adelphoi*, either directly or indirectly. In a sense, Arsinoë was recognizable because Ptolemy II was, though in both cases, inscriptions on statue bases really confirm their identity. Their images often appeared paired in public: Pausanias (1.8.6) says their statues stood in the Athenian agora, near the entrance to the Odeum; at Olympia, there were the statues Callicrates dedicated (see chapter 5); another sculptural pair was dedicated to Poseidon at Kalauria by the Methanians who had just become the Arsinoëans and wanted to publicize their name change.[92] Despite their frequent joint appearance, we should not necessarily assume that these paired statues of Ptolemy II and Arsinoë II represented male and female on the same scale; they were a pair, but not necessarily an equal one (fig. 6.6).[93] Nonetheless, Arsinoë's image helped to define Ptolemy II's, as his did hers.[94]

FIGURE 6.6. Bronze Statuettes of Arsinoë II and Ptolemy II. © British Museum.

Arsinoë's image on cheap, mass-produced *oinochoai* used in her cult seems at first generically Greek. Inscriptions on the *oinochoai* identify her portrait and that of subsequent queens on similar jugs. While the quality of the images on the *oinochoai* (British Museum AN967226001; fig. 6.7) varies tremendously, many do seem individualized and some see a marked resemblance to Arsinoë's coin image.[95] The *oinochoai* show Arsinoë holding her characteristic double cornucopia and a libation bowl, with an altar to her right and a pillar to her left. Despite their superficially Hellenic look, the wine jugs really represent a kind of combination of Greek and Egyptian traditions: faience (itself an Egyptian technology, originally) offering vessels were used in Egyptian cults but Arsinoë's clothing and pose is Greek (though some discern some subtle and varying Egyptian influence, possibly because these objects were produced in workshops run by Greeks but employing Egyptians).[96] Probably closely connected to Arsinoë's image on the *oinochoai* is a charming small head now at the British Museum, also in faience, apparently from

FIGURE 6.7. Oinochoae. © British Museum.

a statuette, possibly used in Arsinoë's cult; while the head is not inscribed, it so closely resembles—particularly when viewed in profile—the better quality of the Arsinoë images on the wine jugs as to make an identification with Arsinoë very probable (fig. 6.8).[97]

Some believe that Egyptian tradition affected Greek-style portraits of Arsinoë and others.[98] The inhabitants of Alexandria and of other places in Egypt certainly saw both styles of portraits. Whether or not the portrait styles seeped into each other, double images of the Ptolemies must have been part of the cultural baggage inhabitants/viewers carried.

Coin Images

Ptolemy I, soon after he took the royal title, ca. 304,[99] became the first of the Successors to put his own image on coins, transforming the nature of Greek coinage by placing the image of a living man on coins. He established a distinctive and lasting tradition of Ptolemaic coin

FIGURE 6.8. Faience head. © British Museum.

portraiture, of which Arsinoë's coin images form a part. His image itself on his own coins and on the later ones, constitutes a marked break with the tradition of Greek male portraiture, itself only a slightly more realistic tradition than that for female portraits. Ptolemy I's coin portrait approaches caricature; minimally it was a new "ideal." He has a long and somewhat bumpy hooked nose; beetling brow; large, protuberant eyes; and a very strong chin that tends upward, so that chin and nose threaten to meet. His image was not literally realistic (he is shown as middle-aged, though he was in his sixties when the first coins appeared, and his coin image never aged). The goal was not literal realism, but the appearance of it.[100]

This is the image that became iconic, the one echoed to varying degrees by subsequent Ptolemies, male and female.[101] The portraits of the dynastic founder Ptolemy I as well as those of Arsinoë II appeared on Ptolemaic coins until the end of the dynasty; these are the only two Ptolemies for whom this is true.[102] Though the image of Arsinoë on later coins (after the reign of her husband Ptolemy II) tended to take on the features of the current queen, she clearly functioned as a model for sub-sequent royal women.[103] Ptolemy II and subsequent rulers who contin-ued these images stressed continuity with the past of the dynasty and thereby increased its unity.[104] Gold coinages in large denominations with royal images of the Ptolemies may have commemorated royal deaths or accessions and could have been handed out as gifts meant to ensure loyalty at the time of a transmission of power.[105]

Whereas dead male heroes had sometimes appeared on Greek coins, mortal women had not appeared at all and yet, late in the fourth century, the first living woman's image on a coin was minted. Again, members of the Ptolemaic dynasty took the lead.[106] Berenice I's head appears on coins from Rhodes and Cos (the site of the birth of her son the future Ptolemy II), possibly dating to the late fourth century.[107] Coins from Ephesus Arsinoë bearing a female image, apparently that of Arsinoë, probably date to the period of her marriage to Lysimachus (see chapter 2). It was not till the reign of Ptolemy II that royal women

FIGURE 6.9. Gold octadrachm of Arsinoë II. Image © The Metropolitan Museum of Art.

appeared on coins produced in Egypt. Arsinoë's image on Egyptian coins,[108] though Greek in style, was not necessarily intended only for a Greek audience; the iconographical program of her coins seems to have been directed at both Greeks and Egyptians.[109]

Some coins show her head alone on the obverse.[110] Arsinoë wears a veil, *stephane* (crown), diadem, a "melon" hairdo, behind her head is a lotus scepter,[111] and ram horns circle her ear (fig. 6.9), apparently associating her with Alexander the Great, the only other person shown with the same attribute.[112] On the reverse of these single-image coins of Arsinoë is either the Ptolemaic eagle or the double cornucopia or the Dioscuri. The legend reads "of Arsinoë Philadelphus." Like her profile on the *oinochoai*, coin images of Arsinoë show her with a long sharp, almost pointed nose, with a curve to it; a chin that, like that of Ptolemy I though in a less pronounced way, threatens to meet her nose; and large protuberant eyes. Unlike her father, her forehead recedes and her lips are pursed and her cheeks full. Whether some or any of these coins were issued during her lifetime is uncertain, particularly because of the chronological ambiguity of the epithet "Philadelphus."[113]

Other coins (called jugate) show (on the obverse) her in profile, behind the profile of her sibling spouse and (on the reverse) Ptolemy I and Berenice I (see chapter 4, fig. 4.1).[114] These paired-coin images became one of the hallmarks of the dynasty that, from Ptolemy II on, imagined itself in interlocking pairs. The beautiful golden coins not only epitomize the double imagery of Ptolemy II and Arsinoë II, but probably commemorate a particular event; the obvious possibilities are their marriage, the initiation of the cult of the *theoi adelphoi*, or Arsinoë's apotheosis as *thea philadelphus*.[115] Viewed simply in terms of the congruence of iconography to event, the double jugate images would best suit either their marriage or the initiation of the *theoi adelphoi*, possibly signifying that they were first coined while Arsinoë still lived.[116] Currently, however, scholarly consensus considers them posthumous, but products of Ptolemy II's reign.[117]

Though the coin images of Arsinoë have often been considered realistic, or at least more realistic than her sculptured portraits in either Greek or Egyptian style, the images with each pair mirroring each other and the other pair, may allude—with their prominent, staring eyes—to Alexander and stress or exaggerate existing similarity of features[118] because this in turn confirms legitimacy and demonstrates continuity with the past.[119] One wants children who look like their father. Theocritus

(17.63) tells us that Ptolemy II was "born in the likeness of his father": resemblance demonstrated legitimacy.[120] The paired jugate images imply that the younger pair is in some sense the reincarnation of the elder.[121] Moreover, the similarity reinforced the power of pairing, of the doubled image of the sibling rulers. That royal pairs resembled each other as well as their parents doubled their right to rule.

On the other hand, the coin portraits of Arsinoë II and her mother, Berenice I, were indeed more individualized, relatively speaking, than earlier images of women, and the images of mother and daughter, though certainly similar, are differentiated.[122] In a sense, the images of Arsinoë and her mother represent a new female ideal, as did Ptolemy I's.[123] Still, perhaps the most striking feature of the two pairs of portraits is that while Ptolemy I's portrait is highly individualized (if somewhat less so than on his individual coins), the other three are far less so. Moreover, their three profiles resemble each other[124] much more than they do Ptolemy Soter.[125]

The Chremonidean War, Arsinoë's Memory, and Her Son

As we have seen, the Chremonidean War (ca. 268–61) pitted a number of Greek city-states supported by Ptolemy II against the power of the Macedonian king, Antigonus Gonatas. Though Arsinoë had died by the time the war began, the Athenians associated her with the policy that led to Ptolemaic involvement, and Ptolemy II and his admiral used the memory of Arsinoë and her cult to promote support for their cause. In roughly the same time period (268/67 until 259), a man called Ptolemy, Son of Ptolemy (known to historians as "Ptolemy the Son" (*Nios*), coruled with Ptolemy II, a position probably terminated because he was also the son of Ptolemy II who, along with Timarchus, rebelled against his father in Asia (Trog. *Prol.* 26). Was Ptolemy II's coregent in fact Arsinoë's son by Lysimachus and did Ptolemy II raise him to coregency in order to, in the course of the war, place him on the Macedonian throne, only to have to remove him when, frustrated by the failure of this supposed plan, he revolted?[126]

Admittedly, there are a number of attractive aspects to this recently revived identification: the apparent coexistence of the coregency and the war;[127] the use of Arsinoë's memory as a propaganda tool in the war, the son of Lysimachus' past interest in regaining his father's throne and Arsinoë's similar concern, not to mention the difficulty in finding a more plausible candidate as Ptolemy II's mystery co-ruler.[128] Nonetheless, the preponderance of available evidence argues against this identification.

Ptolemy II's conduct during the war does not support the conclusion that, whether to honor his sister's memory or to overthrow Antigonus Gonatas or both, he was attempting to put his nephew on the Macedonian throne. Ptolemy II's forces did not invade any part of the Greek peninsula, let alone Macedonia itself, though such activity would surely have been required if he intended the son of Lysimachus to take the throne of his father.[129] Nothing indicates that the son of Lysimachus himself attacked Macedonia. Moreover, had Ptolemy II wished to support his nephew's effort to take control of Macedonia, nothing necessitated that he make him co-regent to do so.

Another obvious problem is that Arsinoë's son was not, in fact, the son of Ptolemy II, though Ptolemy II did have two biological sons by Arsinoë I, the elder named "Ptolemy" (the future Ptolemy III) and may have had other sons by other women. No evidence exists that Ptolemy II adopted his nephew; the only evidence about adoption is that Arsinoë II adopted Arsinoë I's children, most likely at the time of her marriage to her brother (see chapter 4). The possibility has been raised that Arsinoë I's children were initially disgraced after their mother's fall and that Ptolemy III Euergetes was not really his father's expected heir until after the rebellion of the mysterious Ptolemy Nios.[130] There is, however, no good reason to conclude that Arsinoë I's children shared her comparatively modest disgrace or exile; the future Ptolemy III was far too young for his father to hold him accountable for whatever plot his mother may have involved herself in.[131] If, in fact, the plot was mere fiction, it is even less likely that the hard-headed Philadelphus would have disinherited his biological son.

We do, however, know something about the ultimate fate of Arsinoë II's son. A Ptolemy, son of Lysimachus, ruled Telmessus from about 259 on; this man was indeed the son of Arsinoë II.[132] Ptolemy, son of Lysimachus, appears in an inscription at Telmessus in Lycia about 258,[133] indicating that either he had an estate in the area or was a Ptolemaic official. A later inscription from 240/39 (*OGIS* 55 = Austin 1981: no. 271) demonstrates that Ptolemy III Euergetes put the son of Lysimachus in charge of Telmessus. His descendants ruled in the area into the second century

BCE.[134] In other words, presumably because of his mother's influence and his relationship to his uncle (and later his cousin),[135] the son of Lysimachus ultimately ruled a portion of his father Lysimachus' former Anatolian possessions and was able to pass that role on to his descendants.[136] He may well have held other offices within the Ptolemaic empire prior to his arrival in Lycia, but we have no evidence of that. It does seem likely that Philadelphus promised to give Arsinoë's son some position at the time of their marriage, did so, and continued to support him after Arsinoë's death.

In fact, the fate of Arsinoë I, the daughter of Lysimachus, should tell us something about the comparatively modest prospects of her half brother, Lysimachus' son Ptolemy. Defeated and dead fathers did not count for much in Hellenistic power politics. Arsinoë II's influence bought her son better prospects than those of his half sister, but something so grand as coruling with Philadelphus was simply inconceivable for the man whose father had fallen in defeat at Corupedium and who had himself been unable to dislodge either Ceraunus or Antigonus Gonatas from the Macedonian throne. Ptolemy, son of Lysimachus, took his lumps and made the best of it, doing a good job as a petty prince and building a stable seat for his descendants.

Ptolemy II's Failure to Marry Again and the Role of his Royal Courtesans/Mistresses

Athenaeus (13.576e–f), citing Ptolemy III as his source, comments that Ptolemy II had a very large number of female lovers, was particularly inclined to the things of Aphrodite, and then names a number, including Bilistiche. He adds that Polybius (14.11.2) refers to yet another, Cleino, Philadelphus' cupbearer, and explains that many images of her in tunic and holding a rhyton were erected in Alexandria. Ptolemy II assigned a public role (including divinization) to some of these women.[137] *Truphe*, the hallmark of his dynasty, in this context has a sexual aspect as well as a transgressive one: the king broke rules ordinary people had to follow, whether by marrying his sister or divinizing courtesans.[138] His relationships, at least some of them, probably predated the death of Arsinoë II.[139] Arsinoë's demise may, however, have allowed royal mistresses more prominence than was possible while she lived.

Drawing any kind of firm line between royal wives and mistresses is never easy,[140] but Ptolemy II elevated the position of several royal mistresses, not only by his erection of statues and memorials, but also by the creation of cult in association with Aphrodite. Plutarch (*Mor.* 753e–f) tells us that Ptolemy II created temples and holy places to Aphrodite Bilistiche that the Alexandrians maintained even in Plutarch's own day (late first, early second century CE).[141] Thus both Arsinoë and Bilistiche were associated with Aphrodite. While this sort of apparent equation by cult of royal wife and mistress was not unprecedented (see chapter 5), none that we know of were created by the ruler himself,[142] and Bilistiche's cult did not apparently happen at the same time as Arsinoë's cults. Possibly this same Bilistiche competed at Olympia (like Arsinoë and her mother, Berenice I) and may have celebrated a victory soon after Arsinoë's death.[143] A woman of similar name also held the office of *canephore* for Arsinoë's cult.[144] Exactly how to interpret Bilistiche's career is debatable,[145] particularly since we cannot be sure that all these references are to the same woman, but even if they are, it would mean that she was prominent but she did not bear the title *basilissa*. In the absence of an actual royal wife, Bilistiche did seem to acquire a "quasi-institutional" role.[146]

Ptolemy II did not to marry again after Arsinoë's death, even though he was only in his late thirties or early forties when she died (suggesting, among other things, that he was not in need of an heir; see chapter 4) and lived another twenty years. His decision inevitably highlighted Arsinoë; in effect, she remained his consort, albeit a dead one. Naturally Ptolemy II would hesitate to compromise the power of this piece of image-making by having an actual living *basilissa* as well.[147] Even a century after her death, Arsinoë remained so memorable a figure that she had to be included in a second-century CE fictional account of Ptolemy II's fabulous court.[148]

Why did Ptolemy II refuse to take another wife yet choose to elevate some of his mistresses? The role he allotted these women could relate to his preference for showing royal power as "binary."[149] Ptolemy II's refusal to remarry seems more significant, however, than his bent for publicizing and even venerating his mistresses. Single kings were a rarity in the ancient world and unmarried Ptolemies especially so. He prioritized the image of the dead Arsinoë over acquiring a living spouse. He and his court had spent years creating the dual vision of Ptolemaic monarchy made possible by his sibling marriage. Ptolemy II proved more committed to that vision than to any need for a current consort or for additional legitimate children.

Subsequent Ptolemaic Afterlife of Arsinoë

Arsinoë remained a powerful presence as long as her dynasty continued to rule Egypt. Her cult survived at least until the first century BCE. For instance, at Memphis she was venerated along with the chief god Ptah as late as 75 BCE.[150] Loyalty to her (and the Ptolemies) in the Egyptian priestly class persisted: in Memphis, priestly families continued to name their daughters "Arsinoë" or "Berenice" through the first century BCE.[151] After Arsinoë II, every ruling Ptolemaic couple was more or less automatically deified, demonstrating the "charisma of the Ptolemaic family" while insuring the kingdom fertility and prosperity.[152] As we have seen, her image remained on Ptolemaic coins until the end of the dynasty as did Ptolemy I's; his image continued to appear because he was the founder of the dynasty, but the reason hers reappeared generation after generation is less obvious. She was not literally the founding mother of the dynasty but she functioned as its central female icon in a way that her mother, though biologically the founding mother, did not. Memory of her sister Philotera was not comparable. In some cases, worship of the two sisters was combined (*FGrH 613 F5*), but the last reference to Philotera's individual cult dates only to about 260.[153]

The primary reason that Arsinoë became literally and figuratively iconic was that hers was the base from which the position of royal women in the dynasty evolved. Her sibling marriage became the model for all Ptolemaic marriages, whether or not the bride and groom were actual siblings or close kin. Brother-sister marriage became the ideal if not always the reality. Thus the Canopus decree (*OGIS 56*) describes Ptolemy III and Berenice II as the children of Ptolemy II and Arsinoë II, and refers to Berenice II as Ptolemy III's sister and wife, though they were not brother and sister, and Arsinoë II was the mother of neither. From Ptolemy IV on, actual close-kin marriages dominated the dynasty.[154] Arsinoë II's immensely successful cult doubtless contributed to the increasing importance of Ptolemaic women.[155] The paired images initially so characteristic of Ptolemy II and Arsinoë II were endlessly reiterated. While some aspects of the iconographic program connected to Arsinoë (her unusual crown, the double uraeus, the double cornucopia, and her throne names) were assumed by only a few royal Ptolemaic women, the notion that all this pairing implied was that Ptolemaic women as well as men had some sort of public power, were in some ways regnant.

Berenice II appears to build on Arsinoë's model and expand it. Like Arsinoë II, she had royal titulary and an individual cult, but both clearly happened during her lifetime.[156] In the second century, Cleopatra I assumed the regency after her husband's early death and Ptolemaic women began to take an ever more active role in rule, one that reached its height and most intense form in the career of the last of the Ptolemies, Cleopatra VII, who ruled on her own in practice and may have done so, at some periods, in fact.[157] It cannot be chance that, as we have seen, Cleopatra VII borrowed Arsinoë's distinctive headdress and her double cornucopia; whatever these symbols originally meant or had been intended to mean, Cleopatra's appropriation of them surely suggests that she, at least, associated them with rule.

Roman Afterlife of Arsinoë

As Sylvia Barbantani has observed, the reputation and image of the last Ptolemaic ruler, Cleopatra VII, tended to absorb memory and tradition about all other Ptolemaic rulers, a tendency that continued and if anything intensified in the post-ancient period. This is particularly the case because Cleopatra VII had a half sister named Arsinoë (IV). This other Arsinoë attracts attention as a kind of anti-Cleopatra, the good sister victimized by the bad: she initially escaped from Alexandria but ultimately fell into Roman hands, marched in Caesar's triumph, and was exiled to the sanctuary of the temple of Artemis at Ephesus where Marc Antony and Cleopatra had her executed. A tomb, with the skeleton of a young woman, was discovered at Ephesus in the 1990s and has been attributed to Arsinoë IV.[158] Memory of one Arsinoë has tended to eliminate memory of the other.

While Roman emperors were portrayed in Egyptian-style art as pharaohs, as the Ptolemies had been, they never became part of Egyptian tradition, were not really Egyptian rulers but rather men who ruled Egypt. Indeed they seized and carried off to Rome many Ptolemaic and pharaonic monuments. The Arsinoëum, for instance, may have been torn down during the reign of Augustus and certainly its obelisk was removed (Pliny *N.H.* 36.64–69).[159] Aspects of Arsinoë II's cult endured, though she was now understood simply as a protective goddess, not a particular royal woman.[160] Streets in Alexandria and elsewhere retained her name, perhaps also attesting to her continuing popularity.[161] Lingering interest in and reverence for the Ptolemies in the Roman era could function as a kind of allegiance to Egyptian identity and clearly did so. Roman political figures, primarily emperors and members of their families, borrowed some parts of Ptolemaic royal imagery. The emperor Gaius (Caligula) imported the statues of Ptolemy II and Arsinoë II to Rome (the ones now in the Vatican) and gave a statue of the queen to his sister, whom he had certainly deified.[162] The Romans appropriated jugate images. Ironically, Marc Antony and Octavia appeared as a jugate pair on a tetradrachm.[163] Later jugate coins were issued: for instance, there is a gold aureus showing a jugate Nero and Agrippina, ca. 55 CE.[164] Two famous cameos, one in Vienna and one in St. Petersburg, feature jugate images of a man and woman. These paired images have been variously identified (as Olympias and Alexander or as some Ptolemaic or Julio-Claudian pair) and dated from the third century BCE to the first century CE. Most likely very late Hellenistic or early imperial, the cameos use double profile portraits to fabricate an image that stresses the similarity of male and female royals, highlighting their common descent and possibly their shared rule.[165] Another well-known cameo imitates the golden octradrachms that showed the two royal pairs of Ptolemy I and Berenice and Ptolemy II and Arsinoë II: the Gemma Claudia portrays Claudius and Agrippina II on the left and Germanicus and Agrippina I on the right.[166]

Post-Ancient Afterlife

After the ancient period, Arsinoë all but vanishes. An illustrated fifteenth-century manuscript of Justin (now at the Bodleian) does show Lysimachus and Arsinoë sitting serenely at the dinner table while Agathocles, whom they have poisoned, falls to the floor.[167] Generally, though, the dominance of the memory of Cleopatra VII continued. One looks in vain for clear references to Arsinoë II in Western art, although several incidents in her colorful career would seem obvious fodder for the kind of "historical" paintings popular from the sixteenth through the nineteenth centuries. In the middle of the sixteenth century (ca. 1555–60), the

Venetian artist known as Jacopo Tintoretto painted *The Deliverance (or Rescue) of Arsinoë* (now in Gemaeldegallerie Alte Meister, Dresden), but the painting pictures Arsinoë IV's rescue from Alexandria rather than Arsinoë II's flight from Ephesus after the death of Lysimachus. Literary Arsinoës—like the character of that name in Moliere's *The Misanthrope* (1622)—seem simply inspired by generic classicism; after all, a number of women in Greek mythology bore the name.[168] Starting in the late seventeenth century and continuing through the entire eighteenth century, an astonishing number of operas and plays, in a variety of languages, featured a major character—often the title character—named Arsinoë: *Arsinoë*, an opera of Pietronio Franceschini (1676); *Arsinoë* by Tomaso Stanzani (Bologna, 1676); *Arsinoë, Queen Of Cyprus*, an opera by Thomas Clayton (1705);[169] *La grandezza d'animo, or Arsinoë*, an opera by Reinhard Keiser (1710); *La verità nell'inganno ossia Arsinoë*, an opera of Antonio Caldara(1727); *Attala od Arsinoë* a musical drama by Antonio Bioni (1728); *"Arsinoë; Or, the Incestuous Marriage. a Tragedy"* by Andrew Henderson (1752); *Arsinoë*, an *opera seria* of Vincenzo Legrenzio Ciampi (1758); and *Arsinoë*, an *opera seria* by Gaetano Andreozzi (1795). Many of the operas had classical plots and themes and focused on female characters and their affairs of the heart.[170] Arsinoë II's melodramatic life story seems ready made for opera. Much as with Tintoretto's painting, however, these dramatic works largely deal with the "wrong" Arsinoë in the sense that the eponymous character is not based on Arsinoë II, though often she is a royal woman and court intrigue is central to the plot. In some cases, the drama seems inspired by an entirely different historical character whereas in others there is no clear historical reference. Keiser's Arsinoë is based on Berenice's II's mother, Apame; Caldara's Arsinoë is heir to the Assyrian throne and is involved in Bithynian intrigue; Clayton's Arsinoë rules Cyprus, but despite the fact that the Ptolemies in general and Arsinoë II in particular had associations with Cyprus, the plot fits no particular Ptolemaic woman, though the dynastic scheming seems reminiscent of Ptolemaic intrigue;[171] and Andreozzi's Arsinoë is Homeric.

A mid-eighteenth-century exception is *Arsinoë; Or, the incestuous marriage. A Tragedy* by Andrew Henderson. Whether or not it was ever performed, it was printed in 1752. Surprisingly, the incestuous marriage in question turns out to be that of Arsinoë II to Ptolemy Ceraunus, not her marriage to Ptolemy II. Henderson's plot depends heavily on Justin's narrative of the marriage and murders, so naturally he casts Arsinoë as victim and Ceraunus as villain. While Henderson, following Justin's model, attributes political motives to both bride and groom, he also describes both, though Ceraunus more than Arsinoë, as also actually interested in each other sexually. Incestuous desire, Henderson suggests, is wrong because it is excessive and he endlessly preaches the wisdom of *sophrosyne*. Henderson's Arsinoë is not evil, but deluded by love and ambition for her sons. Significantly, Henderson names her maids of honor "Helen" and "Olympias."

We can only speculate as to why, unlike so many other figures of ancient myth or history, Arsinoë II inspired so little literature and art in the early modern period and in the nineteenth century, but incest was almost certainly the problem, particularly if combined with the story of Arsinoë's supposed attempt to seduce Agathocles (Paus. 1.10.3). Whereas the latter alone could have made her an intriguing bad girl like the most famous female Ptolemy, her marriage to her brother flew in the face of Christian tradition. In the nineteenth century, the brother-sister marriage was proof that Arsinoë was an unscrupulous weaver of plots; a power-hungry woman was an unhealthy woman and the reverse, and so she becomes the one who persuades/forces her brother to marry.[172]

In modern times, naming things or people "Arsinoë" often seems little more than a vaguely classical or Egyptian reference. The asteroid Arsinoë (discovered in 1895), a pretty golden mustard–colored butterfly "Vindula Arsinoë" from Australia (perhaps the color suggested royalty), many cats (as revealed by Google), and an erotic comic book series whose covers features a young woman who is usually nude except for a few vaguely Egyptian pieces of jewelry (or, if entirely nude, some pyramids appear in the background) all seem to fall into this general category.

Most historical novels featuring a character named "Arsinoë" turn out, predictably, to focus on Cleopatra VII's sister, but there are a few exceptions. George Ebers, a nineteenth-century German Egyptologist, published a series of historical novels set in Egypt including one, *Arachne: A Historical Romance* (published in English in 1898), in which Arsinoë II is a character. Ebers' Arsinoë I actually is plotting to kill her husband Ptolemy II because he prefers his sister, and Arsinoë II proves a loyal and able partner in rule, though both Philadelphi are severe rulers. Duncan Sprott's two recent novels, *The Ptolemies: A Novel* (2005) and *Daughter of the Crocodile* (2007), feature Arsinoë II as a major character; she proves to be bad to the bone, fulfilling virtually every stereotype about women and political power. Sprott's Arsinoë plots murder with poison and magic (the familiar female weapons) against a long list of victims, is bedeviled by lust for both Agathocles and Ptolemy Ceraunus, and yet said to be mannish and exceptional (Sprott's model for female behavior seems more Athenian than Macedonian) because of her interest in politics. In addition to these works of fiction, a brief Greek popular biography of Arsinoë II has recently appeared.[173]

The only trace in the modern world that probably does recall something associated with Arsinoë II is the Arsinoë Beach Hotel on Cyprus, near Limassol; there were a number of cities named after Arsinoë on Cyprus and while the hotel is not particularly near any of them, that probably does explain the nomenclature.

Important People in the Life
of Arsinoë II

Agathocles son of Lysimachus by an earlier wife and his apparent heir until Lysimachus either ordered or allowed his death.

Antigonus Gonatas the son of Demetrius Poliorcetes, having failed in his first attempt (against Ptolemy Ceraunus) to regain the throne of Macedonia for his family, he succeeded in defeating the invading Gauls and became king of Macedonia. His descendants ruled until the Romans conquered Macedonia. He was the archrival of Ptolemy II.

Arsinoë I daughter of Lysimachus, first wife of Ptolemy II, by whom she had children, including the future Ptolemy III; she was exiled to Coptos.

Berenice I one of the wives of Ptolemy I, by whom she had Arsinoë II, Ptolemy II, and Philotera. She also had children from an earlier marriage.

Callicrates an admiral of Ptolemy II who established a cult for Arsinoë II as Arsinoë Aphrodite at Zephyrium. He was also first priest of the cult of *theoi adelphoi*.

Demetrius I Poliorcetes (the city besieger) son of the Successor Antigonus, a charismatic general and sometime king who was unable to sustain his victories or a hold on his territories.

Eurydice daughter of Antipater, wife of Ptolemy I by whom she had several children, including Lysandra and Ptolemy Ceraunus. She was a cousin of Berenice I.

Lysandra daughter of Ptolemy I and Eurydice, full sister of Ptolemy Ceraunus, wife and later widow of Agathocles.

Lysimachus one of Alexander the Great's bodyguards and one of the Successors, later king of Thrace, parts of Anatolia and Macedonia. He had a number of wives but married Arsinoë II ca. 300.

Philotera daughter of Ptolemy I and Berenice I, full sister of Ptolemy II and Arsinoë II, she never married but was deified posthumously, probably not long before the death of Arsinoë II.

Ptolemy Ceraunus (thunderbolt) a son of Ptolemy I by Eurydice, he long expected to be his father's successor but was rejected in favor of Ptolemy II in 285. He went to the court of Lysimachus where his full sister Lysandra was married to Agathocles. After the death of Agathocles, he went with his sister to the court of Seleucus and served under him until he murdered him and claimed the throne of Macedonia. He married Arsinoë II, promising to treat her sons as heirs, but murdered two instead. Soon after, he was defeated and killed by the invading Gauls.

Ptolemy son of Lysimachus the son of Lysimachus and Arsinoë II, the only survivor of Ptolemy Ceraunus' murder of his siblings, he failed in his attempt to regain control of Macedonia for his family. He probably ended his days in Telmessus as a local ruler, and his descendants succeeded him. Some consider him to have been "Ptolemy the Son" but I do not.

Ptolemy II Philadelphus the son of Ptolemy I and Berenice I, full brother of Arsinoë II, he coreigned with his father and then ruled on his own. He first married Arsinoë I and had children by her, then exiled her and married his full sister, Arsinoë II. He established cults for his parents, himself and Arsinoë II, and for Arsinoë II by herself, after her death.

Ptolemy the Son the mysterious coruler with Ptolemy II from 268/67 to 259, he is referred to as Ptolemy, son of Ptolemy. Some believe that he was Arsinoë's son by Lysimachus, subsequently adopted by his uncle. I think he is more likely a son of Ptolemy II by another woman.

Ptolemy I Soter one of Alexander the Great's bodyguards and one of the Successors, he established a kingdom in Egypt. He married many women, including Eurydice and Berenice I, and was the father of numerous children (including Ptolemy II, Arsinoë II, and Ptolemy Ceraunus). His dynasty endured until the defeat and suicide of the last of his descendants to rule independently, Cleopatra VII.

Seleucus I (Nicator) an officer under Alexander the Great, one of the Successors, founder of the Seleucid dynasty and empire, which included much of the old Persian Empire; he defeated Lysimachus in 281, was murdered by Ptolemy Ceraunus.

Sources and Assessment of Arsinoë II's Career

Sources on the life of Arsinoë II divide neatly into two categories, with only a bit of overlap: those that relate to her life before her return to Egypt sometime after 279, and those that deal with her life after her return. The evidence about Arsinoë II is less than abundant for both periods.

Many of the sources relevant to the first period of her life are Greek, but an important one is Latin. Justin (Marcus Junianus Justinus) created an *epitome* (a short version) of a world history composed by Pompeius Trogus in Latin in the late first century BCE (or early first century CE). Trogus' prologues to each book survive, but Justin, not Trogus, dominates the language of the narrative;[1] moreover, simply by determining what to include and what to omit, he inevitably created a different kind of historical narrative than that of Trogus. Justin's narrative contains many errors but is the only extant narrative for some periods of Hellenistic history.

Justin's treatment of Arsinoë's actions during the reign of Lysimachus differs dramatically from his coverage of her brief marriage to Ceraunus,[2] reflecting the different circumstances in which she found herself on these two occasions. In the first circumstance, Justin represents her as willing to poison her stepson when her husband apparently commands her to do so (17.1.1–12), whereas in the second (17.2.6–8; 24.2.1–3.10) she and her sons are pathetic victims. Justin's narrative never recognizes his switch from portraying her as victimizer to focusing on her as victim; it is as if he has never mentioned her before when he offers his account of her second marriage. One reason for this seeming oddity is that Arsinoë is a minor figure in Justin's account of the death of Agathocles, whereas his description of events involving Arsinoë and Ptolemy Ceraunus is far more detailed and in that account she is a major figure. What is, however, more contradictory is that in the earlier period Justin mentions her in passing as a mere tool of her evil husband whose motivation is not explained, whereas in the later sections, Justin focuses on her and details the reasons for her actions. Justin casts Arsinoë as the tragic heroine and Ceraunus as the villain who gets his comeuppance.[3] Justin's narrative proves problematic in another respect: his contradictory versions of Ceraunus' motivation for marrying Arsinoë (17.2.6–8; 24.2.1–3.10); in one passage Ceraunus at first means well but in the other he is murderous from the start. While the mechanical cause of this problem is most likely that Justin (or Trogus) was combining two traditions,[4] perhaps more important is that his narrative priorities—drama—make the contradiction unimportant to him.

Memnon of Heraclea Pontica (a Greek city on the Black Sea), who probably wrote in the first century CE, composed a history of his city, probably using Nymphis as his source. Nymphis, also from Heraclea, lived in the third century BCE.[5] Memnon's treatment (*FGrH* 434 5.6,8.4–6) of Arsinoë, the only extant narrative source apart from Justin, is consistently harsh: she comes between Lysimachus and Amastris, his Persian wife and sometime ruler of Heraclea; she takes advantage of Lysimachus' old age; she misrules Heraclea via her agent Heracleides of Cyme; she turns Lysimachus against his son Agathocles and causes Agathocles' death by falsely accusing him. Presumably, the Memnon/Nymphis treatment reflects a hostile tradition about both Lysimachus and especially Arsinoë in Heraclea, demonstrating the unpopularity of the couple in Lysimachus' realms in Asia Minor.[6] Memnon may have been similarly hostile in his treatment of Antigonus Gonatas,[7] possibly because the Heracleote patriot disliked any of the kings who tried to limit the independence of his city. The surviving fragments of Memnon's narrative can be useful, so long as one recognizes that he writes partisan history from a very particular perspective.

In addition, three other Greek authors provide critical bits of narrative about Arsinoë's career. As part of a fairly detailed rendition of the career of Lysimachus, Pausanias (1.10.3–5) recounts that Arsinoë feared what Agathocles would do to her children after Lysimachus was dead and therefore plotted against Agathocles but then, apparently making use of a different source, Pausanias claims that she only worked to have

Agathocles killed after he had repulsed her sexual advances and that Lysimachus did not discover what she was up to until after Arsinoë (presumably) had murdered his son, by which point he could do nothing because he had already lost all his *philoi*. Pausanias concludes with an account of the flight of Lysandra, events in Asia Minor, and the death of Lysimachus. Like Justin, Pausanias seems unbothered by the contradictions in his sources. In addition, he seems to believe that Arsinoë married Lysimachus after her half-sister Lysandra had married Agathocles, rather than long before. Pausanias composed a many-volume description of Greece and its monuments, often providing considerable historical background as he did so. His reputation for historical accuracy is not high, and he generally seems hostile to Macedonians (probably because he blamed the decline of Greece on them), but he does preserve several different traditions, probably going back to contemporary sources, about events at the court of Lysimachus.[8]

Strabo, a first-century CE geographer, composed a multivolume geography of the world as he knew it. Like Pausanias, Strabo included considerable historical background. He (13.4.1) remarks that Lysimachus, overwhelmed by internal family disputes, was forced to kill Agathocles. This brief notice intrigues because it suggests good understanding of dynastic politics and because it does not demonize any of the parties involved.

Appian of Alexandria, in the second century CE, wrote a history of the countries and regions included in the Roman Empire, beginning with their early history and ending with their incorporation into the Roman state. His account of the Syrian Wars includes (62–64) some additional material about the deaths of Lysimachus and Seleucus and the interesting observation that Ceraunus left Egypt out of fear. He also (14.1.21) confirms that the city of Ephesus was renamed after Arsinoë II.

Polyaenus (8.57) is our sole source for Arsinoë's supposed trick escape from Ephesus after Lysimachus' defeat and death at Corupedium in 281. Polyaenus was a rhetorician, not a historian, and his stratagem collection makes odd but not necessarily unuseful reading.[9] He claims that Arsinoë eluded capture because she dressed her maid as herself; the maid was killed and she survived. This tale does resemble others he (8.61, 52.7–9) tells, as well as a story of Phylarchus (*ap.* Ath.13.593e). Even if the plot conforms to some sort of *topos* (theme),[10] its essentials could be accurate. Similarity of circumstance could generate similarity of narrative.[11] The bit about the maid cross-dressing as a royal woman could be fiction, but Arsinoë got out of Ephesus somehow, most likely not dressed to look like the wife of Lysimachus. Car chases certainly constitute a *topos* of American movie making, but they really do happen; the *topos* derives from real practice. In a world where women were recognized more by their garments than (thanks to veils and the use of litters) their facial features, the disguised escape makes sense; moreover, many royal women suffered the kind of sudden reversal of fortune that made such escapes necessary.

In addition to these literary sources, some inscriptional and coin evidence has survived that is relevant to Arsinoë's career. Coin evidence seems to confirm some of the information literary sources provide about Arsinoë's control of Ephesus (see chapter 2) and inscriptional evidence tells us that at least one Greek city treated Arsinoë as if she were Lysimachus' sole wife and *basilissa* (*SIG*³ 381) and offers information about the attempts of Arsinoë's son to promote himself as heir (see chapter 2, n. 70). Most important, we know that Arsinoë dedicated the rotunda at Samothrace only because of an inscription (*OGIS15* = *IG* XII 227), though damage to the inscription prevents certainty about which king she was married to at the time.

No extant literary source provides a historical narrative for the period after Arsinoë returned to Egypt, but some tidbits in Greek writers do tell us a little. The scholion for Theocritus 17.128 informs us that Ptolemy II exiled Arsinoë I for plotting against him, married his sister, and had her adopt his children by Arsinoë I, but tells us nothing that enables us to date these events. Pausanias (1.7.1–3) includes the erroneous but interesting statement that Ptolemy II fell in love with his sister and then married her following Egyptian custom, but he also reports that Ptolemy II's children were by his first wife, that she died without children (presumably he means by Ptolemy II, but perhaps not) prior to the Chremonidean War, and that a nome was named after her. Plutarch's works contain two references (*Mor.* 11a 736e–f) and Athenaeus (621a) one to contemporary reaction to Arsinoë's marriage to her full brother.

Coin images of Arsinoë, reliefs, *oinochoai*, and sculpture in the round in both Greek and Egyptian style survive in significant numbers, but most of this material probably postdates her life. Some scholars believe that her distinctive crown and title of King of Upper and Lower Egypt indicate that she coruled and that some examples did appear in her lifetime, but that has not been the general view (see chapter 6).

The main sources for Arsinoë's life while married to Ptolemy II are Egyptian inscriptions and poetry produced in the context of the Alexandrian court during the reign of Ptolemy II, some of it probably during the lifetime of Arsinoë herself, as well as one critical Athenian decree, the decree of Chremonides. The important Egyptian hieroglyphic documents are the Pithom and Mendes stelai.[12] The Pithom stele (CCG 22183) records a number of events between year 6 and year 21 of Ptolemy II including the information that Arsinoë II accompanied Ptolemy II to inspect the eastern borders of Egypt and that, by the time this happened, she was married to her brother. Granted the uncertainty about when the switch was made in dating the years of Ptolemy II's reign, though this document provides a date by which we know they were married, in an absolute sense, that date is not entirely certain.[13] The Mendes stele, like the Pithom, records a series of events, but the regnal date of the first event—the king's visit to the sacred ram of Mendes—has been destroyed. The Mendes stele records that he has married his sister (no new date is offered),[14] then it reports the death of Arsinoë in year 15, refers to Egyptian funerary rites for her, and then sets out a decree of the king, approved by the priests, that her statue would appear with that of the Mendes god, and that her cult image should be placed in every Egyptian nome, with her cult name. More events then follow. The decree of Chremonides (*SIG*[3] 4334–5; see chapter 5) speaks of Ptolemy II acting in accord with the policy of his ancestors and his sister, thus offering official recognition for the first time that a woman had a public policy.

Arsinoë II figures prominently in poetry produced in Alexandria during her brother's reign. Using poetry as evidence for historical events proves complex; it is easy to misread or oversimplify poetic texts. Scholars used to treat much of the poetry from this period as propaganda, produced by spineless sycophants. Now, the quality and complexity of this poetry has gained much more respect, but it does come out of the milieu of the Alexandrian court and the authors were likely all under Ptolemaic patronage in some fashion. Thus poetry that references Arsinoë proves most useful as an indication of how the court wanted her and her actions to be understood. Theocritus (*Id.* 17. 131–4), for instance, concluding an encomium to Ptolemy II, compares his marriage to Arsinoë to the "holy marriage" of the sibling gods Zeus and Hera, just as Plutarch claimed a rhapsode did at the actual wedding (*Mor.*736e–f). Theocritus also (*Id.* 15) describes the experiences of two women at a celebration of Adonia at the palace, under Arsinoë's patronage. A fragment of Callimachus (228 Pf) about the death of Arsinoë and her deification tells us something about popular reaction, how her deification was imagined, and that her funerary rites (at least according to a Greek poet) were Greek. Apollonius Rhodius' account of the court of Alcinous and Arete in book 3 of his epic the *Argonautica* may well allude to the court of Ptolemy II and Arsinoë (see chapter 5). Another poet active during Ptolemy II's reign, Posidippus, is probably the author of the 112 epigrams in the recently discovered (1992) "Milan Papyrus" (P. Mil. Vogl. VIII 309); one of these (AB 78) speaks to Ptolemaic equestrian victories generally and then mentions that "Arsinoë won all three harness victories" in a single year.[15] Nearly everything we know about the cult of Arsinoë Aphrodite that Callicrates created comes from poetic references (Posidippus AB 39.2, 116.6–7, 119.2; Callimachus [frg. 5 Pf]; and Lock of Berenice [frg. 110 Pf]).

Viewed as a whole, the sources on Arsinoë II distinguish themselves not so much by being poor as by being idiosyncratic, particularly in terms of the division in the nature of the sources between the two periods of her life. Apart from the difficulty of making a coherent whole out of the different voices of Greek and Egyptian sources in the second part of her life, another source problem that proves striking is that nearly all the Greek prose sources derive from the era of the Second Sophistic (a Greek cultural revival of the second and third centuries CE). Many writers of that period, committed to an understanding of high classical culture focused on Athens, produced a vision of the Greek past that resembles Victorian readings of the classical past in its insistence on moderation, its focus on Athens in the fifth and fourth century, and consequent discomfort with Macedonia and Macedonians, Hellenistic culture and practice, and those whose lives were characterized by excess, particularly if the people in question were women. Many of these sources contain useful contemporary information, but we need to remember that it is filtered through the values of a different era.

Finally, our sources, especially those relating to the period after Arsinoë's return to Egypt, create a series of tangles about dating. Ptolemaic history is replete with fierce and possibly insolvable chronological problems, rich in documentary sources and court poetry, poor in narrative history. Virtually every date in Arsinoë's career, including her death, is uncertain or disputed; even the order of events is often unknown. Instead of attempting to resolve these intricate problems, hoping to avoid turning her life into a series of technical puzzles, I have tried to take the long view about the events of her life, attempting to arrive at a way of understanding her life that does not depend, at least not heavily, on one particular date or even order of events.

Scholarship about Arsinoë,[16] often echoed in more general and popular publications, took a peculiar turn about a century ago; the repercussions are still with us. Early in the twentieth century, starting with W. W. Tarn in 1913,[17] for a variety of reasons (uncritical reading of hostile ancient sources; the advent of the first wave of feminism with its advocates and detractors; perception of Ptolemy II as effeminate; and discomfort with the notion of brother-sister marriage),[18] a picture of Arsinoë as the all-powerful, nearly omniscient, and unusually violent ruler of Egypt (and perhaps Macedonia as well) emerged. In this view, her husbands, at least Lysimachus and Ptolemy II, were essentially nonentities obedient to her will while Arsinoë actually ruled their kingdoms. At times, it seemed that nothing happened in either kingdom unless Arsinoë made it happen; as Barbantani has observed, this school of thought makes Arsinoë II a kind of "dea ex machina" for developments in virtually the entire Mediterranean basin.[19] Such a view required connecting Arsinoë to events for which no evidence of connection existed, often on the basis of character stereotyping. (She was somehow always uniquely manipulative, murderous, and yet competent when no one else around her was, so if anything that could be described in these terms happened, she must have done it.)[20]

Scholars long continued to relish this implausible image of Arsinoë, often employing a kind of entertainingly florid prose to describe her career. Even as late as the mid-sixties, Eleanor Huzar could term her a "typical Hellenistic tigress queen," echoing Bevan's 1927 judgment, "a Macedonian princess, with not a little of the tigress."[21] Arsinoë the royal dominatrix lasted until, somewhat ironically, relatively early in the second wave of feminism; in 1982, Stanley Burstein cut the scholarly legs out from under this image of a scary but powerful Arsinoë by pointing out how little evidence supported the construct.[22]

Reaction then set in and, unfortunately, often led to another extreme in which Arsinoë was just another royal wife (though oddly, she is often still understood as really scheming and murderous but just somehow not powerful). An extreme version of this approach not only argues that Arsinoë herself had no power but that the gradual increase in political power of Ptolemaic women was an accident based solely on Ptolemy II's use of his wife in royal propaganda.[23] Difficulty persists with developing nuanced consideration of her career. Discussion about her continues to function in terms of oppositional analysis: if Arsinoë is not running the kingdom then she must be a sort of royal housewife. It certainly does not help to assume that those who conclude that Arsinoë had any kind of power at all are somehow insisting that she dominated her brother.[24] Moreover, Arsinoë the ruler or coruler has not disappeared from the scene,[25] and there are those who continue to believe that any plot or plan occurring during her lifetime originated with her or was a consequence of her influence.[26]

To some degree, this treatment of her career resembles scholarly treatment of other royal women. Wikander characterizes such analysis of political women as a "combination of fascinated revulsion and an unconscious wish to denigrate them actively."[27] But even compared to scholarly treatment of other royal women, work about Arsinoë has been and remains curiously personal. The consequence of this long and oddly emotional scholarly debate has often been the development of interpretations that make little sense except in the context of scholarly dispute, academic straw dogs.

For instance, Burstein asserted that the fact that Arsinoë's brother-husband failed to make her son by Lysimachus heir to the Egyptian throne (itself not a certainty) demonstrated Arsinoë's lack of influence over her husband.[28] The problem with this approach is that there is no evidence that Arsinoë ever tried to get her brother to do this, granted that he had at least two sons of his own. If she did and failed, this would certainly mean that there were limits to her influence with her husband but hardly that she had no influence at all. It is only because some scholars long ago imagined that she tried that the issue even comes up.

This brings me to the notion that Ptolemy II's coregent (see chapter 6), the so-called Ptolemy the Son, was not his biological son but Arsinoë's. Tarn first raised this possibility in 1913 as part of his scenario that involved an all-powerful Arsinoë stage managing her brother's reign.[29] The notion had fallen out of favor along with the picture of Arsinoë as mistress of the universe. Subsequent scholarly recognition that Ptolemy son of Lysimachus had become a ruler in Lycia at Telmessus also contributed to this development.[30] Huss, however, in 1998, revived the notion that Lysimachus' son was Ptolemy II's coregent by putting forward much better arguments than Tarn's in support of the identification.[31] Huss's view has won new supporters,[32] though perhaps more because of the strength of his arguments against other possible identifications of Ptolemy's coregent than because of his arguments in favor of the son of Lysimachus. As we've seen, although Huss's arguments have some advantages—they would, for instance, explain where Arsinoë's son was for at least some of the time between his departure from Macedonia around 277/76 and the first time he appeared in Telmessus around 259, a nearly twenty-year period—they do not convince on a number of grounds.[33]

We need to recall why the notion of identifying Arsinoë's son with Ptolemy II's coregent ever developed. It arose out of the now generally rejected picture of Arsinoë as the real ruler of Egypt. It is worrying that it is so difficult to establish the identity of Philadelphus' coruler, but that does not justify concluding that he was Arsinoë's son, simply to solve the problem. If the identification of Ptolemy the Son with Lysimachus' son had not been present in century's worth of scholarship, one wonders if it would have been suggested now.[34] Too little attention has been paid to how odd it was that a man in his late thirties or early forties, a man who proved perfectly able to rule more than another twenty years, took on a coregent, though other Hellenistic precedents for coregency involved aged rulers close to the end of their days. We could surmise that Ptolemy II was in ill health and perhaps expected to die, but there is no evidence of ill health and his comparatively long life suggests the opposite.[35] Nor (see chapter 6) did he need to make Arsinoë's son coregent simply to sponsor him as a candidate for the Macedonian throne. Based on the current evidence, Ptolemy II, despite the fact that he had focused so much energy on unifying the dynasty, complicated the succession by making this mystery man coregent and then again by removing him. No one has come up with really convincing reasons for Ptolemy II's actions,[36] but that doesn't necessitate falling back on outdated ones.

Notes

Introduction

1. See Romm 2011; Waterfield 2011; and Erskine 2003.
2. O'Neil 2000; Carney 2000a: 203–33.
3. See chapter 1.
4. Hammond and Griffith 1979; Hammond 1988a: 1–196; Borza 1992; King 2010: 5.
5. Ogden 2011a: 96; Greenwalt 1989.
6. Ogden 2011a: 94–95 offers a list of such disputes in the Argead and Hellenistic eras.
7. See Carney 2000a: 34–35.
8. Carney 1991; 2000a: 225.
9. Mooren 1983; Walbank 1984; Ma 2003; Austin 1986. Erskine 2003: 103–74 provides overviews of each major Hellenistic dynasty.
10. Walbank 1984: 87.
11. Müller 2011.
12. Schmitt 1991: 82–83.
13. Bingen 1988: 37–38.
14. Pomeroy 1984: 3–40; Savalli-Lestrade 1997 and 2003; Bielman Sánchez 2002 and 2003; Carney 2000a: 203–33 and 2011. Barbantani 2008: 104–5.
15. Billows 1995a; Sherwin-White and Kuhrt 1993: 23–25.
16. Carney 2000a: 225–28.
17. *OGIS* 35; *OGIS* 56.1.47ff; *OGIS* 745. See Vatin 1970: 74f.; Ritter 1965: 116; Tarn 1913: 351, n. 27; Brosius 1996: 18 *contra* Bikerman 1938: 27.
18. Carney 2000a: 232–33; Carney 1995. Roy 1998: 121 goes too far.
19. Kosmetatou 2004a; Carney 2007.
20. Savalli-Lestrade 1997: 417 *contra* Pomeroy 1984: 11.
21. Savalli-Lestrade 1994: 419; 2003: 65.
22. Savalli-Lestrade 1997: 423. See chapter 5.
23. Savalli-Lestrade 2003: 68 uses Arsinoë II as an example.
24. Diodorus' (19.59.4–6) description of Phila, though clearly idealized, speaks to what male dynasts and their advisers wanted in a royal woman. Carney 2000a: 165–69.

25. Robins 1993b: 21–55; Forgeau 2008: 3–24.

26. Delia 1993: 199–200, suggests that the situation could be similar for the Ptolemies.

27. O'Connor and Silverman 1994.

28. Pillonel 2008: 3–4.

29. Pillonel 2008: 3–4.

30. Pillonel 2008: 3.

31. Robins 1993b: 23–27.

32. By the Middle Kingdom, the royal mother is believed to be impregnated by a god (Forgeau 2008: 6–7).

33. Troy 1986: 3–25; Forgeau 2008: 5.

34. Forgeau 2008: 8.

35. Troy 1986: 106.

36. Tyldesley 2012: 5–24.

37. See chapter 4. See also Forgeau 2008: 11–12.

38. Minas 2005: 128–33. Occasionally queens sacrifice by themselves.

39. The vulture hieroglyph means "mother" and the cap refers to Isis as mother of Horus, so to the queen as the mother of a future king—see Stanwick 2002: 35.

40. Forgeau 2008: 9–10.

41. Troy 1986: 131–39.

42. Forgeau 2008: 16–20.

43. Carney 2001: 37–40.

44. Troy 1986: 70; Forgeau 2008: 22.

Chapter 1

1. Blundell 1995: 119; Greenwalt 1988 notes some royal brides married later, doubtless for political reasons.

2. Berve 1926: 2:329–35; Heckel 1992: 222–27, and 2006: 235–38; and Ellis 1993.

3. Huss 2001: 90–91.

4. Satyrus *FGrH* 631 F 2; Curt. 9.8.22; Theoc. 17.26; OGIS I 54, l. 6. Gow 1952: 331; Ogden 1999: 67–68 *contra* Cameron 1995: 245.

5. Errington 1976: 155–57; Heckel 1992: 222 *contra* Ellis 1993: 3; Collins 1997.

6. Heckel 1992: 207, 22006: 235 *contra* Huss 2001: 90.

7. Reames 2008.

8. Heckel 1992: 207; 2006: 236. Ellis 1993: 10.

9. Heckel 2006: 237–38.

10. See Meeus 2008.

11. Seibert 1969: 27–38; Ellis 1993: ix, 26; Bosworth 2002: 57; Meeus 2008: 27–38.

12. Hölbl 2001: 14–34; Huss 2001: 97–250.

13. Casson 2001: 32.

14. *Contra* Ogden 1999: 68.

15. The Satrap Stele of 311 demonstrates that the move to Alexandria had been completed by this date; see Hölbl 2001: 113, n. 20. See also Fraser 1972: 2:11–12, n. 28; Ellis 1993: 54.

16. Pausanias (1.8.6) says it was given to him by the Rhodians; Johnson 2000 *contra* Hazzard 1992.

17. *Suda s.v. "basileia."*

18. Erskine 1995: 38.

19. *FGrH* 239 B 19; Austin 2006: 40.

20. He did name his son by Thaïs "Lagus," (Ath. 13.576e) but this son was born before the death of Alexander (Ogden 2008: 353–54), thus before he had any hope of kingship.

21. Hölbl 2001: 94.

22. Tac. *Hist.* 4. 83. See McKenzie 2008: 40–41.

23. Empereur 1998: 20.

24. Erskine 1995: 40.

25. Ellis 1993: 55; Casson 2001: 31, 34. See Strab. 9.1.20; Diog. Laert. 5.78.

26. Hölbl 2001: 26; McKenzie 2008: 41.

27. Erskine 1995: 40.

28. Theoc. 17.112–16; Erskine 1995: 45; Hunter 2011: 51, Bingen 1988: 46–51.

29. Ferrario 1962 demonstrates that *OGIS* 14 is not valid evidence for her girlhood.

30. Clarysse 2000: 29.

31. Errington 1969; Meeus 2008: 46.

32. Pomeroy 1977 argues for extensive expansion of education for royal women and more specifically asserts (1977: 61) that royal Macedonian women had a "long tradition" of learning. Cole 1981 is more cautious, but she too sees royal women (Cole 1981: 230) as literate. See also Carney 2000a: 28–29.

33. Empereur 1998: 308.

34. Alonso Troncoso 2005a.

35. Pomeroy 1984: 112; Alonso Troncoso 2005a: 101. Suda s.v. "Zenodotus," refers to Zenodotus as teaching the children (*paidas*) of Ptolemy and Diogenes Laertius 5.60 mentions that he taught a princess.

36. See Ogden 1999: 68–69, 2008: 253–55.

37. Bennett s.v. "Lagus," Leontiscus," and "Eirene"; Ogden 2008: 354–55.

38. Ogden 1999: 69.

39. See Ogden 1999: 69.

40. Wheatley 2003; Ogden 2008: 355.

41. Brosius 1996: 78, 184–85.

42. E.g., Berve 1926, 2:52; Brosius 1996: 78.

43. Ogden 1999: 69.

44. Tarn 1929: 138–39; Stephens 2003: 14.

45. Macurdy 1932: 102–4; Heckel 1989 and 2006: 122.

46. Baynham 1994; Heckel 2006: 35–38.

47. Macurdy 1932: 55–58, 104, 114; Ogden 1999: 58–61, 68–73; Carney 2000a: 160–61.

48. Macurdy 1932: 56, 58, 64–65, 103–4; Ogden 1999: 68–73, 173–77; Carney 2000a: 167.

49. Porphyry *FGrH* 260 F 3 10; s.v. Bennett "Meleager"; Heckel 1989: 33, n. 10.

50. Ogden 1999: 69.

51. Heckel 1989: 34.

52. Macurdy 1932: 104–9; Heckel 1989; Ogden 1999: 68–73; Heckel 2006: 71.

53. Schol. for Theoc. 17.34. See Maas 1927: 68–70.

54. The scholiast for Theoc. 17.34 calls her the daughter of "Baga"; rather than emending this name to "Lagus" and making Berenice the first Ptolemaic sibling bride, Bücheler 1875: 59, suggested "Maga," an emendation confirmed by her son's name. See Ogden 1999: 70 *contra* Longega 1968: 116; Bengston 1975; and Green 1990: 190; Hazzard 2000: 90.

55. Ogden 2008: 355 *contra* Nisetich 2005: 36, 59.

56. Bennet s.v. "Magas."

57. Plut. Pyrrh. 4; Schol. Theoc. 17.61; Just. 23.2.6. Heckel 1989: 33, n. 10; Beloch 1928: $4^2$2.179; Seibert 1967: 73; Ogden 1999: 70.

58. Macurdy 1932: 105.

59. Griffiths 1979: 54 suggests this in terms of Ptolemy's mother, but it applies to both mothers.

60. OGIS 14 ca. 299 refers to her as *basilissa*, a title applied only to king's daughters or wives. Carney 1991: 161, n. 45; Ogden 1999: 70.

61. Older scholarship assumed that the kings were serial monogamists and so believed that Berenice did not become a wife until her son's coregency and that Eurydice had to be repudiated first. Hölbl 2001: 24, continues this tradition.

62. Pomeroy 1984: 13.

63. Unlike Thaïs, she was not a courtesan *contra* Kosmetatou 2004b: 18; Ogden 2008: 356. Pausanias 1.6.8 says that Antipater sent Berenice with his daughter, hardly something he would have done for a courtesan.

64. Bennett s.v. "Philotera" assumes that she was born after her sister but before her brother and that the relationship between Ptolemy I and Berenice could not have begun before 317. There is no evidence for any of these assumptions. Regner 1941; Wikander 2002: 188. See chapters 5 and 6.

65. *Parian Marble 120* (archonship of Demetrius) = *FGrH* 239 B.19; Austin 2006: 40 (21.19).

66. Ogden 1999: 70.

67. Heckel 1989: 34.

68. This would have continued to be true after the death of her father Antipater in 319 until the death of her brother Cassander ca. 297.

69. Mitchell 2007: 67–73.

70. Herman 1980–81; see chapter 5.

71. Heckel 1989: 35.

72. Carney 1994: 123–24; Heckel 1989: 34–36.

73. Carney 1992; 2000: 23–27.

74. Cohen 1974: 177–79.

75. *Contra* Heckel 1989: 34–35.

76. Carney 1999.

77. Subsequently, he named a city after his mother-in-law, s.v. Steph. Byz. "Berenikai." Hazzard 2000: 106 denies that any of Ptolemy I's wives had "any power as queen," prizing Diodorus Siculus' failure to mention such power or the absence of it over Plutarch's positive assertion of it.

78. Adams 2008: 94–95. He does see the marriage as signaling the establishment of a *philia* relationship that would continue with Ptolemy II. From Pyrrhus' point of view, the marriage was an important step.

79. Though, as Müller 2009: 25, points out, Demetrius of Phalerum's support suggests that even a very important courtier thought that Ceraunus still had a chance.

80. Buraselis 2005; see also the Introduction.

81. *Contra* Billows 1995: 4. We do not know that he was expelled.

82. Ogden 1999: 72 *contra* Macurdy 1932: 103; Mori 2008: 95. Eurydice's presence in Miletus for her daughter Ptolemais' marriage to Demetrius in 286 (Plut. *Demetr.* 46) is not relevant (*contra* Bevan 1927: 54; Macurdy 1932: 103; Vatin 1970: 63).

83. Diog. Laert. 5.89. Green 1990: 87–88; Ellis 1993: 59–60.

84. Ogden 1999: 71.

85. Fantuzzi 2005 passim, especially 249–50.

86. Golden 2008: 6–8.

87. Barbantani 2010: 228, 230.

88. Fantuzzi 2005: 251–52, 258 suggests that the stress on the Macedonian ethnicity of Ptolemaic victors relates to their ambitions in the Greek peninsula.

89. Adams 2003; Kertész 1999, 2003, 2005.

90. SIG^3 314; Paus. 6.15.9–10, 16.2,9. 17.3, 7–8. Fantuzzi 2005: 251; Bennett 2005: 91. On royal *philoi*, see Thompson 2005: 279–80; see chapter 6 on Bilistiche's victory.

91. P. Mil. Vogl. VIII 309 surfaced in 1992. It contains 112 epigrams and the poetry collection has generally been attributed to him. Gutzwiller 2005.

92. Posidippus AB 87–88. 87 could possibly refer to another Berenice's victories (*contra* Cameron 1995: 244) but 88 demonstrably refers to Berenice I.

93. Bing 2002–3: 253, n. 23, dates Berenice's victory, Ptolemy I's and Ptolemy II's to the same Olympics, those of 284; Bennett 2005: 93, is less certain, but points out that many Ptolemaic victories were tied to critical dynastic events, like the choice of Berenice's son as co-king.

94. Paus. 5.6.7, 6.20.9. See Pomeroy 2002: 22, n. 79.

95. Material evidence does not connect members of the female Macedonian elite to horses, though narrative sources imply that some did ride: Carney 2000a: 69–70, 129–31, and 132–37; Pillonel 2008: 126–28.

96. Hodkinson 2000: 321–23; Pomeroy 2002: 21–23; Palagia 2009: 34–36; Kyle 2007b: 188–96.

97. Nisetich 2005: 59.

98. She was able to dedicate two monuments at Olympia commemorating her victory (Paus. 5.12.5; 6.1.6); Palagia 2009: 34–35.

99. Fantuzzi 2005: 263–64, thinks this explains the absence of reference to Euryleonis, another Spartan female Olympic victor, one not known to be part of a royal family.

Golden 2008: 22, suggests that Berenice also "one-ups" Cynisca by being not the daughter and sister of a king, but the wife and mother of a king.

100. Mantas 1995: 128–29.

101. Nicholson 2005: 2; Fantuzzi 2005: 264–66.

102. Pomeroy 2002: 22, n. 82 for references.

103. *Contra* Plut. Ages. 20.1, Xen. *Ages.* 9.6–7 See Mantas 1995: 128; Kyle 2007a: 141–45; 2007b: 189–96; Golden 2008: 11–12; Nicholson 2005: 3; Hodkinson 2000: 327; Fantuzzi 2004a: 397. The Ptolemies clearly did not share Agesilaus' supposed point of view.

104. Translation: Nisetich 2005: 36.

105. Pomeroy 2002: 21 notes the horsey names of some of Cynisca's female kin. In the *Clouds* (60–64). Aristophanes makes fun of aristocratic names involving horses. Strepsiades' aristocratic wife, significantly, wants one of those for her son.

106. Savalli-Lestrade 2003: 62.

Chapter 2

1. Hieronymus *FGrH* 154 F 10; Just. 17.10; Appian *Syr.* 64. See Ogden 1999: 58, n. 61. Heckel 1978: 224–28, 1992: 273–74, 2006: 153.

2. Translation is Yardley 1994: 123–24.

3. Yardley 1994: 149.

4. See Heckel 1992: 270–71; Lund 1992 and below.

5. Berve 1926: 2:239–41; Saitta 1955; Merker 1979; Heckel 1992: 26775; Landucci Gattinoni 1992: Lund 1992.

6. Porphyry *FGrH* 260 F3.8. Pausanias (1.9.4) and Justin (15.3.1) say he was Macedonian.

7. Lund 1992: 2–5; Heckel 2006: 153.

8. Heckel 1992: 270; Lund 1992: 10–12.

9. Lund 1992: 158–60; Hadley 1974: 55, 63.

10. Lund 1992: 54; Heckel 2006: 155.

11. Paus. 1.9.8; Diod. 20.29.1; Appian (*Syr.* 1.1). Will 1979: 76, 98; Lund 1992: 64. At least two other cities were named after him, but it is not clear he founded them (G. M. Cohen 1995: 114–15, 167).

12. Will 1979: 97–103; Burstein 1986; Lund 1992: 8–206.

13. Geyer 1930: 29; Seibert 1967: 93–96; Lund 1992: 10, 88, 185. Müller 2009: 33 suggests that he became a serial monogamist when he sent Amastris back to Heraclea.

14. Cohen 1973.

15. Ogden 1999: 57–58.

16. Diod. 20.109.6–7; Strabo 12.3.10; Memnon *FGrH* 434 F. 4.4.

17. Memnon *FGrH 434 F. 4.9.* On Lysimachus' continuing relationships with the family, see Lund 1992: 88. Ogden 1999: 57–58 points out that though Memnon says they separated, Amastris did not remarry.

18. Burstein 1976: 83–85; Carney 2000a: 229–32 *contra* Dmitriev 2007: 142–46.

19. Ogden 1999: 59.

20. Ogden 1999: 58–59.

21. Justin (24.3.5) says her two younger sons were sixteen and thirteen at the time of their murder ca. 280, making her oldest son at least seventeen.

22. G. M. Cohen 1995: 41, 45, 177–80; Longega 1968: 31 and n. 88. Whether this meant she had a political role in the city is unknown.

23. *Contra* Rigsby 2005: 111, n. 14.

24. Burstein 1982: 198–99, n. 6. See *contra* G. M. Cohen 1995: 177.

25. G. M. Cohen 1995: 41.

26. G. M. Cohen 1995: 65.

27. Kahrstedt 1910: 266; Koch 1924: 85; Longega 1968: 31; Mørkholm 1991: 81; Davesne 1991: 21–22; Müller 2009: 345–48; Parente 2002: 263–65. The coins are inscribed "ARSI," but Kahrstedt 1910: 266, notes that the legend is an abbreviation for "of the Arsinoëans," not "of Arsinoë.

28. Strabo 10.2.22 says she herself was responsible. See Lund 1992: 251, n. 74; Mueller 2006: 57.

29. Homolle 1896: 508–9; Longega 1968: 27–29, suggest the earlier date, but Burstein 1982: 209; Lund 1992: 194, the later.

30. See Lund 1992: 194 *contra* Longega 1968: 27–30.

31. Carney 1988a: 134–42, and 2000a: 207–9.

32. *Contra* Lund 1992: 194–95.

33. Carney 2004: 190, n. 31; see chapter 3.

34. See Fraser 1960: 48–50; Burstein 1982: 199.

35. Carney 2000a: 226–27, especially n. 125; Müller 2009: 66–67.

36. See Fraser 1960: 51; Burstein 1982: 199; Cole 1984: 22; Lund 1992: 168, for the view that this dedication happened during her marriage to Lysimachus *contra* Roux 1981: 231–39; Frazer 1990: 232–33.

37. Carney 2006: 88–103.

38. Roux 1981: 236, n.15.

39. Kron 1996: 171.

40. Lund 1992: 10–12.

41. Hazzard 2000: 82, n. 10. Müller 2009: 46–57, points out that these two themes, the tyrannical ruler and the seductive and manipulative queen, tend to be linked.

42. Hazzard 2000: 83.

43. Variations of this anecdote appear in several authors (Plut. *Mor.* 606b, 634b; Sen.*de ira* 3.17). Lund 1992: 7, considers them simply a recurrent literary theme *contra* Cameron 1995: 98.

44. Carney 2000a: 223–25; see also chapters 5 and 6.

45. Pomeroy 1984: 18–19, using Arsinoë as her example, argues that women in the ancient world, even royal women, were a "muted group" and that historians must recognize that there are limits to how much ancient sources will tell us, directly, about women.

46. The Delian decree, whatever its date, should be taken with a grain of salt. See Lund 1992: 194 *contra* Longega 1968: 27–29.

47. Carney 2000a: 160–61.

48. Heckel 1989: 34; Carney 2000a: 159–60.

49. Heckel 1989: 34; Ogden 1999: 59; Dmitriev 2007: 138–41 *contra* Pausanias (1.10).

50. Macurdy 1932: 56–57; Seibert 1967: 75–76.

51. Seibert 1967: 97, n. 20, suggests that Lysimachus treated his daughter and son-in-law this way because he hoped to use the "claim" of Alexander's widow Lysandra as a basis for rule in Macedonia; see also Heckel 1989: 35; Ogden 1999: 59.

52. Ogden 1999: 58.

53. See Lund 1992: 45–49.

54. *Contra* Dmitriev 2007: 146–49, who assumes that the success of Berenice's son was sudden and that Lysimachus would have switched heirs simply because one had a closer connection to the Ptolemaic heir than the other.

55. On the conflicting sources and the chronological problems, see Paus. 1.16.2; Heinen 1972: 4; Errington 1990: 157 *contra* Memnon F 8.2, App. Syr 62. Tarn 1913: 125.

56. Lund 1992: Ogden 1999: 61.

57. *Contra* Dmitriev 2007: 135.

58. Lund 1992: 196–97.

59. Robert 1933; Longega 1968: 44; Heinen 1972: 10; Lund 1992: 197–98.

60. Holleaux 1921: 194–95; Robert 1933: 490; Longega 1968: 44; Heinen 1972, 10, 82, n. 314; Bringmann 2000: 88; Müller 2007d: 278.

61. *Contra* Hölbl 2001: 35.

62. Heinen 1972: 4–19; Lund 1992: 184–206; Landucci Gattinoni 1991; Carney 1994: 125–27; for the date, see Walbank 1988: 239.

63. If he had, he would not have mistaken one Ptolemy for the other (he states that Ptolemy Ceraunus actually carried out Lysimachus' execution order). Most historians think, if there is any truth at all to this assertion, that he has confused Ptolemy Ceraunus with Ptolemy son of Lysimachus (Heinen 1972: 10–16; Will 1979: 103–5; Walbank 1988: 297; Lund 1992: 188; Landucci Gattinoni 1992: 210, n. 149; Carney 1994: 126; Ogden 1999: 61; Müller 2009: 39 *contra* Tarn 1913: 124,135; Mori 2008: 95, n. 14).

64. Ogden 1999: 61, thinks that Pausanias misunderstood a plan of Arsinoë's to replace her old husband with the current presumptive heir.

65. Lund 1992: 193–95.

66. *Contra* Longega 1968: 45.

67. Landucci Gattinoni 1992: 211–13, argues that the sources allow for the possibility that Agathocles conspired with Philetaerus and Seleucus. See also Müller 2009: 45.

68. Lund 1992: 198.

69. Lund 1992: 196–98; Ogden 1999: 62, note some actions of Agathocles' that might have generated distrust.

70. Lund 1992: 196–98.

71. Will 1979: 100, believes that he hoped that the campaign Seleucus launched would bring him a kingdom of his own.

72. See Landucci Gattinoni 1990: 111–26; 1992: 214–21.

73. Müller 2009: 42–43.

74. Will 1979: 101.

75. Lund 1992: 199–206.

76. The firm date of the battle depends, ultimately, on the Babylonian Chronicle (see Lund 1992: 201–2).

77. Landucci Gattinoni 1990.

78. Hazzard 2000: 83, does this.

79. The quotation is Hazzard 2000: 83.

80. See further Lund 1992: 199–206.

81. Heinen 1972: 38, takes it as hatred of Arsinoë.

82. Hazzard 2000: 83 terms the tale "unflattering," but nothing in Polyaenus' text supports this view.

83. Ritter 1965: 117, n. 3, 172–73, doubted the historicity of the episode because he considered it too similar to an episode attributed to Mysta, an *hetaira* of Seleucus II, reported both by Phylarchus (*ap.* Ath. 13.593e) and Polyaenus (8.61) himself.

84. Hazzard 2000: 83, simply assumes they were with her; Polyaenus makes no mention of them.

Chapter 3

1. For these events, see Heinen 1972: 37–91; Walbank 1988: 241–58; Errington 1990: 156–61.

2. Nothing more is known of Lysandra and her children. Heinen 1972: 52, n. 192.

3. Müller 2009: 68–69.

4. Walbank 1988: 244. Memnon (*FGrH* 434 F 8.2) claims that Seleucus had promised to restore Ceraunus to rule in Egypt, after the death of Soter, despite the fact that Soter was, by this point, already dead (Heinen 1972: 4–9).

5. Walbank 1988: 243–44.

6. Walbank 1988: 244.

7. Hammond 1988b.

8. Heinen 1972: 76–77; Walbank 1988: 247.

9. Lund 1992: 173; Burton 1995: 124.

10. Carney 2004: 190–93. See also Schaps 1982; Loman 2004; Pillonel 2008.

11. Ritter 1965: 112 *contra* Heinen 1972: 78.

12. Walbank 1988: 241–42 *contra* Heinen 1972: 79. Justin 24.2.2 says merely that the kingdom or kingship belonged to Lysimachus' sons.

13. *Contra* Collins 1997: 464–72.

14. The careers of Parmenio (Diod. 17.5.2; Curt. 7.1.3) and Cleander (Arr. 3.26.3) offer examples.

15. Müller 2009: 72.

16. See discussion in Ogden 1999: 77.

17. Müller 2009: 80.

18. *Contra* Heinen 1972: 81–83; Ogden 1999: 77; Müller 2009: 75. Heinen and Müller believe the departure of the oldest son Ptolemy caused Ceraunus to adopt a more

murderous plan because the original agreement was shattered. Ceraunus, however, could equally well have used his control of the younger brothers against the eldest, by making them hostages.

19. There is no mention of a marriage for Ceraunus; even when he had expectations of the Egyptian throne, it would have been unusual for him to marry before he was king. Justin 17.2.14, 24.1.8 probably refers to the daughter of another Ptolemy (Hammond 1988b: 407).

20. Memnon *FGrH* 434 F. 5.6 claims that a Ptolemy actually killed Agathocles, on Lysimachus' orders. As we have noted (see chapter 2, n.64), many have concluded that though Memnon specifies Ptolemy Ceraunus, this is a mistake, and that it was actually the son of Lysimachus. Heinen 1972: 81–83; Will 1979: 103–5; Roux 1981: 237, believe that the son of Lysimachus feared Ceraunus because of his supposed youthful murder. Memnon's confusion, however, compromises his credibility and it is hard to see a distinction between Arsinoë and her son here; surely both had reason to fear Ceraunus' vengeance.

21. Carney 2000a: 123–28, 129–31, 188–89, 229.

22. *Contra* Heinen 1972: 81–83; Errington 1990: 159.

23. Longega 1968: 65ff; Heinen 1972: 81 *contra* Ritter 1965: 121f. Longega 1968: 66, implausibly suggested she got the title because she ruled Cassandria.

24. Müller 2009: 76–81; Carney 2000a: 232–33.

25. Ritter 1965: 114. *Contra* Granier 1931: 120, it did not mean she coruled with Ceraunus.

26. Philo *On Spec. Laws* 3.22; Sen. *Apocol.* 8; Plut. *Them.* 32; Nep. *Cim.* 1.2; Ar. *Nub.* 1372. Karabélias 1989; Modrzejewski 1964: 59–60; Vérilhac and Vial 1998: 91–101; Buraselis 2008: 292; Rowlandson and Takahashi 2009: 106–9.

27. Ogden 1999: 9–10, 14–15.

28. Ogden 1999: 78, 124–25.

29. Justin (24.3.3) makes it clear that it did not happen at Cassandria (*contra* Hazzard 2000: 84) and that Arsinoë returned to Cassandria after the wedding and arranged the ceremonial procession. See Müller 2009: 76, n.371.

30. Arslan and Özen 2000 proposed that coins from a hoard found in Thrace bearing the inscription "Basileos Ptolemaiou" were minted by Ptolemy Ceraunus and that some show Arsinoë on the obverse. See Müller 2009: 348–53 *contra*. The coins are more likely those of another Ptolemy; so too a dedication at Delos (Heinen 1972: 83–84).

31. Killing children in their mother's arms is a *topos* (literary theme), especially in Justin (9.7.12, 38.8.4): Roux 1981: 237.

32. Chaniotis 1997; Spawforth 2007: 91. See also chapter 5.

33. Carney 2000a: 203–7.

34. Walbank 1988: 248; Carney 2000a: 188–89, 206.

35. A. Cohen 1995.

36. Carney 2006a: 85–87.

37. Carney 2006a: 84–85.

38. Polyaen. 6.7.2. Carney 2004: 190, n. 31; Müller 2009: 73, n.352, *contra* Macurdy 1932: 103; Loman 2004: 45.

39. Macurdy 1932: 115; Heinen 1972: 12.

40. Burton 1995: 140, suggests that a reference to Hecuba in Theocritus (15.139) might, for those in the know, have recalled aspects of the life of Arsinoë.

41. Lund 1992: 173.

42. Müller 2009: 58–67 *contra* Cole 1984: 22, n. 179.

43. Walbank 1988: 248, n. 4.

44. Burstein 1982: 200.

45. Walbank 1988: 248–49 *contra* Heinen 1972: 82.

46. Tarn 1926: 161; Rice 1983: 41, *contra* Walbank 1988: 248, n. 4, 254, n. 2, although see Walbank 1988: 258.

47. Walbank 1988: 252.

48. Strootman 2005, especially 105–7, 112–13; Tarn 1913: 139–66; Walbank 1988: 251–58; Gabbert 1997: 26–28.

49. *Contra* Hazzard 2000:98.

Chapter 4

1. Müller 2009: 89.

2. Berenice was alive when Pyrrhus married Antigone ca. 299, still alive in 284, if that was the date of her Olympic victory (see chapter 1), and probably still living when her son began to rule on his own in 283/82. (Bennet s.v. "Berenice I"). The cult of the *theoi soteres* (see below) is usually associated with the first Ptolemaea in 279 and thus many presume that Berenice was dead by 279 (e.g., Hölbl 2001: 94).

3. Foertmeyer 1988: 91, argues that by the time of the great procession (Callixeinus (*FGrH* 627 F2 34), Berenice was dead and had a cult building, but the date of the procession is contested (and chapter 5). Theoc. *Id*. 17.123–24 has Aphrodite revivify her and turn her into a deity. Gutzwiller 1992a: 363–65, especially n. 20, considers a lifetime deification of Berenice I possible but not certain. See also Tondriau 1948b: 2–3 and 1948a: 14; Fraser 1972: 1: 197.

4. See chapter 3 and Huss 2001: 307, n. 22.

5. On his reign, see Huss 2001: 251–331; Hölbl 2001: 35–45, 54–76; McKechnie and Guillaume 2008. Hazzard 2000 is extremely tendentious.

6. Ager 2003: 37.

7. Samuel 1993: 183; Barbantani 2007: 71–72 *contra* Hazzard 2000: 1. See also chapter 5.

8. Tunny 2001: 132–33.

9. Errington 2008: 120.

10. Barbantani 2010: 238–39.

11. Rice 1983: 39; Ogden 1999: 74; Bennett 2003, consider 285 or early 284 likely.

12. *P. Brit. Mus.* Inv. 589; see Vatin 1970: 78.

13. Amastris, Lysimachus' Persian wife, married him about the right time to produce a child of the apparent age of Arsinoë I (see chapter 2), but *contra* Bennett 2003: 66, she is not likely the mother.

14. In theory, Arsinoë II could have been her mother, but this is extremely unlikely Macurdy 1932: 109; Bennett s.v. "Arsinoe I."

15. Müller 2009: 92.

16. Ogden 1999: 74.

17. Fraser 1972: 1:347, 369; Rice 1983: 39; Tunney 2000: 83.

18. Müller 2009: 94 takes this possibility seriously; see also Bennett s.v. "Arsinoë I."

19. Bennett s.v. "Ptolemy III" gives a wide range of 285–75, but 283–79 makes more sense.

20. Ager 2005: 6.

21. Burstein 1982.

22. E.g., Macurdy 1932: 110.

23. Rice 1983: 39.

24. Rice 1983: 39 notes that Pithom stele seems to say that Philadelphus journeyed to Pithom in the sixth year of his reign, probably signifying that he had no consort at the time. If Ptolemy II's Grand Procession was the first celebration of the Ptolemaea, then at the time of the festival in 279, he had no wife, implying that he had already rejected Arsinoë I and had not yet married Arsinoë II (see chapter 5).

25. *Contra* Bennett s.v. "Arsinoë I" and 2003: 68–70, who maintains that the Cypriote inscription KAI 43, dated 275/74, refers to Arsinoë I in a way that shows she cannot have been rejected at the time.

26. Olympias; Cleopatra, her daughter; Cleopatra, the last wife of Philip II; Cynnane, sister of Alexander (Carney 2000a: 123, 127, 74, and 131). Perdiccas' sister Atalante was also killed (Diod. 18.37.2).

27. Macurdy 1932: 110.

28. Macurdy 1932: 121; Burstein 1982: 202, n.25. Ogden 1999: 78, thinks the phrase the scholiast used implies this and cites Harrison 1968–71: 1:83–84. Wikander 2002: 187, seems to consider it a decision made during Arsinoë's lifetime, a kind of antipolygamous move meant to consolidate the royal clan. Buraselis 2005: 96, says it happened before Arsinoë's death.

29. Stele CCG 70031, the stele of Senu-sher or Senenshepsu (Lloyd 2002: 123), a steward of a queen Arsinoë at Coptos, has long been assumed to refer to Arsinoë I in exile (Petrie 1896: 20–22), but Quaegebeur 1970: 212, 215–16 and 1978: 249; and Lloyd 2002: 123–25, have argued compellingly that Arsinoë II is meant. See *contra* Traunecker 1992: 256.

30. Ogden 1999: 74, who, however, assumes that the Coptos inscription refers to Arsinoë I.

31. Carney 1987; Ager 2005, 2006, 2007; Carney 2010.

32. On the basis of CCG 22183 (the Pithom Stele), Ager 2003: 39, says early 273 but Bennett s.v. "Arsinoë II": n. 14, noting problems with counting Ptolemy II's regnal years, concludes that the date could be November 274 or 272.

33. A relationship probably exists between the marriage and the revolt of Magas, Ptolemy II's half brother and governor of Cyrene, but which precipitated which is difficult to say Will 1979: 149; Tarn 1913: 26.

34. Rowlandson and Takahashi 2009: 106 reject the use of the term *incest* because of its moral presumptions; I may use "incestuous" or "incest" to describe someone else's interpretation of the practice.

35. Ogden 2011a: 99, provides a list of all the Ptolemaic close kin marriages.

36. See Ager 2005 for references as well as Buraselis 2008; Rowlandson and Takahashi 2009: 110.

37. Carney 1987: 435; Ager 2005: 16.

38. Cérny 1954: 23; Hopkins 1980: 311–13.

39. Frandsen 2009: 9; Rowlandson and Takahashi 2009: 110.

40. Carney 1987: 423, n. 8; Shaw 1992: 283; Buraselis 2008: 296–97 (a few have doubted that there were any full sibling royal marriages (see Buraselis 2008: 24, n. 14.). Buraselis believes that pharaonic practice was known to Ptolemy II, via Manetho.

41. Hawass et al. 2010.

42. Robins 1993a: 70.

43. Forgeau 2008: 11–12.

44. Hölbl 2001: 95; Quaegebeur 1998: 93; Huss 2001: 309; Buraselis 2008: 298. See also chapter 6.

45. *Contra* Hazzard 2000: 88 the passage does not condemn such marriages but simply notes they were unprecedented.

46. Ager 2005: 2.

47. Buraselis 2008: 292, examples.

48. Ager 2005: 2.

49. Ager 2005: 2–3.

50. Fraser 1972: 1:117–18; Carney 1987: 428; Ager 2005: 27 *contra* Buraselis 2008: 292. Hazzard wrongly believes (2000: 40) that these later views must have depended on contemporary hostile tradition.

51. Plutarch's passive verb could refer to opinion in Ptolemy II's day or could be more general but is not obviously related to Athens *contra* Hazzard 2000: 39.

52. A fragment of Callimachus may allude to Sotades' poem (Ogden 2008: 381).

53. Plutarch *Mor.* 11a merely has him imprisoned. See Launey 1945: 44.

54. Launey 1945; Fraser 1972: 1:117–18; Cameron 1990; Weber 1998–99: 162–65; Kosmetatou 2004b: 31 *contra* Ogden 2008: 373.

55. Longega 1968: 74; Fraser 1972: 1:117–18; Carney 1987: 428; Cameron 1995: 98; Ager 2005: 27 are skeptical about the seriousness of his remark.

56. Weber 1998–99: 162–65, 173. She points out that artists killed by kings were all "notorious grousers," mavericks, not voices of the people.

57. Diod. 1.27.1–2; Paus. 1.7.1; Memnon *FGrH* 434 F8.7; Philo *On Spec. Laws* 3.23–25; Seneca *Apocol.* 8.3; Sextus Empiricus *Pyr.* I. 152, III.205, 234.

58. Kornemann 1923: 17–45; Bengtston 1975: 117, argued that the model for Ptolemaic brother-sister marriage was Persian, but see *contra* Ogden 1999: 108, n. 59.

59. Huebner 2007: 24. Rowlandson and Takahashi 2009: 112 *contra* Murray 1970: 166, who suggests Hecataeus.

60. Remijsen and Clarysse 2008: 55–56; Rowlandson and Takahashi 2009: 113–14.

61. Modrzejewski 1964; Hopkins 1980. See now Huebner 2007; Fischer 2007; Remijsen and Clarysse 2008; and Rowlandson and Takahashi 2009. Huebner 2007 denies the existence of brother sister marriage, but see *contra* Remijsen and Clarysse 2008; Rowlandson and Takahashi 2009.

62. Hazzard 2000: 93, argues that some Greek sources call Arsinoë the king's sister to avoid calling her his wife; they may, however, have simply considered the former relationship the more important.

63. Fraser 1972: 1: 118.

64. Carney 1987: 429.

65. *Contra* Bevan 1927: 60; Seibert 1967: 82. Menopause happened between forty and fifty (Amundsen and Diers 1970).

66. Ogden 1999: 74.

67. Scholiast for Theoc. 17. 129.

68. Longega 1968: 73, amusingly assumes that this meant it cannot have been a love match (see chapter 6).

69. Wilcken 1896: 1283; Kornemann 1923: 20; Bengston 1975: 117.

70. Carney 1987: 424, n. 11.

71. Ager 2005: 15, especially n. 80.

72. Tarn 1913: 262; Beloch 1928: 4, 1, 242, 582; Bevan 1927: 60–61; Macurdy 1932: 118; Vatin 1970; Thompson 1973: 120; Pomeroy 1984: 7.

73. Burstein 1982.

74. Tarn 1926: 161; Will 1979: I, 149 try. Magas, Berenice's son, for instance, was a threat to the coherence of the Ptolemaic dynasty. See Buraselis 2008: 300; Ogden 2011a: 100. Droysen 1878: 3: 265. Hazzard 2000: 87 *contra* Macurdy 1932: 118.

75. Carney 1987: 433–34; Hauben 1983: 106. I do not mean to suggest (*contra* Ager 2005: 19), that he had to marry his sister but rather that, if he wished to marry, the diplomatic situation made it advantageous to marry her rather than a Seleucid.

76. Burstein 1982: 211–12; Ogden 1999: 75 *contra* Hazzard 2000: 88–89. Ptolemy II executed one son of Eurydice for trying to start a rebellion in Cyprus and Argaeus, perhaps another son of Eurydice, for conspiracy (Paus. 1.7.1–2).

77. Ogden 1999: 79. See further chapter 5.

78. Carney 1994: 130–31; 2000: 228–32.

79. *Contra* Modrzejewski 1964: 270–73; 1993; 1998: 573–76.

80. Ogden 1999: 73–116.

81. Ogden 2011a: 100.

82. Ager 2005:17 *contra* Carney 1987: 432.

83. Carney 1987: 430 stresses the importance of continuity in terms of Ptolemaic image making.

84. Griffiths 1979: 77.

85. Ager 2005: 18.

86. Kosmetatou 2002: 109–10, points out that court poetry stressed the links between living and dead Ptolemies, often paired links.

87. Hauben 1989: 447.

88. Müller 2009: 130–31 *contra* Hazzard 2000: 90.

89. Hazzard 2000: 93.

90. *Contra* Carney 1987: 432, Ptolemy II and Arsinoe could have wanted to appeal to both Egyptians and Greeks (Ager 2005: 17).

91. Ager 2005: 17, n.95.

92. Buraselis 2008: 292, n. 4, sees the passage about their marriage at the end of the poem as a kind of "consummation" of Ptolemy II's divine character.

93. Callimachus Fr. 392 Pf; another fragmentary poem, probably by Posidippus, AB 114 (see discussion in Gutzwiller 2005: 5–6, n. 17) seems to put Arsinoë's wedding in the context of Hera's, as an anonymous poem does as well (Stephens 2005: 243–44; Griffiths 1979: 54–55).

94. *OGIS* 26, 27. See also Hauben 1970: 34–36.

95. Kosmetatou 2004b: 24.

96. Theocritus, to emphasize this, links the marriage to dynastic cult (Griffiths 1979: 61–62). Stephens 2003: 168–69, notes that Hecataeus speaks of them ruling together in harmony.

97. Fraser 1972: 1: 216–17, 2: 367; Longega 1968: 98–99; Anastassiades 1998: 135–37; Burstein 1982: 201, n. 21; Koenen 1994: 51; Buraselis 2008: 291, n. 2; Wallenstein and Pakkanen 2009: 159, believe that she got the epithet around the time of her marriage, based on Theocritus *Id.* 17.128–30. Thompson 1973: 55–57, connects the epithet to the cult of the *adelphoi*. Sauneron 1966: 97, prefers to associate it with her posthumous cult. Whether the epithet also suggests a connection to divine marriages, like that of Zeus and Hera, is uncertain (Criscuolo 1990; Muccioli 1994). When it began to be applied to Ptolemy II is even less clear; the first evidence is second century BCE (Müller 2009: 280, n. 808).

98. Müller 2009: 281, suggests a similarity with the epithet "Soter."

99. Kosmetatou 2004b: 24, sees the divine aspect as justification whereas Hazzard 2000: 85–90, sees it as the sole reason Ptolemy decided on it.

100. Carney 1987: 434; Ager 2005: 20.

101. Ager 2005: 22–27, especially ns. 139, 140.

102. Ager 2005: 23–24.

103. Ager 2005: 25–26 *contra* Hazzard 2000: 67.

104. See Ager 2005: 26–27.

105. Ager 2005: 1.

106. Ogden 1999: 77; Ogden 2011a: 100. Ager 2005: 20, speculates that Arsinoë might have offered to marry Magas, ruler of Cyrene and Arsinoë's uncle, if her brother did not offer her marriage himself.

107. Carney 1994: 130, n.29.

108. Golden 1981: 324–25.

Chapter 5

1. Pomeroy 1984: 19.

2. Herman 1997; Weber 1997.

3. Chaniotis 1997; see chapter 3.

4. Nielsen 1994: 19–20.

5. Nielsen 1994: 16.

6. Kuttner 1999; Nielsen 1994: 15–16.

7. Barbantani 2007: 68–69.

8. McKenzie 2008: 41–55; see chapter 1.

9. Nielsen 1994: 14–24, 130–54, 280–82. Evidence is a scanty mix of archaeological material (though much remains under water), comparative material from the palaces of Ptolemaic governors outside Egypt, and literary descriptions (though many of these postdate the reign of Ptolemy II, e.g., the "Letter of Aristeas"; see chapter 6 and Hunter 2011 *contra* Nielsen 1994: 19–25.) The description of the palace of Aetes in Colchis in Apollonius' *Argonautica* (3.164ff.) may have been influenced by the palace of Ptolemy II (Nielsen 1994: 133, 179; Pfrommer 1996: 136, 140).

10. Erskine 1995: 38; Hoepfner 1996: 6.

11. Ashton 2004: 15.

12. The gardens may have been used for audiences and banquets (Pfrommer 1996: 136, 140).

13. Diod. 3.36.3–37.8; *P. Cair. Zen.* I 59075. See Fraser 1972: 2: 782, n.200. McKenzie 2008: 49 suggests that there was a royal game preserve elsewhere.

14. Strab. 17.8 (793–94); Ath. 14.654c. Nielsen 1994: 24.

15. Hoepfner 1996: 93–94.

16. Müller 2009: 156–384, especially 156–75.

17. Nielsen 1994: 18.

18. Herman 1997: 207, 223.

19. Barbantani 2008: 131.

20. McKenzie 2008: 32–34, 37, 48.

21. Empereur 1998: 76–77; Pfeiffer 2008: 293; Ashton 2004: 26–27.

22. Stephens 1998: 167.

23. Quaegebeur 1971; 1988; Pomeroy 1984: 19.

24. Troy 1986: 139; Grzybek 2008. Women occasionally ruled during the pharaonic period, typically when there was a scarcity of adult males.

25. Athenaeus, a third-century-CE author, describes some passages from Callixeinus (writing in the late third century BCE), based on material found in Ptolemaic archives. See Goukowsky 1995: 79.

26. Dunand 1981: 16. Walbank 1996: 121. Wikander 1992: 147. Wikander (1992: 148–49) sees this festival as somewhat interactive—Ptolemy II projected the ideals of kingship and the audience responded.

27. Walbank 1996: 1123; Wikander 1992: 148.

28. Goukowsky 1995: 79.

29. Walbank 1996: 124.

30. Wikander 1992: 149; Erskine 1995: 44.

31. For 279/78 or 275/74: Fraser 1972: 1:231; Huss 2001: 321–23; Buraselis 2008: 300. For 279/78: Rice 1983: 38–43; Walbank 1996: 121; Thompson 2000: 367–81; Kosmetatou 2004b: 121; Marquaille 2008: 54–55. For 275/74: Foertmeyer 1998; Hölbl 2001: 39.

For 271/70: Dunand 1981: 13; Goukowsky 1995: 80. Hazzard 2000: 66, alone argues for 262.

32. Thompson 2000: 381; Müller 2009: 203. The "rulers" could be Ptolemy II and Arsinoë II or Ptolemy I and Ptolemy II.

33. Rice 1983: 38–43; Müller 2009: 203–4. Foertmeyer 1988: 102–4, wonders if Callixeinus or Athenaeus simply omitted Arsinoë.

34. McKenzie 2008: 48.

35. Ath. 196a–197cl; Nielsen 1994: 22–23; McKenzie 2008: 49.

36. Mooren 1975: 53–60; Hölbl 2001: 58.

37. Fantuzzi 2004a: 390, 394–95.

38. Savalli-Lestrade 2003: 61–65.

39. Nielsen 1994: 23–24, 136, discussing the royal Nile barge of Ptolemy IV, assumes a physical division into male and female areas but see Carney 2010: 51.

40. Savalli-Lestrade 1997: 430.

41. Wikander 2002: 185–91.

42. Burstein 1982: 212; Troxell 1983: 59.

43. Burton 1995: 7–40; Selden 1998.

44. Selden 1998: 312, 353; Burton 1995: 3.

45. Schmitt 1991: 79–83, 86.

46. Burton 1995: 140.

47. Bing 2002–3: 242, 253, concludes that only 272 (127th Olympiad) and 276 (126th) are possible, but her marriage may not have happened until after 276, as we have seen.

48. Golden 2008: 9–10.

49. Carney 2004. See also Schaps 1982; Loman 2004, especially 45–48; Stephens 2005: 240–41; Pillonel 2008.

50. The identity of those buried in the royal tombs remains contested. See Carney 2004: 187, n. 15.

51. Carney 2001: 27–33; Dodson and Hilton 2004: 140.

52. See Carney 2001: 33–35 for references.

53. Pillonel 2008: 129.

54. The Pithom stele (the source for this trip) endorses a public role for the queen in defense, though not necessarily corule, as Nilsson 2010: 286, believes.

55. Stephens 2005: 241–42.

56. Hölbl 2001: 145.

57. Nisetich 2005: 25. See Stephens 2004: 163–70 and 2005: 236–43; Barbantani 2005; 2007; 2008.

58. Bing 2002–3: 257; Stephens 2004: 167.

59. Stephens 2004: 168; Bing 2002–3: 258–60.

60. Stephens 2004; 167–68 *contra* Barbantani 2008: 117.

61. Bing 2002–3: 260; Barbantani 2005: 149.

62. Fantuzzi 2004a: 379; Austin et al. 2002. See also Stephens 2004: 163–70, 2005: 236–43; Barbantani 2005: 149, 2008: 116–19.

63. Lelli 2002 and Stephens 2005: 238–41, suggest that the Arsinoë image may be claiming Egypt as "spear-won" land. See *contra* Bing 2002–3: 259–60.

64. Kuttner 1999: 110–13 argues that the Thmuis mosaic images of an older and younger woman, both with warship crowns, represented Arsinoë II and Berenice II and were connected to Ptolemaic naval power, possibly to Arsinoë Aphrodite Euploia, protectress of sailors and seafarers (see below).

65. See Carney 2006: 50–52; 2011: 197–98.

66. Moran 1992: 91; Robins 1993b: 32–34; Arnold 1996: 12.

67. Carney 2000a: 135–36.

68. Macurdy 1932: 119; Pomeroy 1984: 18.

69. *SIG*³ 4334–35. See Austin 2006: 130–33; Barbantani 2008: 111–13; Heinen 1972: 213; Habicht 1992: 71–73 and 1997: 365, favor of 268/67. Meritt 1981: 78–99; Gabbert 1987: 230–35; Dreyer 1999: 331–51, prefers 265/64.

70. Hauben 1992: 162; O'Neil 2008: 68–71, conclude that even if she died in 269/68 (Grzybek 1990: 103–7), she was probably dead by the time of the war, but only by a month or two. Habicht 1992: 72–73, wonders if Chremonides knew she was dead. See chapter 6.

71. Habicht 1992.

72. Gauthier 1985: 49; Barbantani 2008: 111.

73. Decrees honoring Hellenistic kings that also mention their wives are not parallel. See Longega 1968: 27ff; Barbantani 2008: 111.

74. The contrasting discussions of Burstein 1982 and Hauben 1983 are the most useful.

75. Müller 2009: 150–52.

76. Hauben 1992: 162.

77. *Contra* Burstein 1982: 210.

78. *Contra* Will 1979, 1: 222; Heinen 1972: 97–100, 132–39; Hazzard 2000: 39.

79. See Wallenstein and Pakkanen 2009: 157–64, and chapter 6.

80. Fantuzzi 2004a: 282–83.

81. Habicht 1992: 143.

82. O'Neil 2008: 66.

83. Habicht 1992: 72.

84. Fantuzzi 2004a: 281.

85. See Frazer 1990, especially 227–33. Construction of the two buildings may have overlapped, even if Arsinoë's dedication began to be built in the 280s and Ptolemy II's not till the 270s.

86. So Tarn 1913; 1926; Macurdy 1932: 11–20; Longega 1968: 93–95; Anastassiades 1998: 130.

87. Walbank 1988: 279.

88. Carney 2000a: 209–25, 2000b: 21–24; Mirón-Pérez 1998a and 1998b.

89. Tondriau 1948a: 14.

90. Carney 2000b: 30–31; Müller 2006: 79–94.

91. Müller 2006: 76–79. Ogden 2011a: 98–99 suggests a possible Argead precedent.

92. Carney 2000b: 31, n.53. *OGI* 61 offers evidence of a city cult at Scepsis for the same pair even earlier, probably in 311.

93. Phila's civic cult appeared in the period between Demetrius' salvation of Athens and his departure for his campaign. The cults of his *hetairai* probably date ca. 304–3 BCE. (Wheatley 2003; Müller 2010).

94. Carney 2000a: 325, n. 117.

95. Carney 2000b: 32–33.

96. Fraser 1972: 1:236–37, 246.

97. Price 1984a; 1984b. Müller 2010 sees Demetrius Poliorcetes' cults and those of the women connected to him as part of his attempt to craft a distinctive royal image.

98. Carney 2000b: 34. Is it the individual woman as Aphrodite or Aphrodite in the form of the woman? Ogden 2011a: 97, believes the latter is the case if the goddess's name appears first, the former if it is second.

99. Loraux 1992. See also Mirón-Pérez 1998b: 230–35; Tondriau 1948a: 1–2, 12–13, 20–21. Athenaeus 13.566c associates beauty with rule.

100. Neumer-Pflau 1982: 55–60.

101. Carney 2000b: 36–40. See chapter 6 on the cults of Ptolemy II's courtesans.

102. Gutzwiller 1992a: 263–68.

103. Wikander 2002: 188.

104. P. Hibeh II 199. Ii 12, 15–17, says that the cult was founded in the fourteenth year of Ptolemy II's reign. What absolute date this would be is disputed because of the change in the reckoning of his regnal years. Consensus now supports 273 or 272/71. Fraser 1972: 1:21; Hauben 1983: 113, n. 57; Grzybek 1990: 160; Koenen 1994: 51f; Hazzard 2000: 89–90, argue that their joint deification and marriage happened in the same year, 273. Huss 2001: 323–25; Bing 2002–3: 244; Buraselis 2008: 298–99, date the cult to 272/71. Longega 1968; 95–102; Cadell 1998: 3; Thompson 2005: 271, all conclude it was lifetime. See also Samuel 1962: 25–28; Sauneron 1966: 83–109; Burstein 1982: 201, n. 21.

105. Pfeiffer 2008: 400–402, discusses the possibility that they had an earlier cult.

106. Hauben 1992: 161.

107. Koenen 1994: 62–63.

108. Fraser 1972: 1:228; Grimm 1998: 73; Pfeiffer 2008: 398.

109. Fantuzzi 2004a: 389. Bing 2002–3: 248–49. Fantuzzi 2004b: 35, argues that the dedication confirmed the theme that competitive success was a prerogative of the dynasty.

110. Hauben 1970 40–41.

111. Hoepfner 1971: 45–49.

112. Barbantani 2008: 131. See also Hauben 1970: 37–40.

113. Barbantani 2008: 132.

114. Callimachus F 228 pictures Philotera as already deified at the time of the death and deification of Arsinoë II. See also Pfeiffer 1922: 14–37. Thompson 1988: 127, 131, seems to understand her cult as beginning before Arsinoë's (see chapter 6), but Hölbl 2001: 103, thinks her cult followed that of Arsinoë.

115. See chapter 1; Schol. Theocritus 17.121–3d; Macurdy 1932: 127–28; Ogden 1999: 79; Wikander 2002: 188–89; Müller 2009: 299.

116. Reymond 1981: 60–70; Hölbl 2001: 103.

117. Regner 1941: 1287. Wikander 2002: 188, thinks that the dedication means that she was alive as late as 279/78. Wallenstein and Pakkanen 2009: 157, n. 6, say early 270s.

118. See Wikander 2002: 191, n. 16.

119. Reymond 1981: 60–70; Hölbl 2001: 120, n. 159.

120. *Contra* Wikander 2002: 188–89, her unmarried state was surely the decision of her father and/or brother.

121. PP VI 14574; Strab. 16.4.5. There was a city founded by her brother and named after her near the Red Sea (Fraser 1972: 1:177–78 and 2:299.) and also two eponymous villages in the Fayum and a deme Philotereios in Ptolemais (Regner 1941: 1293).

122. Hölbl 2001: 103.

123. Wikander 2002: 189.

124. Berenice, the nine-year-old daughter of Ptolemy III, was also deified. See Wikander 2002: 187–88.

125. McKenzie 2008: 52.

126. Bing 2002–3: 260–66 would add Posidippus AB 37 and an epigram of Hedyllus (Ath. 11.497d = 4 G-P).

127. Stephens 2005: 246 *contra* Fantuzzi 2004a: 385–86.

128. Bing 2002–3: 257–57.

129. See Hauben 1983: 113, n.59. Hölbl 2001: 104.

130. Gutzwiller 1992a: 366 and 1992b: 198–209; Burton 1995: 134. Barbantani 2005 discusses a Hellenistic hymn that celebrates Aphrodite as patroness of the sea and goddess of marriage. She stresses the connection between harmonious marriage and dynastic legitimacy and stability. Gutzwiller 1992b: 199–202, sees the two aspects as linked by the "image of the sea of love" and a connection between calm seas and sexual moderation.

131. Savalli-Lestrade 1997: 43.

132. Müller 2009: 268.

133. Pomeroy 1984: 30–38; Burton 1995: 133–34. See also Fraser 1972: 1:197. On the Isis/Aphrodite association, see chapter 6.

134. Hauben 1983: 111–14.

135. Savalli-Lestrade 2003: 68.

136. Walbank 1984: 96–97.

137. Earlier discussions have considered only the evidence for the date of this particular cult, not the broader pattern for lifetime private cults established by *philoi*. Robert 1966 has shown that the Zephyrium cult must have preceded her individual cult (see chapter 6). Evidence from poetic references to the cult is problematic (Posidippus AB 39.3; AB 116) and may in any case relate to the date of the poem, not the date of the cult (Hauben 1970: 44–45; Bing 2002–3: 257). Neumer-Pflau 1982: 57; Gutzwiller 1992a: 365; McKenzie 2008: 52 consider the cult a development of her lifetime.

138. Hauben 1970; Bing 2002–3.

139. Tarn 1926: 158; Mitford 1938: 32; Fraser 1967: 40 favor the idea that his primary connection was to Arsinoë. Ferguson 1911: 175, n.2, suggested that another Ptolemaic admiral Patroclus owed his career to Arsinoë.

140. Hauben 1970: 63. Beloch 1928: 4: 244, 582–84, 586, implausibly argued that Samos remained in Arsinoë's control after Lysimachus' death and that she later transferred the island to her brother.

141. Hauben 1970: 67.

142. Bing 2002–3: 246.

143. Stephens 2005: 248. Gutzwiller 1992b: 209, suggests that Arsinoë was the real founder of the cult.

144. See references in Kosmetatou 2004a: 227.

145. Robert 1966: 201–2.

146. Burton 1995: 147.

147. Hauben 1983: 114.

148. Gutzwiller 1992a: 366; Thompson 1973: 120. See further chapter 6.

149. Burton 1995: 3; Foster 2006: 143.

150. *Contra* Hazzard 2000: 39, who considers this kind of patronage trivial.

151. See Foster 2006. The date is uncertain; the festival could come before or after the establishment of any of her various cults. Gow 1952: 2.265; Skinner 2001: 203–6; Foster 2006: 143, n. 33, favor the date of 272. Griffiths 1979: 119; Reed 2000: 319, associate it with the death and deification of Berenice I, but the date of that event is also uncertain.

152. Reed 2000: 324; Stephens 2003: 246. Reed 2000: 340 raises the possibility that it was part of a state cult.

153. Fraser 1972: 1:207. Griffiths 1979: 119 says the festival "celebrates a fantasy of female power and self-sufficiency." Whitehorne 1995 sees the entire poem as a kind of justification for sibling marriage.

154. Reed 2000: 321–33; Stephens 2003: 155.

155. Von Hesberg 1996: 94; Whitehorne 1995: 74; Reed 2000: 324.

156. Pomeroy 1984: 34; Gutzwiller 1992a: 365, speak of her as the patron of the "sexually passionate" wife. Griffiths 1979: 65–66 concludes that aspects of the myth would appeal to the Ptolemaic royal image; in Egypt, victory over death and the idea of regeneration tied to sacred marriage obviously recalled Isis and Osiris.

157. Whitehorne 1995; Skinner 2001: 13–14. Fabric, especially for women, functioned as a sign of status and class.

158. Foster 2006: 135.

159. Whitehorne 1995: 74–75.

160. Griffiths 1981: 247–73; Gutzwiller 1992a: 364.

161. Cameron 1995: 434. See also Fraser 1972: 1:207; Thompson 1973: 66–67.

162. Fraser 1972: 1:207. Hunter 1995: 20, thinks the Ptolemies may have spread the Samothrace cult.

163. Hölbl 2001: 101.

164. Barbantani 2008: 132–34; Bertazzoli 2002; Müller 2009: 238–42.

165. Pomeroy 1977: 61, who assumes that Arsinoë functioned as a patron of Theocritus, points out this precedent.

166. Gow 1952: 2:291–92. Hunter 1996b: 123–24.

167. Bousquet 1949: 110–12; Cameron 1995: 211–12.

168. Nielsen 1994: 16, 131.

169. Goldhill 1991: 272–73; Hunter 1993: 152.

170. Barbantani 2008: 133–34 brings up this possibility.

171. Hunter 1993: 161.

172. Barbantani 2008: 110.

173. Lelli 2002 collects most of them.

174. Fantuzzi 2004a: 377.

175. Barbantani 2008: 122.

176. Barbantani 2010: 227–28.

177. Griffiths 1981: 25–89 refers to Theocritus, but this view could also apply to Apollonius.

178. See Hunter 1993: 152–69.

179. *Contra* Mori 2008: 128–39.

180. Foster 2006: 137–44.

181. Mori (2001: 90, n. 17; 2008: 97) notes that a scholiast believed that Hesiod considered Arete the sister of her husband Alcinous, but as Hunter 1993: 161, observes, Apollonius says nothing about this and Homer (*Od.* 7.54–68) makes Arete Alcinous' niece.

182. Bertazzoli 2002; Müller 2009: 239, see this as evidence for patronage; Barbantani 2008: 132–34, has doubts.

183. This reading depends on the reconstruction of a line and a scholiast's comment. See Cameron 1995: 141–42; Stephens 2005: 244, n. 61; Mori 2008: 29, n.56.

184. Cameron 1995: 142. Pausanias (9.31.1) reports a statue of her on Mount Helicon depicting her as a muse.

185. See Griffiths 1979: 52, 88; Basta Donzelli 1984, especially 311–12, for Helen also as protector of seafarers; Gutzwiller 1992a: 367, especially n. 26, for references to the "revamped" marriage as model.

186. Griffiths 1981: 251, who also attributes Theocritus' sympathetic reading of female experience to a female patron. Foster 2006: 147, discusses how Theocritus praises her by comparing her to Arete, Circe, and Helen.

187. Mori 2008: 27.

188. Ogden 2008: 358.

189. See Burton 1995: 4, for references. Theocritus' poetry reflects considerable interest in women and their world: see Skinner 2001, Reed 2000.

190. Quack 2008: 277 notes that the Mendes Stele describes her Egyptian opening of the mouth ceremony, something not possible if Callimachus is literally correct, but possible if the ceremony was performed, for instance, to a coffin, as it sometimes was.

191. Pfeiffer 1926: 171. The translation of these fragments is Nisetich 2001: 123–27.

192. Pfeiffer deduced the date of July 9 from a Callimachus fragment (228.6) that associates the apotheosis of Arsinoë with the full moon (see Grzybek 1990: 109–12). On the exact day in July, see further Cameron 1995: 160–61, Koenen 1994: 51–52, especially n. 61.

193. Hazzard 1987 concludes that while this change was made almost immediately after he took office in terms of the Macedonian calendar, it was not implemented in the Egyptian system until about 267, thus leading to documents with dates two years apart.

194. See von Oppen 2010 (who favors the later dating) for a recent discussion with references. Criscuolo 1991; Hölbl 2001: 38, 40, 288 n. 29; Cadell 1998; Huss 2001: 310, n. 41; Ager 2003: 40; Austin 2006: 59; reject the new dating. Hazzard 1987; Grzybek 1990; Hauben 1992: 160–62: Koenen 1994: 51–52; Cameron 1995: 160–61, accept the new dating and Habicht 1992: 72 seems to accept it.

195. Mori 2008: 8–18.

196. See Mori 2008: 52–59, 140–86.

197. Knight 1995: 247–51; Mori 2001 *passim* but especially 88. Mori 2001: 91; 2008: 127–39, is less persuasive in suggesting that Arete's advocacy for Medea was somehow a criticism of Arsinoë for advocating personal favorites. The text offers no criticism, direct or indirect, of Arete.

198. Mori 2008: 91, concludes that the *Argonautica* consistently portrays men who accept female assistance in a positive way and the women who offer such assistance as deserving public honor.

199. Gutzwiller 1992a: 364.

200. Mori 2008: 92; Hunter 1995: 22.

201. On Hellenistic kings and masculinity, see Roy 1998; Mori 2008: 101.

Chapter 6

1. Pomeroy 1984: 55–59; Minas 1998; Bailey 1999.

2. Preference for the earlier or later date for the death of Arsinoë (see chapter 5) does not necessarily affect views about whether the cult was lifetime or posthumous. Thompson (1973: 71) dates the cult 267/66, thus after either date. Hauben 1992: 161, though preferring the later death date, deduces that the cult and canephorate was created in the year following her death. Bing 2002–3: 257, citing Hauben 1970: 161, dates the cult to 268/67, whereas Hölbl 2001: 103, following Cadell 1998: 3, dates it to March 269, leaving open the possibility that, if Arsinoë died in 268, the cult was not posthumous. Müller 2009: 366, sees the evidence of both the Mendes stele and Callimachus (frg. 228 Pf) that the cult was posthumous but Van Oppen 2010: 7–9, argues that the cult was established within her own lifetime, possibly at the same time as the cult of the *theoi adelphoi*.

3. Thompson 1973: 120; Gutzwiller 1992a: 366.

4. Collombert 2008.

5. Koenen 1994: 66–69; Clarysse and Vandorpe 1998; Hölbl 2001: 103, n. 163.

6. Mendes Stele, Z lines 12–14. See Hölbl 2001: 113, n. 23, for references. There are pharaonic examples of deified pharaohs shown worshipping themselves (Hölbl 2001: 101, n. 146).

7. Hölbl 2001: 101.

8. Hölbl 2001: 102; Quaegebeur 1970: 191 and 1971: 262–70.

9. Hölbl 2001: 101.

10. Thompson 1973: 58.

11. Quaegebeur 1988: 45–46.

12. Quaegebeur 1998: 83.

13. Thompson 1988: 127–32.

14. Thompson 1988: 132.

15. See Peremans 1987: 340–43.

16. Thompson 1988: 132.

17. Ronchi 1968; Burstein 1982: 211, believe that originally she shared the temple with her deified parents.

18. Fraser 1972: 2:75, n. 173; Ghisellini 1998.

19. Ronchi 1968 discusses a fragmentary poem probably inscribed on the base of the obelisk.

20. Hölbl 2001: 103; McKenzie 2008: 50.

21. Fraser 1972: 1:25 and 2:72–73.

22. McKenzie 2008: 51.

23. Pfrommer 2002: 55–75, offers a reconstruction of the planned monument, though he believes it was never built.

24. See McKenzie 2008: 386, n. 147.

25. See Pfeiffer 2008: 399.

26. Minas 1998: 45–56; Hölbl 2001: 104.

27. Barbantani 2005: 147.

28. Hauben 1989: 460; Quaegebeur 1988: 41.

29. A partially preserved civic decree regulating public aspects of the celebration is a major source for the festival (Satyrus *FGrH* 631 = P. Oxy. 2465, fr.2, col.I.1–9). See Robert 1966: 206–8; Fraser 1972: 1:229–32; Thompson 1973: 71–77,118–19; Pollitt 1986: 273; Müller 2009: 280–300. The description of the festival that follows is largely based on Thompson's widely accepted reconstruction *contra* Plantzos 1991–92: 120.

30. Thompson 1973: 73–74, thinks the date possibly related to Isis or even to the death of Arsinoë.

31. Thompson 1973: 120, unconvincingly suggests that these jugs were a way for citizens to accept the brother-sister marriage of Ptolemy II. Hölbl 2001: 103, imagines an element of "coercion" in the festival.

32. Thompson 1973: 74.

33. Plantzos 1991–92: 120; Ashton 2001a: 51.

34. Thompson 1973: 52. Fraser 1972: 1:241–43, suggested that the cults of Ptolemaic queens were ultimately absorbed into that of Tyche.

35. Thompson 1973: 53–54.

36. Savalli-Lestrade 2003: 70.

37. Hölbl 2001: 103, n. 155.

38. Hölbl 2001: 104.

39. Plantzos 1991–92: 129–31.

40. Savalli-Lestrade 2003: 72.

41. See Carney 2000a: 207–9.

42. Mueller 2006: 36.

43. G. M. Cohen 1995: 28; Mueller 2006: 3, 37–38.

44. G. M. Cohen 1995: 28, uses Arsinoë Ephesus as an example.

45. Cheshire 1982: 109; Fantuzzi 2004a: 380. Thompson 1973: 75, suggests a connection to sites of her worship but also a desire to combine her powers with those of other deities.

46. See Gill 2007: 98, for an example.

47. Mueller 2006: 10–11, notes that though "Cleopatra" was a more common name than "Arsinoë" for Ptolemaic rulers, settlements named after Arsinoë, Berenice, and Ptolemais were the most common.

48. Marquaille 2008: 175–95. See also chapter 5, G. M. Cohen 1995; Mueller 2006: 142–59. Le Rider 1968: 234, 239, notes that in Crete, Cyprus, and the central Aegean Ptolemaic foundations were named only after Arsinoë.

49. See Gill 2007 for discussion.

50. Bagnall 1976: 238; Mueller 2006: 36–37.

51. See Kyrieleis 1975: 78–94; Brunelle 1976: 10–29; Prange 1990 on her Greek-style portraits.

52. So Kyrieleis 1975: 87; Prange 1990: 200–202.

53. Pollitt 1986: 250.

54. Quaegebeur 1988: 47, 75; Stanwick 2002: 98–99, figs 4–5; Ashton 2004: 18–19.

55. Sauneron 1966: 84–85; Stanwick 2002: 15–18; Ashton 2004: 19–20, 36, fig. 2.

56. See Stanwick 2002: 117, fig. 116 for references. See also Kyrieleis 1975: 82.

57. Quaegebeur 1978; Minas 2005: 127–34; Ashton 2001b: 148–52.

58. Of the forty-seven cases in extant Egyptian art where Arsinoë is both identified by an inscription and her head is preserved, forty-five show her with this distinctive headgear (Dils 1998: 1299). See also Nilsson 2010: 58–222.

59. Quaegebeur 1971; Dils 1998: 1300–304. Figure 6.3 shows a temple relief from the chapel of Ptolemy II San el-Hagar, now in the British Museum, AN602557001. Arsinoë wears her crown and Ptolemy II the double crown of Upper and Lower Egypt.

60. Dils 1998: 1303–4.

61. Quaegebeur 1988: 45. Dils 1998: 1301.

62. See Dils 1998: 1301–3, who concludes that it is impossible to say. Quaegebeur's views varied (see Dils 1998: 1303, n. 13). Nilsson 2010 is certain that this was a lifetime attribute.

63. Quaegebeur 1978: 257–58, thinks that the stele of Memphis seems to indicate that her posthumous deification established her titulature and maybe her special crown as well.

64. Dils 1998: 1309, 1311, 1326. Dils argues that royal women wear the crown when acting as priests and comments (1311) that the women wearing the crown all "participated in royal power," though conceding that it is not easy to explain why these same women sometimes wear a traditional queen's crown and sometimes that of Arsinoë.

65. See general discussion in Dils 1998: 1304–15; see also Nilsson 2010.

66. Quaegebeur 1978: 260, argues that the depictions (including her crown) and titles given Arsinoë in Egyptian documents give her the character of a sovereign, but Quaegebeur 1998: 83, wonders whether her crown is royal or divine. Dils 1998: 1326, connects it to the exercise of royal power. Nilsson 2010: 496, does as well.

67. Nilsson 2010. See below.

68. Forgeau 2008: 20.

69. Ashton 2001a: 40; 2003: 98. The inscribed Egyptian-style statuette of Arsinoë in the Metropolitan, for instance, has a double cornucopia (Ashton 2001a: 47). Cleopatra VII also carries the double cornucopia, suggesting her desire to be linked to Arsinoë II (Ashton 2001a: 48).

70. Plantzos 1991–92: 124–25 *contra* Rice 1983: 202–8.

71. See Müller 2009: 374–79. Rice 1983: 42; Plantzos 1991–92: 125, associate it with her posthumous cult. Ager 2005: 24, n. 144 links it to *truphe* and her sibling marriage. Thompson 1973: n. 279; Ashton 2001a: 51, connect cornucopias carried by queens on the *oinochoai* to the role of royal women as the mothers of all Egypt, providers of abundance.

72. Ashton 2001a: 40.

73. Quaegebeur 1978: 259. For instance, Ahhotep, Ahmes Nefertari, Tetisheri.

74. Ashton 2001b: 152.

75. Troy 1986; Hölbl 2001: 85.

76. Quaegebeur 1970: 204–6, 1978: 45, 47.

77. Quaegebeur 1970: 205, 1978: 258–59, says there is no proof of the title during her lifetime, but in 1998: 83, he wonders. Pomeroy 1984: 19, considers the title probably posthumous; Hölbl 2001: 85, is certain the title was posthumous. Nilsson 2010: 400 and *passim*, argues for a lifetime date for the title, based on analysis of the iconography of reliefs including the title.

78. Quaegebeur 1970: 205, argues that the names of Taoseret and Hatshepsut were preserved in Manetho.

79. Quaegebeur 1970: 207, suggests that the titles she bore were inspired by the god's wife Ammon, but this alone does not seem an adequate explanation.

80. Pomeroy 1984: 19.

81. *Contra* Pomeroy 1984: 19.

82. Hazzard 2000: 98, implausibly argues that the title given to her by Egyptian clerics was insignificant, that they simply did what the king asked, and that he did not understand its significance. If he did not understand its meaning, why impose it?

83. Quaegebeur 1970: 205–6, 208–9, concludes that she shared sovereignty with her brother and connects it to her role in naval policy.

84. Dillon 2010: 1.

85. Smith 1988: 43–48, notes that royal women's Greek-style images did not use many of the iconographic symbols of divinity, the exception being Arsinoë's ram's horns on coins (see below). His view, however, seems to assume more secure identifications of royal women's portraits in the Greek style than his own subsequent discussion justifies.

86. Kyrieleis 1975: 82–84; Brunelle 1976: 10–29; Prange 1990: 197–211; Hölbl 2001: 120, n. 162.

87. A further source of confusion is that some portrait statues, particularly of priestesses, may show them wearing garments similar to those of goddesses (Dillon 2010: 20).

88. See, for instance, Prange 1990: 202.

89. Museum of Fine Arts Boston, Accession Number 96.712. The electronic catalog notes that the head has been identified as either a goddess or Arsinoë II.

90. British Museum, AN403182001, a head from Halicarnassus. Another portrait head in the British Museum, AN785680001, has an even more hesitant description, "The head resembles images identified as the Ptolemaic queens Arsinoë II, III and Berenike II, but may represent a goddess or private individual as there is no diadem carved."

91. The Metropolitan Museum of Art currently gives that label to Accession Number 2002.66, but the electronic catalog description adds "the face is stamped with enough individuality to identify it as a portrait. In all probability, it represents a member of the Ptolemaic dynasty." The description notes that the head has recently been identified as Arsinoë II and suggests a connection to Arsinoë's cult.

92. See Wallenstein and Pakkanen 2009: 155–56, for references.

93. Smith 1988: 91, suggests that the large bronze statuette pair in the British Museum (Pl 70.6), identifiable as Arsinoë and Ptolemy II, are a model for what lost large portrait pairs looked like; Arsinoë's image is not only smaller but on a somewhat smaller scale. On the other hand, the Egyptian-style Vatican Ptolemy II and Arsinoë II are of similar scale.

94. Roy 1998: 119, argues that the Hellenistic king's masculinity was defined by the prominent role given the queen in statuary and otherwise. Whether or not this was universally so, it certainly applies to the Ptolemies.

95. Thompson 1973: 78, sees these images as showing "startling fidelity" to the coin images. She also notes that "realistic" portraits were an innovation in Greek ceramics and presumably connected to the developing cults of Ptolemies.

96. Thompson 1973: 82, 104–5; Pollitt 1986: 273.

97. British Museum AN462132001. See Higgs in Walker and Higgs 2001: 46. The particularly nice fragment of an Arsinoë head from a jug now in the Metropolitan Museum (Accession number 26.7.1017) seems quite comparable.

98. Kyrieleis 1975.

99. Brunelle 1976: 11; Hölbl 2001: 21.

100. Smith 1988: 90.

101. Thompson 1973: 78–79, observes that no other dynasty's portraits were "as unflattering as the Ptolemies," a feature she partially connects to veristic Late Period Egyptian portraits.

102. Kyrieleis 1975: 78, notes that their coin types are similar.

103. Svoronos 1904: 252; Kahrstedt 1910: 270; Kyrieleis 1975: 78; Prange 1990: 208–11.

104. Kyrieleis 1975: 155, followed by Troxell 1983: 58–59; Smith 1988: 28; Mørkholm 1991: 103.

105. Smith 1988: 14. Müller 2009: 354, argues that the mnaieia were intended only for court circles as a kind of memorial, but that smaller denominations, even gold drachmas, served a wider audience.

106. Müller 2009: 335–80.

107. Kahrstedt 1910: 261–63, dates the Cos coins ca. 309 BCE and the coins from Rhodes ca. 304 BCE; see also Koch 1924: 71–72; Brunelle 1976: 12–13; Plantzos 1991–92: 128. See further Müller 2009: 344, n. 1192.

108. On Arsinoë's coin images, see Koch 1924: 80–88; Kyrieleis 1975: 78–94; Parente 2002; Müller 2009: 365–80.

109. Kyrieleis 1975: 78–80; Cheshire 1982 *contra* Smith 1988: 14.

110. See general description in Müller 2009: 366–70.

111. Cheshire 1982.

112. Arsinoë's horns are usually assumed to be those of Ammon, like Alexander's (Smith 1988: 40; Müller 2009: 370), but Brunelle 1976: 17 interprets the horns as earrings, possibly related to the Mendes cult.

113. See discussion in Müller 2009: 365–66. Kyrieleis 1975: 79, considers the tetra-drachms with the Ptolemaic eagle lifetime issues (*contra* Parente 2002: 260–62) but those with the double cornucopia posthumous. Müller 2009: 366, plausibly argues that the coins with the Dioscuri on the reverse are particularly likely to be posthumous because their connection to her apotheosis. See also Mørkholm 1991: 102, 294. General opinion increasingly treats the coins with her individual image as posthumous.

114. For general discussion and references, see Müller 2009: 353–64.

115. So Müller 2009: 354.

116. Scholars supporting a lifetime date: Kahrstedt 1910: 267, Longega 1968; Brunelle 1976: 11–12; Burstein 1982: 21; Pollitt 1986: 273. Pollitt believed that they were issued by Ptolemy II soon after he established the cult of the *theoi adelphoi*, arguing that the inscriptions on the two sides of the coins read together translate "a coin of the divine siblings."

117. Koch 1924: 83–85; Thompson 1973: 81–82; Smith 1988: 91; Mørkholm 1991: 103; Johnson 1999: 53; Parente 2002: 260–62. See also Davis and Kraay 1973, figs. 15–19; and Troxell 1983.

118. Thompson 1973: 82. Müller 2009: 359, considers the double portraits a kind of iconographic code.

119. Smith 1988: 49–52, notes how many Ptolemaic royal epithets stressed ideal family relationships as did the repetition of family names.

120. Stanwick 2002: 46. Stanwick also notes the resemblance between early Ptolemaic royal images and thirtieth dynasty images, again a similarity signaling legitimacy. He also (Stanwick 2002: 66), points to the great lengths Ptolemy II went to in order to move the obelisk of Nectanebo to the front of the Arsinoëum.

121. Griffiths 1979: 77–78.

122. *Contra* Kyrieleis 1975: 80 but also Brunelle 1976: 13–14, who claims, implausibly, that Berenice's eyes look toward heaven and Arsinoë's do not.

123. Brunelle 1976: 14; Smith 1988: 91.

124. They have wide eyes, a swollen area between eye lid and brow, tendency to obesity, and noticeable Adam's apple, even in women (Brunelle 1976: 14). I would add that noses tend to be thin and hooked.

125. Brunelle 1976: 15, explains the difference by alleging that Soter's is in the style of the Successors, as a "man of action," whereas the other three are in the style of the Epigoni, weaker, less dramatic.

126. See Bennett, s.v. "Ptolemy the Son"; Huss 1998; Ogden 1999: 79–80; Gygax 2000; Tunny 2000. See also Heckel 1989: 35. Holleaux 1904: 408–19; Tarn 1910: 221–22; Crampa 1969: 113–20; Mastrocinque 1979: 82ff; Burstein 1982: 205–8.

127. Habicht 1992: 72–73.

128. See recent but differing discussions in Bennett s.v. "Ptolemy the Son"; Müller 2009: 105–11; von Oppen 2010: 9–11.

129. Marquaille 2008: 47.

130. Bennett s.v. "Ptolemy III" argues, on the basis of an inscription *IG* XII 3,464, that Ptolemy III spent time in exile in Thera, presumably because of his mother's plot. The inscription refers to a Ptolemy, son of King Ptolemy, grandson of King Ptolemy, who was raised among the Theraeans. Obviously, it could be another Ptolemy.

131. Ogden 1999: 79.

132. It has become *communis opinio*. See Holleaux 1942; Segré 1938: 181–208; Bagnall 1976: 106–9; Wörrle 1978; Billows 1995b: 101.

133. Segré 1938: 183; Wörrle 1978: 218; Kobes 1996: 147.

134. Holleaux 1921: 183–97; Segré 1938: 181–208; Wörrle 1978: 218–25; Holleaux 1942: 365–404; Roos 1950: 60–63; Billows 1995b: 100–102. See Hill's discussion (Hill 1933: 229–30; followed by Billows 1995b: 102) of the iconographic similarities between his coins and those of Lysimachus. See also Bagnall 1976: 106–9; Billows 1995b: 100–104, 110.

135. Billows 1995b: 101.

136. Billows 1995b: 101 *contra* Wörrle 1978: 225; Bagnall 1976: 234.

137. Ogden 1999: 73, 278–79, and 2008.

138. Ogden 2011a: 96–97.

139. Ogden 2008: 382 *contra* Kosmetatou 2004b: 35.

140. See Ogden 1999: 215–72.

141. Fraser 1972: 1:240 n. 401.

142. *Contra* Kosmetatou 2004b: 32.

143. Cameron 1990; Hauben 1992: 162.See Ogden 2008: 366, on the dates of her two Olympic victories. Kosmetatou 2004b: 30, deduces that her victories were funded by Ptolemy II.

144. Edgar 1920: 99; Criscuolo 2003: 319; Kosmetatou 2004b: 20, 33, doubt that the king's mistress was the canephore whereas Pomeroy 1984: 57; Ogden 1999: 262; Hazzard 2000: 85; Ogden 2008: 268, consider the canephore and the mistress identical.

145. Cameron 1990: 295–304; Kosmetatou 2004b; Mori 2008: 101; Ogden 2008: 365–79.

146. Kosmetatou 2004b uses this term in her title.

147. Müller 2009: 246.

148. The narrative is known as "'The Letter of Aristeas." Johnson 2005: 13, n. 17, points out that the inclusion of Arsinoë, granted the comparatively short duration of her marriage to Ptolemy II, "is part of the portrayal of the quintessential Philadelphus of history."

149. Ogden 1999: 262–63, is unconvincing in suggesting it related to Aphrodite's role as a patroness of courtesans and, granted that there is no evidence for enduring hostility to the sibling marriage (see chapter 4), the prominence of Bilistiche and others had little to do with a desire to suggest that the sibling marriage was sexless, *contra* Ogden 2008: 381.

150. Quaegebeur 1988: 42, 45.

151. Thompson 1988: 132.

152. Hölbl 2001: 109.

153. Greek literary tradition preserves reference to the worship of the two sisters together (*FGrH* 613 F5). Seals show Philotera and Arsinoë together (Quaegebeur 1988: 45). Priests often wore seal rings with images of members of the dynasty, and they could also be gifts given to *philoi* (Thompson 1973: 80). The Metropolitan Museum has a seal impression of a priest of Arsinoë and Philotera (Accession number 10.130.1563). See Quaegebeur 1971: 246, n. 42; Thompson 1988: 131; Huss 1994: 99, n. 115. Thompson 1988: 127, 131, understands Philotera's cult as beginning before Arsinoë's and later either disappearing (after two generations) or being joined to hers.

154. Ager 2005: 4–8 provides a list.

155. Stanwick 2002: 36.

156. Hölbl 2001: 105, 85, especially n. 27. See also Llewellyn-Jones and Winder 2011.

157. Pomeroy 1984: 20–28.

158. Hilke 1990: 43–56.

159. Fraser 1972: 1:25; Nilsson 2010: 54.

160. The latest reference is dated to 154 CE; see Thompson 1973: 60, 73.

161. Thompson 1973: 75.

162. Cat. Number 22683 at the Vatican, a colossal statue of "Drusilla-Arsinoe," from Rome, the Sallustian gardens, reign of Caligula 37–41 BC.

163. Wood 2000, fig. 3, dates the coin to 40–35 BCE, early in their marriage, though Antony had already established a relationship with Cleopatra VII. Wood 2000: 15, observes that such portraits "could create a resemblance between people who were not related" and were common practice in Hellenistic and Roman imperial art. Clearly, an image originally generated in a circumstance in which the married couple were related has something to do with this.

164. Wood 2000: fig. 132.

165. See Carney 2006a: 114–16; Kyrieleis 1975: 80–81; Brunelle 1976: 26–28. Plantzos 1997: 1123–26.

166. See Wood 2000: 306–8, fig. 95. She suggests that it was a gift at the time of the wedding of Claudius and Agrippina II, meant to indicate their connection to the antityrannical (i.e., anti-Tiberius) older couple.

167. Accession number: Shelfmark: MS. Auct. F. 2. 29; ID number; Auct.F.2.29_roll173K_frame5.

168. The nurse of Orestes (Pind. *Pyth.* 11. 16–20); daughter of Leucippus and possible mother of Asclepius by Apollo (Paus. 2.26.7); daughter of Phegeus, king of Psophis, and wife of Alcmaeon; one of the Minyades (Plut. *Mor.* 299e); one of the Nysiads (Hyg. *Fab.* 182).

169. It derived from Franceschini's 1677 work (Nicoll 1922: 260).

170. Nicoll 1922: 280 and *passim*.

171. The dynastic scheming sounds Ptolemaic, but the specifics don't really fit; on the other hand, Arsinoë II certainly had association with Cyprus. Dorisbe, a princess, has arranged for the murder of Queen Arsinoë of Cyprus, in retaliation for the death of the princess's father. However, Ormondo saves Arsinoë, and the two subsequently fall in love. Although Dorisbe is also enamored with Ormondo, she is instead the object of

Feraspe's (the captain of Arsinoë's militia) affection. A second attempt on Arsinoë's life is made, but she survives, only to learn that Ormondo, who ends up in prison, is descended from royal lineage. Dorisbe, who tries to kill herself, is later forgiven, and she is united with Feraspe. The opera concludes with Arsinoë and Ormondo preparing to marry. See White 1983; Fiske 1986.

172. Müller 2005: 41, 43. Henderson (1752: 50) connects incest to a different sort of original sin (Adam and Eve are assumed to be siblings and so we are told "the Mother of Mankind" married her brother).

173. Zographou 2005.

Appendix

1. Yardley 2003.

2. Barbantani 2008: 105.

3. Tarn 1913: 135. Heinen 1972: 75, seems unhappy that she is shown with no negative traits in this section of the narrative.

4. Müller 2009: 71–72.

5. Mathisen 1979: 71–72.

6. Longega 1968: 55 thinks that this means she was disliked everywhere.

7. Mathisen 1978: 72–74.

8. See Carney 2006: 135 for references. His treatment of Olympias also includes unique but hostile material.

9. Wheeler 2010 provides a general assessment of his work and authority.

10. Ritter 1965: 117, n. 3, 172–73, doubted the historicity of the episode because he considered it an example of a *topos* about disguised flight. Heinen 1972: 37, suggests that Polyaenus' source is Duris.

11. Wheeler 2010: 38, argues that the historicity of incidents in Polyaenus should be judged on a case-by-case basis.

12. Quack 2008: 275–83. Collombert 2008: 94, points that these stelai record and thus perpetuate local royal benefactions.

13. On the stele, see references in Fraser 1972: 2:298–99; Collombert 2008: 83, n. 1, 94. For an English translation, see Naville 1902–3; Roeder 1959 gives a German translation. See also Sethe 1904–16: 2, 81–104. Rice 1983: 41 understands the date as June 273, Ager 2003: 39 says early 273, but see Bennett s.v. "Arsinoë" n. 14 on the dating crux: the stele records a visit to Heroopolis on 3 Thoth year 12 = 2 November 274 (if Egyptian year 12 is based on coregency accession) or = 1 November 272 (if Egyptian year 12 is based on true accession). See also O'Neil 2008: 68.

14. Sethe vol. 2: 28–54; Roeder 1959: 168–88; de Meulenaere and McKay 1976: 173–77.

15. See Gutzwiller 2005.

16. See overviews in Carney 1987; Barbantani 2008: 104–110; Müller 2009: 7–14.

17. Tarn 1913: 290–91.

18. Müller 2005.

19. Barbantani 2008: 106.

20. Barbantani 2008: 106, for instance, points to this example: Tarn 1913: 291, insists that there is "no doubt" that Callimachus wrote the Hymn to Delos at Arsinoë's request. Similarly, Longega 1968: 92, credits Arsinoë for Ptolemy II's friendly relations with Rome.

21. Huzar 1966: 337; Bevan 1927: 57.

22. Burstein 1982.

23. Hazzard 2000.

24. Hazzard 2000: 96–98, for instance, insists that Pomeroy 1984: 18–19, claimed that Arsinoë had the dominant role in the kingdom as compared to her brother, whereas what Pomeroy suggests is that she was powerful, not dominant.

25. Lelli 2002, for instance.

26. Hölbl 2001: 36, for instance, comments that "if we believe the account of events in Paus. 1.7.1, the execution of two of his 'brothers by Philadelphus early in his reign may well stem back to Arsinoe II's influence," though Pausanias says nothing at all about her having a role in the elimination of the two men. He mentions only Ptolemy II.

27. Wikander 2002: 186, who argues for an approach that examines these women in the context of the royal family and dynasty.

28. Burstein 1982: 207.

29. Tarn 1913: 190–93; Tarn 1926: 155–62.

30. Holleaux 1942: 365–404; Segré 1938: 181–208; Roos 1950: 54–63; Wörrle 1978: 218–225.

31. Huss 1998: 229–50.

32. For instance, Bennet s.v. "Ptolemy Nios." Ogden 1999: 79–80, also endorses the identification of Nios with Arsinoë's son but had not seen Huss' arguments.

33. See chapter 6 and Tunny 2000.

34. Huss not only identifies Lysimachus' son with Ptolemy the Son and with Ptolemy of Telmessus, but also with a number of other Ptolemies active in the mid-third-century eastern Mediterranean: a son of Ptolemy II who was in Miletus reporting to Ptolemy II about political conditions and probably representing the king. Around 262 (I.*Milet* 3, 139, ls. 1–10 + Welles 1934:71, no.14), the man *P. Haun* 6 refers to as the Ptolemy "the brother of the king" mentioned in a letter dating to 246/45, and a Ptolemy, son of Philadelphus, who commanded a guard at Ephesus, and was killed by Thracian mercenaries (Athenaeus 13.593a–b).

35. Tunny 2001: 120–30 points out that ill health could explain the coregency, but finds evidence only for gout and overweight, not hypothyroidism. Hazzard's suggestion (2000: 42–43) that hyperthyroid problems caused psychosis is without support; royal crankiness hardly requires this diagnosis.

36. Heckel 1989: 35, admits as much.

Glossary

amphimetric disputes between groups of children with the same father but different mothers

apomoira tax on vineyards and garden land assigned to fund the cult of *thea philadel-phus* in 263

basileia rule or kingdom or monarchy

basileus king

basilikoi paides royal youths (sometimes called "pages") of Macedonian and Hellenistic king who served the king, guarded him, and hunted with him

basilissa royal woman, a title first used about 306

canephore "basket carrier" priestess; the cult of *thea philadelphus* had one

Diadochi the Successors, the former generals of Alexander the Great who fought over his empire after his death; some of them established kingdoms of their own

dikera the double cornucopia, a distinctive attribute of Arsinoë II in Greek and Egyptian art

Epigoni the sons of the Diadochi, the second generation of Hellenistic kings

genos race or clan

hetaira, ai female companion/s, a term usually applied to courtesans

hetairos, oi male companion/s of the king, in Macedonia a group who fought near and with the king, on horseback

kleos fame or repute, the pursuit of *kleos* was an important Greek and Macedonian value, going back to the Homeric epics

Lagid/s the descendants of Lagos, also called the Ptolemies

Late Period twenty-fifth to thirty-first dynasties in the pharaonic period

Middle Kingdom twelfth to thirteenth dynasties in the pharaonic period

New Kingdom eighteenth to twentieth dynasties in the pharaonic period

oikos house, household, also house in sense of royal family

oinochoai wine jugs

Old Kingdom third to sixth dynasties in the pharaonic period

philos, oi friend/s, often used in Hellenistic period about the associates of kings (and queens). In effect, *philoi* replaced *hetairoi* in the Hellenistic period.

pompe a procession, in this book used to refer to the famously elaborate one during the reign of Ptolemy II (see chapter 5)

Soter, soteres savior/s, an epithet applied to Ptolemy I and various other Hellenistic rulers, alluding to the ability of kings to rescue and benefit individuals and cities

stephane circlet worn by some goddesses and some royal women

temenos piece of land dedicated to a god, a temple area

Bibliography

Acosta-Hughes, B., E. Kosmetatou, and M. Baumbach (eds.). 2004. *Labored in Papyrus Leaves: Perspectives on an Epigram Collection Attributed to Posidippus (P. Mil. Vogl. VIII 309)*. Washington, DC.

Adams, G. W. 2008. "The Unbalanced Relationship between Ptolemy II and Pyrrhus of Epirus." In McKechnie and Guillame, 91–102.

Adams, W. L. 2003. "Other People's Games: The Olympics, Macedonia and Greek Athletics." *Journal of Sport History* 30: 205–17.

Ager, S. L. 2003. "An Uneasy Balance: From the Death of Selukos to the Battle of Raphia." In A. Erskine 2003, 35–50.

———. 2005. "Familiarity Breeds: Incest and the Ptolemaic Dynasty." *JHS* 125: 1–34.

———. 2006. "The Power of Excess: Royal Incest and the Ptolemaic Dynasty." *Anthropologica* 48: 165–86.

———. 2007. "Response to Michael M. J. Fischer's 'Ptolemaic Jouissance and the Anthropology of Kinship: A commentary on Ager "The Power of Excess: Royal Incest and the Ptolemaic Dynasty."'" *Anthropologica* 49: 301–10.

Albersmeier, S., and M. Minas. 1998. "Ein Weihrelief Für die Vergöttlichte Arsinoe II." In W. Clarysse, A. Schoors, and H. Willems (eds.), *Egyptian Religion: The Last Thousand Years: Studies Dedicated to the Memory of Jan Quaegebeur*. Leuven, 1: 3–29.

Alonso Troncoso, Víctor. 2005a. "La 'paideia' de los primeros Ptolomeos." *Habis* 36: 99–110.

———. 2005b. "La paideia del principe y la ideolgia helenistica de la realeza." In V. Alonso-Troncoso (ed.), *Didochos tes Basileias: La figura del successor en la realeza helenistica*. Madrid, 185–203.

Amundsen, D. W., and C. J. Diers. 1970. "The Age of Menopause in Classical Greece and Rome." *Human Biology* 42: 79–86.

Anastassiades, A. 1998. "ΑΡΣΙΝΟΗΣ ΦΙΛΑΔΕΛΦΟΥ: Aspects of a Specific Cult in Cyprus." *Report of the Department of Antiquities, Cyprus*: 129–40.

Arnold, D. 1996. *The Royal Women of Amarna*. New York.

Arslan, Melih, and Ayça Özen. 2000. "A Hoard of Unpublished Bronze Coins of Ptolemy Ceraunus." *AJN* Ser. 2 12: 59–66, pl. 9–11.

Ashton, Sally-Ann. 2001a. *Ptolemaic Royal Sculpture from Egypt: The Interaction between Greek and Egyptian Traditions.* British Archaeological Reports International Series 923.

———. 2001b. "Identifying the Egyptian Style Ptolemaic Queens." In Walker and Higgs, 148–55.

———. 2003. *The Last Queens of Egypt.* Harlow, UK.

———. 2004. "Ptolemaic Alexandria and the Egyptian tradition." In A. Hirst, and M. S. Silk (eds.), *Alexandria, Real and Imagined* (Publications for the Centre for Hellenic Studies, King's College, London). London, 15–40.

Austin, M. M. 1986. "Hellenistic Kings, War, and the Economy." *CQ* 36: 450–66.

———. 2006. *The Hellenistic World from Alexander to the Roman Conquest.* Cambridge.

Austin, C., G. Bastianini, G., and C. Gallazzi (eds.). 2002. *Posidippi Pellaei quae supersunt omnia.* Milan.

Bagnall, R. S. 1976. *The Administration of the Ptolemaic Possessions outside Egypt.* Leiden.

Bailey, D. M. 1999. "The Canephore of Arsinoe Philadelphos: What Did She Look Like?" *ChrÉg* 147: 156–60.

Barbantani, Silvia. 2004. "Osservazioni sull'inno ad Afrodite-Arsinoe dell'antologia 'Pgoodspeed' 101." In R. Pretagostini and E. Dettor (eds.), *La cultura ellenistica: l'opera letteraria e l'esegesi antica: atti del Convegno COFIN 2001.* Università di Roma "Tor Vergata," 22–24 settembre 2003. Rome, 137–53.

———. 2005. "Goddess of Love and Mistress of the Sea: Notes on a Hellenistic Hymn to Arsinoe-Aphrodite (P.Lit.Goodsp. 2, I-IV)." *AncSoc* 35: 135–65.

———. 2007. "The Glory of the Spear: A Powerful Symbol in Hellenistic Poetry and Art. The Case of Neoptolemus 'of Tlos' (And Other Ptolemaic Epigrams)." *Studi Classici e Orientali* 53: 67–138.

———. 2008. "Arsinoe II Filadelfo nell'interpretazione storiografica moderna, nel culto e negli epigrammi del P. Mil. Vogl. VIII 309." In L. Luigi Castagna and C. Riboldi (eds.), *Amicitiae templa serena: studi in onore di Giuseppe Aricò.* Milan, 103–34.

———. 2010. "Idéologie Royale et Littérature de Cour Dans L'Égypte Lagide." In I. Savalli-Lestrade and I. Cogitore (eds.), *Des Rois Au Prince: Pratiques du Pouvoir Monarchique dans l'orient Hellénistique et Romain (IVe Siècle avant J.-C.-IIe Siècle Après J.-C.).* Grenoble, 227–51.

Barringer, J. M. 2003. "Panathenaic Games and Panathenaic amphorae under Macedonian Rule." In O. Palagia and S. V. Tracey (eds.), *The Macedonians in Athens 322–229 BC.* Proceedings of an International Conference held at the University of Athens. May 24–26 2001. Oxford, 243–56.

Basta Donzelli, G. 1984. "Arsinoe simile ad Elena (Theocritus Id. 15,110)." *Hermes* 112: 306–16.

Baynham, E. 1994. "Antipater: Manager of Kings." In I. Worthington (ed.), *Ventures into Greek History.* Oxford, 331–56.

Beloch, K. J. 1928. *Griechische Geschichte*. Vol. 4, 2d ed. Leipzig.

Bengston, H. 1975. *Herrschergestalten des Hellenismus*. Munich.

Bennett, C. J. 2003. "Three Notes on Arsinoe I." In A. K. Eyma and C. J. Bennett (eds.), *A Delta Man in Yebu*. 64–70.

———. 2005. "Arsinoe and Berenice at the Olympics." *ZPE* 154: 91–96.

———. n.d. "Egyptian Royal Genealogy." Available at http://www.tyndalehouse.com/egypt.

Bertazzoli, V. 2002. "Arsinoe II e la protezione della poesia: una nuova testimonianza di Posidippo." *ARF* 4: 145–53.

Bertholet, F., A. Bielman Sánchez, and R. Frei-Stolba (eds.). 2008. *Egypte—Grèce—Rome: les différents visages des femmes antiques: travaux et colloques du séminaire d'épigraphie grecque et latine de l'IASA 2002–2006*. Bern.

Berve, H. 1926. *Das Alexanderreich auf prosopographischer Grundlage*. Vols. 1 and 2. Munich.

Bettarini, L. 2005. "Posidippo e l'epigramma epnicio: Aspetti linguistici." In M. Di Marco et al. (eds.), *Posidippo e gli altri: Il poeta, il genere, il contesto cultural et letterario*. Atti dell'incontro di studio, Roma, 14–15 maggio 2004. Pisa, 9–22.

Bevan, E. 1927. *The House of Ptolemy*. Chicago.

Bianchi, R. S. 1988. "The Pharaonic Art of Ptolemaic Egypt." In R. S. Bianchi (ed.), *Cleopatra's Egypt: Age of the Ptolemies*. New York, 55–80.

Bickerman, E. J. 1938. *Institutions des Séleucides*. Paris.

Bielman Sánchez, A. 2002. *Femmes en public dans le monde hellénistique IVe-Ier s. av. J.-C.* Paris.

———. 2003. "Régner au feminine. Réflexions sur les reines attalides et séleucides." In F. Prost (ed.), *L'Orient Mediterréen de la mort de la Alexandre aux compagnes de Pompée: cités et royaumes à la époque hellénistique*. Rennes, 1–64.

Bikerman, E. 1938. *Institutions des Séleucides*. Paris.

Bilde, P. (ed.). 1994. *Aspects of Hellenistic Kingship*. Studies in Hellenistic Civilization 7. Aarhus.

Billows, R. A. 1995a. "The Succession of the Epigonoi." *SyllClass* 6: 1–11.

———. 1995b. *Kings and Colonists. Aspects of Macedonian Imperialism*. Leiden.

Bing, P. 1988. *The Well-Read Muse: Present and Past in Callimachus and the Hellenistic Poets*. Göttingen.

———. 2002–3. "Posidippus and the Admiral: Kallikrates of Samos in the Milan Epigrams." *GRBS* 43: 243–66.

Bingen, J. 1988. "Ptolémée Ier Sôter ou La quête de la légitimité." *Bulletin de la Classe des lettres de l'Académie Royale de Belgique* 5, 74: 34–51.

———. 2002. "Posidippe: Le Poète et Les Princes." In J. Bingen (ed.), *Un poeta ritrovato: Posidippo di Pella*. Giornata di studio, Milano, 23 November 2001. Milan, 47–59.

Blundell, Sue. 1995. *Women in Ancient Greece*. Cambridge, MA.

Borza, E. 1992. *In the Shadow of Olympus: The Emergence of Macedon*. Princeton.

Bosworth, A. B. 2002. *The Legacy of Alexander: Politics, Warfare, and Propaganda under the Successors*. Oxford.

Bouché-Leclerq, A. 1903. *Histoire des Lagides*. Vol. 1. Paris.

Bousquet, J. 1949. "Callimaque, Hérodote et le Trône de l'Hermès de Samothrace." In *Mélanges d'archéologie et d'histoire offerts a Charles Picard a l'occasion de son 65e anniversiare*. Vol. 1. Paris, 105–31.

Bringmann, K. 1993. "The King as Benefactor: Some Remarks on Ideal Kingship in the Age of Hellenism." In A. Bulloch, E. S. Gruen, A. A. Long and A. Stewart (eds.), *Images and Ideologies: Self-definition in the Hellenistic World*. Berkeley, 7–24.

———. 1997. "Die Rolle der Königinnen, Prinzen under Vermittler." *Actes du Xᵉ Congrès International d'Épigraphie grecque et latine*. Nîmes, 4–9 October 1992. Paris, 169–73.

———. 2000. *Geben und Nehmen. Monarchische Wohltätigkeit und Selbstdarstellungin Zeitalter des Hellenismus*. Berlin.

Brosius, M. 1996. *Women in Ancient Persia (559–331 B.C.)*. Oxford.

Brown, B. 1981. "Novelty, Ingenuity, Self-aggrandizement, Ostentation, Extravagance, Gigantism, and Kitsch in the Art of Alexander the Great and His Successors." In M. Barasch and L. Sandler Freeman (eds.), *Art, the Ape of Nature: Studies in Honor of H.W. Janson*. New York, 1–13.

Brown B. R. 1984. "Art History in Coins: Portrait Issues of Ptolemy I, II." *Studi Adriani Alessandria e il mondo ellenistico-romano. Studi in onore di Achille Adriani*. Rome, 405–17.

Brunelle, Edelgard. 1976. *Die Bildnisse der Ptolemaërinnen*. Frankfurt.

Bücheler, F. 1875. "De bucolicorum graecorum aliquot carminibus." *RhM* 30: 33–61.

Buraselis, K. 2005. "Kronprinzentum und Realpolitik. Bemerkungen zur Thronan-wartschaft, Mitregentschaft und Thronfole unter den ersten vier Ptolemäern." In V. Alonso-Troncoso (ed.), *Didochos tes Basileias: La figura del successor en la realeza helenistica*. Madrid, 91–102.

———. 2008. "The Problem of the Ptolemaic Sibling Marriage: A Case of Dynastic Acculturation?" In McKechnie and Guillame, 291–302.

Burkert, W. 1993. "Concordia Discors: The Literary and Archaeological Evidence on the Sanctuary at Samothrace." In N. Marinatos and R. Hägg (eds.), *Greek Sanctuaries: New Approaches*. London, 178–91.

Burstein, S. M. 1976. *Outpost of Hellenism: The Emergence of Heraclea on the Black Sea*. University of California Classical Studies. Vol. 14. Berkeley.

———. 1980. "Lysimachus and the Greek Cities of Asia Minor: The Case of Miletus." *AncW* 3: 73–79.

———. 1982. "Arsinoe II Philadelphos: A Revisionist View." In W. L. Adams and E. N. Borza (eds.), *Philip II, Alexander the Great, and the Macedonian Heritage*. Washington, DC, 197–212.

———. 1986. "Lysimachus and the Cities: The Early Years." *AncW* 14:19-24.

Burton, J. B. 1995. *Theocritus' s Urban Mimes: Mobility, Gender, and Patronage*. Berkeley.

Cadell, H. 1998. "A quelle date Arsinoé II Philadelphe est-elle décédée?" In H. Malaerts (ed.), *Le Culte du souverain dans l'Égypte ptolémaïque au IIIe siècle avant notre ère*. Leuven, 1–3.

Cameron Alan. 1990. "Two Mistresses of Ptolemy Philadelphus." *GRBS* 31: 287–311.

———. 1995. *Callimachus and His Critics*. Princeton.

Carney, E. D. 1987. "The Reappearance of Royal Sibling Marriage in Ptolemaic Egypt." *PP* 237: 420–39.

———. 1988a. "Eponymous Women: Royal Women and City Names." *AHB* 2.6: 134–42.

———. 1988b. "The Sisters of Alexander the Great: Royal Relicts." *Historia* 37: 385–404.

———. 1991. "'What's In a Name?' The Emergence of a Title for Royal Women in the Hellenistic Period." In S. B. Pomeroy (ed.), *Women's History and Ancient History*. Chapel Hill, 154–72.

———. 1992. "The Politics of Polygamy: Olympias, Alexander and the Death of Philip II." *Historia* 41: 169–89.

———. 1993. "Foreign Influence and the Changing Role of Royal Women in Macedonia." *Ancient Macedonia* 5,1: 313–23.

———. 1994. "Arsinoë before She Was Philadelphus." *AHB* 8.4: 123–31.

———. 1995. "Women and *Basileia*: Legitimacy and Female Political Action in Macedonia." *CJ* 90,4: 367–91.

———. 1999. "The Curious Death of the Antipatrid Dynasty." *Ancient Macedonia* 6,1: 209–16.

———. 2000a. *Women and Monarchy in Macedonia*. Norman, OK.

———. 2000b. "The Initiation of Cult for Royal Macedonian Women." *CP* 95: 21–43.

———. 2001. "Women and Military Leadership in Pharaonic Egypt." *GRBS* 42: 25–40.

———. 2004. "Women and Military Leadership in Macedonia." *AncW* 35: 184–95.

———. 2005. "Women and *Dunasteia* in Caria." *AJP* 126.1: 65–91.

———. 2006. *Olympias, Mother of Alexander the Great*. New York.

———. 2007. "The Philippeum, Women, and the Formation of a Dynastic Image." In W. Heckel, L. Tritle and P. Wheatley (eds.), *Alexander's Empire: Formulation to Decay*. Claremont, CA, 27–60.

———. 2008. "The Role of the *Basilikoi Paides* at the Argead Court." In Howe, T. and J. Reammes (eds.), *Macedonian Legacies: Studies in Ancient Macedonian History and Culture in Honor of Eugene N. Borza*. Claremont CA, 145–64.

———. 2010. "Putting Women in Their Place: Women in Public under Philip II and Alexander III and the Last Argeads." In E. D. Carney and D. Ogden (eds.), *Philip II and Alexander the Great, Father and Son, Lives and Afterlives*. Oxford, 43–53.

———. 2011. "Being Royal and Female in the Early Hellenistic Period." In A. Erskine and L. Llewellyn-Jones 2011, 195–220.

Casson, L. 2001. *Libraries of the Ancient World*. New Haven.

Cérny, J. 1954. "Consanguineous Marriages in Pharaonic Egypt." *JEA* 40: 23–29.

Chaniotis, A. 1997. "Theatricality beyond the Theater: Staging Public Life in the Hellenistic World." In B. le Guen (ed.), *De la scène aux gradins*, Palas 47. Toulouse: 219–59.

Cheshire, W. 1982. "Zur Deutung eines Szepters der Arsinoe II. Philadelphos." *ZPE* 48: 105–11.

Chugg, A. 2005, "The Journal of Alexander the Great." *AHB* 19.3–5: 155–75.

Clarysse, W. 2000. "The Ptolemies Visiting the Egyptian Chora." In L. Mooren (ed.), *Politics, Administration and Society in the Hellenistic and Roman World: Proceedings of the International Colloquium*. Bertinoro 19–24 July 1997. Leuven, 29–53.

Clarysse, W., and K. Vandorpe. 1998. "The Ptolemaic Apomoira." In H. Melaerts, (ed.), *Le culte du souverain dans l'Égypte ptolémaïque*. Leuven, 5–42.

Cohen, A. 1995. "Alexander and Achilles—Macedonians and 'Myceneans.'" In J. B. Carter and S. P. Morris (eds.), *The Age of Homer: A Tribute to Emily Townsend Vermeule*. Austin, 483–505.

Cohen, G. M. 1973. "The Marriage of Lysimachus and Nicaea." *Historia* 22: 354–56.

———. 1974. "The Diadochoi and the New Monarchies." *Athenaeum* 52: 177–79.

———. 1995. *The Hellenistic Settlements in Europe, the Islands, and Asia Minor.* Hellenistic Culture and Society, 17. Berkeley.

Cole, S. G. 1981. "Could Greek Women Read and Write?" In H. P. Foley (ed.), *Reflections of Women in Antiquity*. New York, 219–46.

———. 1984. *Theoi Megaloi: The Cult of the Great Gods at Samothrace*. Leiden.

Collins, N. L. 1997. "The Various Fathers of Ptolemy I." *Mnemosyne* 50: 436–76.

Collombert, P. 2008. "La 'stèle de Saïs' et l'instauration du culte d'Arsinoé II dans la chôra." *AncSoc* 38: 83–101.

Crampa, J. 1969. *Labraunda*. Vol. 3.1. Lund.

Criscuolo, L. 1990. "*Philadelphos* nella dinastia lagide." *Aegyptus* 70: 89–96.

———. 1991. "Review of Grzybek 1990." *Aegyptus* 71: 282–89.

———. 1998. "Il dieceta Apollonios e Arsinoe." In H. Melaerts (ed.), *Le culte du souverain dans l'Égypte ptolémaïque*. Leuven, 61–72.

———. 2003. "Agoni politica all corte di Alessandria: Riflessioni su alcuni epigrammi di Posidipo." *Chiron* 33: 311–33.

Davesne, A. 1991. "Les monnaies ptolémaïques d'Ephèse." In H. Malay (ed.), *Erol Atalay Memorial*. Izmir, 21–31.

Davies, M. 1995. "Theocritus' *Adoniazusae*." *G&R* 42: 152–58.

Davis, N., and C. M. Kraay. 1973. *The Hellenistic Kingdoms: Portrait Coins and History*. London.

Delev, Petar. 2000. "Lysimachus, the Getae, and Archaeology." *CQ* 50,2: 384–401.

Delia, D. 1993. "Response to Samuels' The Ptolemies and the Ideology of Kingship." In P. Green (ed.), *Hellenistic History and Culture*. Berkeley, 196–210.

Derchain, P. 1985. "Une mention méconnue de Ptolémée 'le Fils.'" *ZPE* 61: 35–36.

Devine, A. M. 1989. "The Generalship of Ptolemy I and Demetrius Poliorcetes at the Battle of Gaza (312 B.C.)." *AncW* 20: 29–38.

Dillery, J. 1999. "The First Egyptian Narrative History: Manetho and Greek Historiography." *ZPE* 127: 93–116.

Dillon, Matthew. 2000. "Did Parthenoi Attend the Olympic Games? Girls and Women Competing, Spectating, and Carrying Out Cult Roles at Greek Religious Festivals." *Hermes* 128: 457–80.

Dillon, S. 2007. "Portraits of Women in the Early Hellenistic Period." In P. Schultz and R. von den Hoff (eds.), *Early Hellenistic Portraiture: Image, Style, Context*. Cambridge, 63–83.

———. 2010. *The Female Portrait Statue in the Greek World*. Cambridge.

Dils, P. 1998. "La Couronne d'Arsinoé II Philadelphe." In W. Clarysse, A. Schoors, and H. Willems (eds.), *Egyptian Religion: The Last Thousand Years: Studies Dedicated to the Memory of Jan Quaegebeur*. Vol. 2. Leuven, 1309–30.

Dmitriev, S. 2007. "The Last Marriage and the Death of Lysimachus." *GRBS* 47: 135–49.

Dodson, Aidan, and Dyan Hilton. 2004. *The Complete Royal Families of Ancient Egypt*. London.

Donzelli, G. B. 1984. "Arsinoe simile ad Elena." *Hermes* 112: 306–16.

Dreyer, B. 1999. *Untersuchungen zur Geschichte Athens in Spätklassischer Zeit (322- ca. 230 v.Chr.* Historia Einzelschriften 137. Stuttgart.

Droysen, J. G. 1878. *Geschichte des Hellenismus*. Gotha.

Dunand, F. 1973. *Le culte d'Isis dans le basin oriental de la Méditerranée 1: Le culte d'Isis et les Ptolémées*. Leiden.

Dunland, F. 1981. "Fête Et Propagande À Alexandria Sous Les Lagides." In F. Dunand (ed.) *La Fête, Pratique et Discours*. Paris, 13–40.

Edson, C. F. 1934. "The Antigonids, Heracles, and Beroea." *HSCP* 45: 213–35.

Ellis, W. M. 1993. *Ptolemy of Egypt*. London.

Empereur, J-Y. 1998. *Alexandria Rediscovered*. New York.

Errington, R. M. 1969. "Bias in Ptolemy's History of Alexander." *CQ* 19: 233–42.

———. 1990. *History of Macedonia*. Berkeley.

———. 2008. *A History of the Hellenistic World 323–30 BC*. Malden MA.

Erskine, A. 1995. "Culture and Power in Ptolemaic Egypt: The Museum and Library of Alexandria." *G&R* 42: 38–48.

———. (ed.). 2003. *A Companion to the Hellenistic World*. Oxford.

Erskine, A., and L. Llewellyn-Jones (eds.). 2011. *Creating the Hellenistic World*. Swansea.

Fantuzzi, Marco. 2004a. "Posidippus and the Ideology of Kingship." In M. Fantuzzi and R. Hunter (eds.), *Tradition and Innovation in Hellenistic Poetry*. Cambridge, 377–403.

———. 2004b. "Sugli epp. 37 e 74 Austin-Bastianini del P. Mil. Vogl. VIII 309." *ZPE* 146: 31–35.

———. 2005. "Posidippus at Court: The Contribution of the *Hippika* of P. Mil. Vogl. VIIII 309 to the Ideology of Ptolemaic Kingship." In Gutzwiller 2005: 249–68.

Ferguson, W.S. 1911. *Hellenistic Athens*. London.

Ferrario, F. 1962. "Arsinoe-Stratonice. A proposito di una iscrizione ellenistica." *RendIstLomb* 96: 78–82.

Feucht, E. 1998. "Ein Bildnis der Neith als Schlangengöttin." In W. Clarysse, A. Schoors, and H. Willems (eds.), *Egyptian Religion: The Last Thousand Years: Studies Dedicated to the Memory of Jan Quaegebeur*. Vol. 1. Leuven, 105–15.

Fischer, M. J. 2007. "Ptolemaic Jouissance and the Anthropology of Kinship: A Commentary on Ager 'The Power of Excess: Royal Incest and the Ptolemaic Dynasty.'" *Anthropologica* 49, 2: 295–99.

Fiske, Roger. 1986. *English Theatre Music in the Eighteenth Century*. Oxford.

Foertmeyer, Victoria. 1988. "The Dating of the Pompe of Ptolemy II Philadelphus." *Historia* 37: 90–104.

Foraboschi, D. 1987. "Arsinoe seconda, Filadelfo e la monetazione romana." *Numismatica e antichità classiche. Quaderni ticinesi* 16: 149–59.

Forgeau, A. 2008. "Les reines dans l'Égypte pharaonique: statut et représentations." In Bertholet et al. 2008, 3–24.

Foster, J. A. 2006. "Arsinoe II as Epic Queen: Encomiastic Allusion in Theocritus, Idyll 15." *TAPA* 136: 133–48.

Frandsen, P. J. 2009. *Incestuous and Close-Kin Marriage in Ancient Egypt and Persia: An Examination of the Evidence.* Copenhagen.

Fraser, P. M. 1960. *Samothrace, The Inscriptions on Stone.* Vol. 2, pt. 1. New York.

———. 1967. "Current Problems Concerning the Early History of the Cult of Sarapis." *Opuscula Atheniesia* 7: 23–45.

———. 1972. *Ptolemaic Alexandria.* Vols. 1–3. Oxford.

Frazer, A. 1969. "The Propylon of Ptolemy II at the Sanctuary of the Great Gods at Samothrace." *AJA* 73: 235.

———. 1982. "Macedonia and Samothrace: Two Architectural Late Bloomers." In B. Barr-Sharrar and E. N. Borza (eds.), *Macedonia and Greece.* Studies in the History of Art 10. Washington DC, 191–203.

———. 1990. "The Propylon of Ptolemy II." In K. Lehmann and P. W. Lehmann (eds.), *Samothrace, Excavations Conducted by the Institute of Fine Arts of New York University.* Vol. 10. Princeton.

Fredricksmeyer, E. A. 1990. "Alexander and Philip: Emulation and Resentment." *CJ* 85: 300–315.

Gabbert, J. J. 1987. "The anarchic Dating of the Chremonidean War." *CJ* 82, 3: 230–35.

———. 1997. *Antigonos II Gonatas. A Political Biography.* London.

Gauthier, P. 1985. *Les cités greques et leur bienfaiteurs.* Paris.

Geyer, F. 1930. *Makedonien bis zur Thronbesteigung Philipps II.* Munich.

Ghisellini, E. 1998. "Ipotesi di localizzazione dell'Arsinoeion di Alessandria." *Numismatica e antichità classiche: quaderni ticines* 27: 209–19.

Gigante Lanzara, V. 2003. "Per Arsinoe." *PP* 58, 332: 337–46.

Gill, D. W. J. 2007. "Arsinoe in the Peloponnese: The Ptolemaic Base on the Methana Peninsula." In T. Schneider & K. Szpakowska (eds.), *Egyptian Stories: a British Egyptological Tribute to Alan B. Lloyd.* Alter Orient und Altes Testament 347. Munster, 87–110.

Goceva, Z. 2002. "Le culte des grands Dieux de Samothrace à la période hellénistique." *Kernos* 15: 309–15.

Golden, Mark. 1981. "Demography and the Exposure of Girls at Athens." *Phoenix* 35: 316–31.

———. 2008. *Greek Sport and Social Status.* Austin.

Goldhill, S. 1991. *The Poet's Voice.* Cambridge.

Goukowsky, Paul. 1995. "Sur La 'Grande Procession' de Ptolémée Philadelphe." In C. Brixhe (ed.), *Hellenika symmikta: histoire linguistique, epigraphie.* Vol. 2. Paris, 79–81.

Gow, A. S. F. 1952. *The Greek Anthology: Theocritus.* Vols. 1 and 2. Cambridge.

Graf, F. 1984. "Women, War, and Warlike Divinities." *ZPE* 55: 245–54.

Granier, F. 1931. *Die makedoische Heeresversammelung.* Munich.

Green, P. 1990. *Alexander to Actium: The Hellenistic Age.* London.

Greenwalt, W. S. 1988. "The Age of Marriageability at the Argead Court." *CW* 82: 93–97.

——. 1989. "Polygamy and Succession in Argead Macedonia." *Arethusa* 22: 19–45.

Griffiths, F. T. 1979. *Theocritus at Court.* Leiden.

——. 1981. "Home before Lunch: the Emancipated Woman in Theocritus." In H. P. Foley (ed.), *Reflections of Women in Antiquity.* Philadelphia, 247–74.

Grimm, G. 1998. *Alexandria. Die erste Königsstadt der hellenistischen Welt. Bilder aus der Nilmetropole von Alexander dem Grossen bis Kleopatra VII.* Mainz.

Gruen, E. S. 1985. "The Coronation of the Diadochoi." In J. W. Eadie and J. Ober (eds.), *Craft of the Ancient Historian: Essays in Honor of Chester G. Starr.* Lanham, MD, 253–71.

Grzybek, E. 1990. *Du calendrier macédonien au calendrier ptolémaïque. Problémes de chronologie hellénistique.* Basel.

——. 2008. "Le pouvoir des reines lagides: son origine et sa justification." In Bertholet et al. 2008, 25–38.

Gutzwiller, K. 1992a. "Callimachus' *Lock of Berenice*: Fantasy, Romance and Propaganda." *AJP* 113: 359–85.

——. 1992b. "The Nautilus, the Halcyon, and Selenaia: Callimachus's Epigram 5 Pf. = 14 G.-P." *ClAnt* 11: 194–209.

—— (ed.). 2005. *The New Posidippus: A Hellenistic Poetry Book.* Oxford.

Gygax, M. D. 2000. "Ptolemaios, Bruder des Königs Ptolemaios III. Euergetes, und Mylasa: Bemerkungen zu I. Labraunda Nr. 3." *Chiron* 30: 353–66.

——. 2002. "Zum Mitregenten des Ptolemaios II. Philadelphos." *Historia* 51.1: 49–56.

Habicht, C. 1992. "Athens and the Ptolemies." *ClAnt* 11: 68–90.

——. 1997. *Athens from Alexander to Antony.* Cambridge, MA.

Hadley, R. A. 1974. "Royal Propaganda of Seleucus I and Lysimachus." *JHS* 94: 50–65.

Hainsworth, J. B. 1991. *The Idea of Epic.* Berkeley.

Hallett, C. H. 2005. *The Roman Nude: Heroic Portrait Statuary, 200 BC–AD 300.* Oxford.

Hammond, N. G. L. 1988a. "From the Death of Philip to the Battle of Ipsus." In Hammond and Walbank 1988, Oxford, 1–196.

——. 1988b. "Which Ptolemy Gave Troops and Stood as Protector of Pyrrhus' Kingdom?" *Historia* 37: 405–13.

——. 2000. "The Continuity of Macedonian Institutions and the Macedonian Kingdoms of the Hellenistic Era." *Historia* 49, 141–60.

Hammond, N. G. L., and G. T. Griffith. 1979. *A History of Macedonia.* Vol. 2. Oxford.

Hammond, N. G. L., and F. W. Walbank. 1988. *A History of Macedonia.* Vol. 3. Oxford.

Harrison, A. R. W. 1968–71. *The Law of Athens.* Vols. 1 and 2. Oxford.

Hauben, H. 1970. *Callicrates of Samos: A Contribution to the Study of the Ptolemaic Admiralty.* Studia Hellenistica 18. Leuven.

———. 1983. "Arsinoè II et la politique extérieure lagide." In E. Van 't Dack, P. Van Dessen, and W. Van Gucht (eds.), *Egypt and the Hellenistic World*. Louvain, 97–127.

———. 1989. "Aspects Du Culte Des Souverains À L'Epoque Des Lagides." In L. Criscuolo and G. Giovanni (eds.), *Egitto e storia antica dall'ellenismo all'età araba. Bilancio di un confronto*. Atti del colloquio internazionale, Bologna, 31 August–2 September 1987. Bologna, 441–67.

———. 1992. "La chronologie macédonienne et ptolémaïque mise à l'épreuve:à propos d'un livre d'Erhard Grzybek." *ChrÉg* 67: 143–71.

Hawass, Z., et al. 2010. "Ancestry and Pathology in King Tutankhamun's Family." *Journal of the American Medical Association* 303,7: 638–47.

Hazzard R. A. 1987. "The Regnal Years of Ptolemy II Philadelphos." *Phoenix* 41: 140–58.

———. 1992. "Did Ptolemy I Get His Surname from the Rhodians in 304?" *ZPE* 93: 52–56.

———. 2000. *Imagination of a Monarchy: Studies in Ptolemaic Propaganda*. Toronto.

Heckel, W. 1978. "The *Somatophylakes* of Alexander the Great: Some Thoughts." *Historia* 27: 224–28.

———. 1982. "The Early Career of Lysimachos." *Klio* 64: 373–81.

———. 1989. "The Granddaughters of Iolaus." *Classicum*: 32–39.

———. 1992. *The Marshals of Alexander's Empire*. London.

———. 2006. *Who's Who in the Age of Alexander the Great*. Malden, MA.

Heinen, H. 1972. *Untersuchungen zur Hellenistischen Geschichte des 3. Jahrhunderts v. Chr. Zur Geschichte der Zeit des Ptolemaios Keraunus und zum Chremonideischen Kriege*. Historia Einzelschrift 20. Wiesbaden.

———. 1978. "Aspects et problèmes de la monarchie ptolémaïque." *Ktema* 3: 177–99.

Henderson, A. 1752. *Arsinoe; or, the Incestuous Marriage. A Tragedy*. London.

Herman, G. 1980–81. "The 'Friends' of the Early Hellenistic Rulers: Servants or Officials?" *Talanta* 12–13: 103–49.

———. 1997. "The Court Society of the Hellenistic Age." In P. Cartledge, P. Garnsey, and E. Gruen (eds.), *Hellenistic Constructs: Essays in Culture, History, and Historiography*. Berkeley, 199–224.

Herz, P. 1992. "Die Frühen Ptolemaier Bis 180 V. Chr." In R. Gundlach and H. Weber (eds.), *Legitimation und Funktion des Herrschers: vom ägyptischen Pharao zum neuzeitlichen Diktator*. Stuttgart, 51–97.

Hesberg, H. von. 1996. "Privatheit und Öffentlichkeit der frühhellenistischen Hofarchitektur." In Hoepfner and Brands 1996, 84–96.

Hilke, T. 1990. "Arsinoë IV, eine Schwester Kleopatras VII, Grabinhaberin des Oktogons von Ephesos? Ein Vorschlag. (Arsinoë IV, a Sister of Cleopatra VII, Grave Owner of the Octagon in Ephesus? Ein Vorschlag)." *JÖAI* 60: 43–56.

Hill, G. F. 1933. "Ptolemaios, Son of Lysimachos." *Klio* 26: 229–30.

Hodkinson, S. 2000. *Property and Wealth in Classical Sparta*. Swansea.

Hodkinson, S. 2004. "Female Property Ownership and Empowerment in Classical and Hellenistic Sparta." In T. J. Figueira (ed.), *Spartan Society*. Swansea, 103–36.

Hoepfner, W. 1971. *Zwei Ptolemaierbauten. Das Ptolemaierweighgeschenk in Olympia und ein Bauvorhaben in Alexandria*. Berlin.

———. 1990. "Von Alexandria Über Pergamon Nach Nikopolis. Städtebah und Stadtbilder Hellenistischer Zeit." *Akten des XIII. Internationalen Kongresses fur Klassicische Archaiologie*. 13: 275–85.

———. 1996. "Zum typus der Baseileia und der königlichen Andro:nes." In Hoepfner and Brands 1996, 1–43.

Hoepfner, W., and G. Brands (eds.). 1996. *Basileia: Die Paläste Der Hellenistischen Könige*. Mainz.

Hölbl, G. 2001. *A History of the Ptolemaic Empire*. London.

Holleaux, M. 1904. "Ptolemaios Lysimachou." *BCH* 28: 408–19.

———. 1921. "Ptolemaios Epigonos." *JHS* 41: 183–98.

———. 1942. "Ptolémée de Telmessos." *Etudes d'epigraphie et d'histoire greques* 3: 365–404.

Homolle, T. 1896. "Inscriptions de Delos." *BCH* 20: 508–9.

Hopkins, K. 1980. "Brother-Sister Marriage in Roman Egypt." *Comparative Studies in Society and History* 22: 303–54.

Huebner, S. 2007. "'Brother-Sister Marriage' in Roman Egypt: A Curiosity of Human-kind or a Widespread Family Strategy." *JRS* 97: 21–49.

Hunter, R. L. 1993. *The Argonautica of Apollonius: Literary Studies*. Cambridge.

———. 1995. "The Divine and Human Map of the *Argonautica*." *SyllClass* 6: 13–27.

———. 1996a. "Mime and Mimesis: Theocritus, *Idyll* 15." In M. A. Harder, R. F. Reguit and G. C. Wakker (eds.), *Theocritus*. Hellenistica Groningana, Vol. 2. Groningen-give, 149–69.

———. 1996b. *Theocritus and the Archaeology of Greek Poetry*. Cambridge.

———. 2003. *Theocritus: Encomium of Ptolemy Philadelphus*. Berkeley.

———. 2004. "Poems for a Princess." In M. Fantuzzi and R. Hunter (eds.), *Tradition and Innovation in Hellenistic Poetry*. Cambridge, 83–88.

———. 2011. "The Letter of Aristeas." In A. Erskine and L. Llewellyn-Jones 2011, 47–60.

Huss, W. 1994. *Der makedonische König und die ägyptischen Priester : Studien zur Geschichte des ptolemaiischen Ägypten*, Historia Einzelschriften 85. Wiesbaden.

———. 1998. "Ptolemaios der Sohn." *ZPE* 121: 229–50.

———. 2001. *Ägypten in hellenistischer Zeit 332–30 V. Chr*. Munich.

Huxley, G. L. 1980. "Arsinoe Lokris." *GRBS* 21: 239–44.

Huzar, E. 1966. "Egyptian Influences on Roman Coinage in the Third Century BC." *CJ* 61: 337–46.

Iossif, P. 2005. "La dimension publique des dédicaces "privées" du culte royal ptolémai-que." In V. Dasen and M. Piérart (eds.), *Idia kai demosia. Les cadres"privés" et "publiques" de la religion grecque antique*. Kernos suppl. 15. Liège, 235–57.

Iwas, W. 1981. "Aphrodite Arsinoe Philadelphos." *ActaArchHung* 29: 385–91.

Johnson, C. G. 1999. "The Divinization of the Ptolemies and the Gold Octradrachms Honoring Ptolemy III." *Phoenix* 53: 50–56.

———. 2000. "Ptolemy I's *Epiklesis Soter*: Origin and Definition." *AHB* 14, 3: 102–6.

———. 2002. "*OGIS* 98 and the Divinization of the Ptolemies." *Historia* 51: 112–16.

Johnson, Sara Raup. 2005. *Historical Fictions and Hellenistic Jewish Identity: Third Maccabees in Its Cultural Context.* Berkeley.

Kahrstedt, U. 1910. "Frauen auf antiken Münzen." *Klo* 10: 261–314.

Karabélias, E. 1989 "Inceste, marriage et strategies matriomoniales dans l'Athènes Classique." In T. Gerhard (ed.), *Symposion 1985. Vorträge zur griechischen and Hellenistischen Rechtsgeschichte.* Ringberg, 24 –26 July 1985. Cologne, 233–51.

Kertész, I. 1999. "New Aspects in the Connections between Macedonia and the Ancient Olympic Games." *Ancient Macedonia* 6: 579–84.

———. 2003. "Studies on Ancient Sport History." *Acta Antiqua Academiae Scientarium Hungariae* 43: 47–58.

———. 2005. "When Did Alexander I Visit Olympias?" *Nikephoros* 18: 115–26.

King, Carol J. 2010. "Macedonian Kingship and other Political Institutions." In J. Roisman and I. Worthington (eds.), *A Companion to Ancient Macedonia.* Oxford, 373–91.

Klapisch-Zuber, C. 2002. "'Kin, Friends, and Neighbors': The Urban Territory of a Merchant Family in 1400." In P. Findlen (ed.), *The Italian Renaissance: The Essential Readings,* Oxford, 97–123.

Knight, V. 1995. *The Renewal of Epic: Responses to Homer in the "Argonautica" of Apollonius.* Leiden.

Koch, W. 1924. "Die ersten Ptolemäerinnen nach ihren Münzen." *ZfN* 54: 67–106.

Koenen, L. 1983. "Die Adaptation Ägyptischer Königsideologie am Ptolemäerhof." In E. van't Dack, P. van Dessel, and W. van Gucht (eds.), *Egypt and the Hellenistic World.* Leuven, 143–90.

———. 1994. "The Ptolemaic King as a Religious Figure." In A. Bulloch, E. S. Gruen, A. A. Long, and A. Stewart (eds.), *Images and Ideologies: Self-definition in the Hellenistic World.* Berkeley, 25–115.

Kornemann, E. 1923. "Die Geschwisterehe im Altertum." *Mitteilungen der Schlesischen Gesellschaft für Volkskunde* 24: 17–45.

Kosmetatou, Elizabeth. 2002. "Remarks on a Delphic Ptolemaic Dynastic Group Monument." *Tyche* 17: 103–11.

———. 2004a. "Constructing Legitimacy: The Ptolemaic Familiengruppe as a Means of Self-Definition in Posidippus' *Hippika.*" In Acosta-Hughes et al. 2004, 225–46.

———. 2004b. "Bįllistiche and the Quasi-Institutional Status of Ptolemaic Royal Mistress." *Archive fur Papyrusforschung und verwandte Gebiete* 50: 18–36.

Kron, U. 1996. "Priesthoods, Dedications and Euergetism. What Part Did Religion Play in the Political and Social Status of Greek Women?" In P. Hellström and B. Alroth (eds.), *Religion and Power in the Ancient Greek World.* Proceedings of the Uppsala Symposium. Uppsala, 139–82.

Krug, A. 1984. "Ein Bildnis der Arsinoe II. Philadelphos." *Alessandria e il mondo ellenistico-romano. Studi in onore di Achille Adriani.* Vol. 1. Rome, 192–200.

Kuttner, A. 1999. "Hellenistic Images of Spectacle, from Alexander to Augustus." In B. Bergmann and C. Kondoleon (eds.), *The Art of Ancient Spectacle.* New Haven, 97–124.

Kyle, D. G. 2003. "The 'Only Woman in all Greece': Kyniska, Agesilaus, Alcibiades, and Olympia." *Journal of Sport History* 30: 183–203.

———. 2007a. "Fabulous Females and Ancient Olympias." In G. P. Schaus and S. R. Wenn (eds.), *Onward to the Olympics: Historical Perspective on the Olympic Games*. Waterloo, Ontario. 131–52.

———. 2007b. *Sport and Spectacle in the Ancient World*. Malden, MA.

Kyrieleis, H. 1975. *Bildnisse der Ptolemäer*. Archäologische Forschungen 2. Berlin.

Landucci Gattinoni, F. 1990. "La morte di Antigono e di Lisimaco." In M. Sordi (ed.), *Dulce et decorum pro patria mori: la morte in combattimento nell'antichità*. Milan, 111–26.

———. 1991. "Lisimaco e l'omicidio del figlio Agatocle." In M. Sordi (ed.), *L'immagine dell'uomo politico: vita pubblica e morale nell'antichità*. Pubbl. della Univ. Cattolica del Sacro Cuore Scienze storiche 17. Milan, 109–21.

———. 1992. *Lisimaco di Tracia: Un sovrano nella prospettiva delprimo ellenismo*. Milan.

Lasserre, F. 1959. "Aux origines de l'Anthologie: I: Le Papyrus P. Brit. Mus. Inv. 589 (Pack 1121)." *RhM* 102: 222–47.

Launey, M. 1945. "Études d'histoire hellénistique: L'Exécution de Sotadès et l'expédition de Patroklos dans la mer Égée (266 av. J.-C.)." *REA* 2: 33–45.

Lelli, E. 2002. "Arsinoe II in Callimaco E Nelle Tetimonianze Letterarie Alessandrine (Teocrito, Posidippo, Sotade e Altro)." *Appunti romani di filogia* 4: 5–29.

Le Rider, G. 1968. "Les Arsinoéens de Crète." In C. M. Kraay and G. K. Jenkins (eds.), *Essays in Greek Coinage, Presented to Stanley Robinson*. Oxford, 229–40.

Leschorn, W. 1998. "Griechicische Agone in Makedonien und Thrakien: Ihre Verbreitung und politisch-religiöse Bedeutung in der römischen Kaiserzeit." In U. Peter (ed.), *Stephanos Nomismatikos: Edith Schönert-Geiss zum 65. Beburtstag*. Berlin, 399–415.

Lévêque, P. 1978–79. "Idéologie et pouvoir sous les dux premiers Lagides." *AttiCAntCl* 10: 99–122.

Linfert, A. 1987. "Neue Ptolemäer. Ptolemaios II. und Arsinoe II." *MDAI(A)* 102: 279–82.

Llewellyn-Jones, L., and S. Winder. 2011. "A Key to Berenike's Lock? The Hathoic Model of Queenship in Early Ptolemaic Egypt." In Erskine and Llewellyn-Jones 2011, 247–69.

Lloyd, A. B. 2002. "The Egyptian Elite in the Early Ptolemaic Period: Some Hieroglyphic Evidence." In D. Ogden (ed.), *The Hellenistic World: New Perspectives*. London, 117–36.

Loman, P. 2004. "No Woman No War: Women's Participation in Ancient Greek Warfare." *G&R* 51: 34–54.

Longega, G. 1968. *Arsinoe II*. Rome.

Loraux, N. 1992. "What Is a Goddess?" In P. Schmitt Pantel (ed.), *A History of Women*. Vol. 1. Cambridge, MA, 11–44.

Lorton, D. 1971. "The Supposed Expedition of Ptolemy II to Persia." *JEA* 57: 160–64.

Lund, H. 1992. *Lysimachus, A Study in Early Hellenistic Kingship*. London.

Luppe, W. 2003. "Ein Weih-Epigramm Poseidipps auf Arsinoe." *ArchPF* 49, 1: 21–24.

Ma, John. 2003. "Kings." In Erskine 2003, 177–95.

Maas, P. 1927. "Antigonas Thugater." *RivFil* 5: 68–70.

Macurdy, G. H. 1932. *Hellenistic Queens*. Baltimore.

Maehler, H. 2004. "Alexandria, the Museion, and Cultural Identity." In A. Hirst and M. Silk (eds.), *Alexandria, Real and Imagined*. Aldershot, UK, 1–14.

Mantas, K. 1995. "Women and Athletics in the Roman East." *Nikephoros* 8: 125–44.

Mari, M. 1996. "Le Olimpie macedoni di Dion tra Archelao e l'età romana." *RivFil* 126: 137–69.

Marquaille, C. 2008. "The Foreign Policy of Ptolemy II." In McKechnie and Guillaume, 39–64.

Mastrocinque, A. 1979. *La Caria e la Ionia meridionale in epoca ellenistica (323–188 A.C.*). Rome.

Mathisen, R. W. 1978. "The Activities of Antigonos Gonatas 280–277 BC and Memnon of Herakleia." *AncW* 1: 71–74.

Matthews, V. J. 2000. "Sex and the Single Racehorse: A Response to Cameron on Equestrian Double Entendres in Posidippus." *Eranos* 98: 32–38.

McKechnie, P., and P. Guillame (eds.). 2008. *Ptolemy II Philadelphus and His World*. History and Archaeology of Classical Antiquity. Leiden.

McKenzie, J. 2008. *Architecture of Alexandria and Egypt, 300–7000*. New Haven.

Meeus, A. 2008. "The Power Struggle of the Diadochoi in Babylon 323 BC." *AncSoc* 38: 39–82.

Meritt, B. D. 1981. "Mid-Third Century Athenian Archons" *Hesperia* 50: 78–99.

Merker, I. L. 1979. "Lysimachus—Macedonian or Thessalian." *Chiron* 9: 31–36.

Meulenaere, H. de, and P. McKay. 1976. *Mendes II*. Warminster.

Meyer, M. 1992–93. "Mutter, Ehefrau und Herrscherin. Darstellungen der Königin auf Seleukidischen Münzen." *Hephaistos* 11–12: 107–32.

Minas, Martina. 1998. "Die κανηφόρος: Aspekte des ptolemäischen Dynastiekults." In Melaerts, H. (ed.), 1998. *Le culte du souverain dans l'Égypte ptolémaïque*. Leuven, 43–60.

———. 2005. "Macht und Ohnmacht. Die Repräsentation ptolemäischer Königinnen in ägyptischen Tempeln." *ArchPF* 51: 127–54.

Mirón-Pérez, M. D. 1998a, "Cómo convertirse en diosa: Mujeres y divinidad en la Antigüedad Clásica." *Arenal* 5, 1: 23–46.

———. 1998b. "Olimpia, Euridice y el origen del culto en la Grecia helenistica." *Florentia Iliberritana* 9, 215–35.

———. 2000. "Transmitters and Representatives of Power: Royal Women in Ancient Macedonia." *AncSoc* 30, 35–52.

Mitchell, L. 2007. "Born to Rule? Succession in the Argead Royal House." In W. Heckel, L. Tritle, P. Wheatley (eds.), *Alexander's Empire: Formulation to Decay*. Claremont, CA, 61–74.

Mitford, T. B. 1938. "Contributions to the Epigraphy of Cyprus: Some Hellenistic Inscriptions" *Archiv für Papyrusforschung und verwandte Gebiete* 13: 28–37.

Modrzejewski, J. 1964. "Die Geschwisterehe in der hellenistischen Praxis und nach römischem Recht." *Zeitschrift der Savigny-Stiftung für Rechtsgeschichte* 81: 52–82.

Mooren, L. 1975. *The aulic titulature in Ptolemaic Egypt. Introduction and Prosopography.* Brussels.

———. 1977. *La hiérarchie de la court Ptolémaïque: Contribution à l'étude des institutions et des classes dirigeantes à l'époque hellénistique.* Leuven.

———. 1983. "The Nature of the Hellenistic Monarchy." In E. van t'Dack, P. Van Dessen, and W. Van Gucht (eds.), *Egypt and the Hellenistic World.* Studia Hellenistica 27. Leuven, 205–40.

———. 1985. "The Ptolemaic Court System." *ChrÉg* 60: 214–22.

Moran, W. L. 1992. *The Amarna Letters.* Baltimore.

Mori, A. 2001. "Personal Favor and Public Influence: Arete, Arsinoë II, and the *Argonautica.*" *Oral Tradition* 16,1: 85–106.

———. 2008. *The Politics of Apollonius' Rhodiius' Argonatuica.* Cambridge.

Mørkholm, O. 1991. *Early Hellenistic Coinage from the Accession of Alexander to the Peace of Apamea (336–188 BC).* P. Grierson and U. Westermark (eds.). Cambridge.

Muccioli, F. 1994. "Considerazioni generali sull'epiteto PHILADELPHOS nelle dinastie ellenistiche e sulla sua applicazione nella titolatura degli ultimi Seleucidi." *Historia* 43: 402–22.

Mueller, K. 2006. *Settlements of the Ptolemies: City Foundations and New Settlement in the Hellenistic World.* Studia Hellenistica 43. Leuven.

Müller, S. 2005. "Die Geschwisterehe Arsinoës II. Und Ptolemaios II. Im Spiegel der Forschung von 1895 bis 1932: Ein Verstoss gegen das normative Paarmodell." *Ariadne* 48: 41–49.

———. 2006. 'Alexander, Harpalos und die Ehren für Pythionike und Glykera: Überlegungen zu den Repräsentationsformen des Schatzmeisters in Babylon und Tarsos,' In V. Lica (ed.), *Philia, Festschrift für G. Wirth*, Vol. 48. Galati, 41–49.

———. 2007a. *Das Königspaar in der monarchischen Repräsentation des Hellenismus— Arsinoë II and Ptolemaios II.* Habilitation Hannover.

———. 2007b. "Im Interesse des oikos: Handlungsräume der antiken makedonischen Königgen." *Feministiche Studien* 2: 258–70.

———. 2007c. "Festliche Götterassimilation im Hellenismus: Ein Zwang zur kollektiven Kostümierung der Hofgesellschaft?" In G. Mentges, D. Neuland-Kitzerow, and B. Richard (eds.), *Uniformierung in Bewegung: Vestimentäre Praktiken Zwischen Vreinheitlichung, Kostümierung und Maskerade.* Munster, 143–57.

———. 2007d. "Luxus, Sittenverfall, Verweichlichung und Kriegsuntüchtigkeit: Dies Codes der Dekadenz in den antiken Quellen." In C. F. Hoffstadt, F. Peschke, A. Schulz-Buchta, M. Nagenborg (eds.), *Dekadenzen.* Bochum/ Freiburg, 13–52.

———. 2009. *Das Hellenistische Königspaar in der medialen Repräsentation— Ptolemaios II und Arsinoë II.* Beiträge zur Altertumskunde 263. Berlin.

———. 2010. "Demetrios Poliorketes, Aphrodite und Athen." *Gymnasium* 117: 559–73.

————. 2011. "Herrschftslegitimation in den frühhellenistischenen Dynastien." In Lambach, D. (ed.), *Politische Herrschaft jenseits des Staates: Zur Transformation von Legitimität in Geschichte und Gegenwart.* Wiesbaden, 151–76.

Munn, M. 2006. *The Mother of the Gods, Athens, and the Tyranny of Asia: A Study of Sovereignty in Ancient Religion.* Berkeley.

Murray, O. 1970. "Hecataeus of Abdera and Pharaonic Kingship." *JEA* 56: 141–71.

————. 2008. "Ptolemaic Royal Patronage." In McKechnie and Guillaume 200, 9–24.

Naville, E. 1902–3. "La Stèle de Pithom." *ZAS* 40: 66–75.

————. 1903. *The Store-City of Pithom and the Route of the Exodus.* London.

Neumer-Pflau, W. 1982. *Studien zur Ikonographie and gesellschaftlichen Funktion hellenistischer Aprhodite-Statuen.* Bonn.

Nicholson, N. J. 2005. *Aristocracy and Athletics in Archaic and Classical Greece.* Cambridge.

Nicoll, A. 1922. "Italian Opera in England: The First Five Years." *Anglia—Zeitschrift für englische Philologie* 46: 257–81.

Nielsen, I. 1994. *Hellenistic Palaces: Tradition and Renewal.* Aarhus.

————. 1997. "Royal Palaces and Type of Monarchy: Do the Hellenistic Palaces reflect the Status of the King?" *Hephaistos* 15: 137–61.

————. 2001. "The Gardens of Hellenistic Palaces." In I. Nielsen (ed.), *The Royal Palace Institution in the First Millennnium BC: Regional Development and Cultural Interchange between East and West.* Aarhus, 165–88.

Nilsson, M. 2010. *The Crown of Arsinoë II. The Creation and Development of an Imagery of Authority.* Ph.D. diss., University of Gothenburg.

Nisetich, F. 2001. *The Poems of Callimachus.* Oxford.

————. 2005. "The Poems of Posidippus." In Gutzwiller 2005, 17–64.

Nourse, Kyra. 2002. *Women and the Early Development of Royal Power in the Hellenistic East.* Ph.D. diss., University of Pennsylvania.

O'Connor, D., and D. P. Silverman (eds.). 1994. *Ancient Egyptian Kingship.* Leiden.

Ogden, D. 1999. *Polygamy, Prostitutes and Death.* London.

————. 2008. "Bilistiche and the Prominence of Courtesans in the Ptolemaic Tradition." In McKechnie and Guillaume, 353–85.

————. 2011a. "The Royal Families of Argead Macedon and the Hellenistic World." In B. Rawson (ed.), *A Companion to Families in the Greek and Roman Worlds.* Chichester, UK, 92–107.

————. 2011b. "How to Marry a Courtesan in the Macedonian Courts." In A. Erskine and L. Llewellyn-Jones 2011, 221–46.

Oikonomides, A. N. 1984. "The Death of Ptolemy 'the Son' at Ephesos and P. Bouriant 6." *ZPE* 56: 148–50.

O'Neil, J. L. 2000. "The Creation of the New Dynasties after the Death of Alexander the Great." *Prudentia* 32.2, 118–37.

————. 2008. "A Re-Examination of the Chemonidean War." In McKechnie and Guillaume, 65–89.

Oppen de Ruiter, B. van. 2010. "The Death of Arsinoe II Philadelphus: The Evidence Reconsidered." *ZPE* 174: 139–50.

Palagia, O. 2009. "Spartan Self-Presentation in the Panhellenic Sanctuaries of Delphi and Olympia in the Classical Period." In N. Kaltsas (ed.), *Athens—Sparta. Contributions to the Research on the History and Archaeology of the Two City-States.* New York, 32–40.

Papakonstantinou, Z. 2003. "Alcibiades in Olympia: Olympic Ideology, Sport, and Social Conflict in Classical Athens." *Journal of Sport History* 30: 173–82.

Parente, A. R. 2002. "Ritrattistica e simbologia sulle monete di Arsinoe II." *Numismatica e antichità classiche: quaderni ticinesi* 31: 259–78.

Peremans, W. 1987. Les Lagides, les éites indigènes et la monarchie bicèphale." In E. Levy (ed.), *Le système palatial en Orient en Grece et à Rome.* Actes du Colloque de Strasbourg, 19–22 June 1985. Leiden, 327–43.

Petrie, W.M.F. 1896. *Koptos.* London.

Pfeiffer, R. 1922. *Kalimachosstudien.* Munich.

———. 1926. "Arsinoe Philadelphos in der Dichtung." *Die Antike* 2: 161–74.

Pfeiffer, S. 2008. "The God Serapis, His Cult, and the Beginnings of the Ruler Cult in Ptolemaic Egypt." In McKechnie and Guillaume 200, 387–408.

Pfrommer, M. 1996. "Fassade und Heiligtum; Betrachtungen Zur Architektonischen Repräsentation Des Vierten Ptolemäers." In Hoepfner and Brands 1996, 97–108.

———. 2002. *Königinnen Vom Nil.* Mainz.

Pillonel, C. 2008. "Les reines hellénistiques sur les champs de bataille." In Bertholet et al. 2008, 117–45.

Plantzos, D. 1991–92. "Ektheosis Arsinoes: On the Cult of Arsinoe Philadelphos." *Archaiognosia* 7: 119–34.

———. 1997. "Hellenistic Cameos: Problems of Classification and Chronology." *BICS* 41: 115–31, Pls. 22A–27A.

Pleket, H. W. 1975. "Games, Prizes, Athletes and Ideology." *Arena (= Stadion)* 1: 49–89.

Pollitt, J. J. 1986. *Art in the Hellenistic Age.* Cambridge.

Pomeroy, S. B. 1977. "Technikai kai Mousikai: The Education of Women in the Fourth Century and in the Hellenistic Period." *AJAH* 2: 51–68.

———. 1984. *Women in Hellenistic Egypt from Alexander to Cleopatra.* New York.

———. 2002. *Spartan Women.* Oxford and New York.

Prange, M. 1990. "Das Bildnis Arsinoes II. Philadelphos (278-270 V. Chr.)." *MDAI(A)* 105: 197–211.

Price, S.R.F. 1984a. "Gods and Emperors: The Greek Language of the Roman Imperial Cult." *JHS* 104: 79–95.

———. 1984b. *Rituals and Power: The Roman Imperial Cult in Asia Minor.* Cambridge.

Quack, J. F. 2008. "Innovations in Ancient Garb? Hieroglyphic Texts from the time of Ptolemy Philadelphus." In McKechnie and Guillaume 2008, 275–89.

Quaegebeur, J. 1970. "Ptolémée II en adoration devant Arsinoé II divinisée." *BIFAO* 69: 191–217.

———. 1971. "Documents Concerning a Cult of Arsinoe Philadelphos at Memphis." *JNES* 3: 239–70.

———. 1978. "Reines Ptolémaïques et Traditions Égyptiennes." In H. von Maehler and V. M. Strocka (eds.), *Das ptolemäische Ägypten.* Mainz, 245–62.

———. 1988. "Cleopatra VII and the Cults of the Ptolemaic Queens." In R. S. Bianchi (ed.), *Cleopatra's Egypt: Age of the Ptolemies.* New York, 41–54.

———. 1998. "Documents Égyptiens Anciens et Nouveaux Relatifs À Arsinoé Philadelphe." In H. Melaerts (ed.), *Le Culte du souverains dans l'Egypte Ptolemaique au IIIe siecle avant notre ere, actes cu colloque international.* Brussels, 73–108.

Rankin, H. D. 1987. *Celts in the Classical World.* London.

Reames, J. 2008. "Crisis and Opportunity: The Philotas Affair . . . Again." In T. Howe and J. Reammes (eds.), *Macedonian Legacies: Studies in Ancient Macedonian History and Culture in Honor of Eugene N. Borza.* Claremont, CA, 165–81.

Reed, Joseph D. 2000. "Arsinoe's Adonis and the Poetics of Ptolemaic Imperialism." *TAPA* 130: 319–51.

Regner, J. 1941. "Philotera." *RE* 20, 1: 1285–94.

Remijsen, S., and W. Clarysse. 2008. "Incest or Adoption? Brother-Sister Marriage in Roman Egypt Revisited." *JRS* 98: 53–61.

Reymond, E. A. E. 1981. *From the Records of a Priestly Family from Memphis,* Ägyptologische Abhandlungen 38. Wiesbaden.

Rice, E. E. 1983. *The Grand Procession of Ptolemy Philadelphus.* Oxford.

Rigsby, K. J. 2005. "Agathopolis and Doulopolis." *Epigraphica Anatolica. Zeitschrift für Epigraphik und historische Geographie Anatoliens* 38: 109–15.

Ritter, H. W. 1965. *Diadem und Königsherrschaft.* Vestigia 7. Munich.

Robert, L. 1933. "XL.—Inscription de Ptolémée, Fils de Lysimaque." *BCH* 57: 485–91.

———. 1966. "Sur un décret d'Ilion et sur un papyrus concernant des cultes royaux." In A. E. Samulel (ed.), *Essays in Honor of C. Bradford Welles.* American Studies in Papyrology 1. New Haven, 175–211.

Robins, G. 1993a. "The God's Wife of Amun in the 18th Dynasty in Egypt." In A. Cameron and A. Kuhrt (eds.), *Images of Women in Antiquity.* London, 65–78.

———. 1993b. *Women in Ancient Egypt,* Cambridge, MA.

Roeder, G. 1959. *Die Ägyptische Götterwelt.* Zurich.

Romm, J. S. 2011. *Ghost on the Throne: The Death of Alexander the Great and the War for Crown and Empire.* New York.

Ronchi, G. 1968. "Il papiro Cairense 65445 (vv. 140–154) e l'obelisco di Arsinoe II." *Studi classici e orientali. Pisa: Istituti Editoriali e Poligrafici Internazionali.* 17: 56–75.

Roos, A.G. 1950. "Remarques sur un édit d'Antiochos III, roi de Syrie." *Mnemosyne* 3: 54–63.

Roux, G. 1981. "The History of the Rotunda." In J. R. McCredie, G. Roux, G. Shaw, S.M. and J. Kurtisch (eds.), *Samothrace.* Vol. 7. Princeton, 231–39.

Rowlandson, J and Takahashi, R. 2009. "Brother-Sister Marriage and Inheritance Strategies in Greco-Roman Egypt." *JRS* 99: 104–39.

Roy, J. 1998. "The Masculinity of the Hellenistic King." In L. Foxhall and J. Salmon (eds.), *When Men Were Men: Masculinity, Power and Identity in Classical Antiquity.* London, 11–35.

Saitta, G. 1955. "Lisimaco di Tracia." *Kokalos* 1: 62–153.

Samuel, A. E. 1962. *Ptolemaic Chronology.* Munich.

———. 1993. "The Ptolemies and the Ideology of Kingship." In P. Green (ed.), *Hellenistic History and Culture.* Berkeley, 168–210.

Sauneron, S. 1966. "Un document égyptien relatif à la divinization de la reine Arsinoé II." *BIFAO* 60: 83–109.

Savalli-Lestrade, I. 1997. "Il Ruolo Pubblico Delle Regine Ellenistiche." In S. Allessandrì (ed.), *Historie. Studie Offerti Dagli Allievi a Giuseppe Nenci in Occasione del Suo Settantesimo Compleanno*. Galatina, Italy, 415–32.

———. 2003. "La Place Des Reines À La Cour Et Dans Le Royaume À L'Époque Hellénistique." *Les femmes antiques entre sphere privée et sphere publiques: actes du diplome d'études avancées*. Universités de Lausanne et Neuchatel. Bern, 59–76.

Scanlon, T. F. 1997. *Olympia and Macedonia: Games, Gymnasia and Politics*. Dimitria Annual Lecture. Toronto.

Schaps, D. M. 1982. "The Women of Greece in Wartime." *CP* 77: 193–213.

Schmitt, H. H. 1991. "Zur Inszenierung des Privatlebens des Hellenistischen Herrschers." In J. Seibert (ed.), *Hellenistische Studien. Gedenkschrift für H. Bengston*. Münchener Arbeiten zur Alten Geschichte 5. Munich, 77–86.

Segre, M. 1938. "Iscrizioni di Licia." *Clara Rhodos* 9: 179–208.

Seibert, J. 1967. *Historische Beiträge zu den Dynastischen Vergingungen in Hellenistischer Zeit*. Historia Einzelschriften 10. Wiesbaden.

———. 1969. *Untersuchungen zur Ptolemaios I*. Munich.

Selden, D. L. 1998. "Alibis." *ClAnt* 17, 2: 289–412.

Sethe, K. 1904–16. *Hieroglyphische Urkunden der griechische-römischen Zeit*. 3 vols. Leipzig.

Shaw, B. D. 1992. "Explaining Incest: Brother-Sister Marriage in Graeco-Roman Egypt." *Man* 27: 267–99.

Sherwin-White, S., and A. Kuhrt. 1993. *From Samarkhand to Sardis: A New Approach to the Seleucid Empire*. Berkeley.

Skinner, M. B. 2001. "Ladies' Day at the Art Institute: Theocritus, Herodas, and the Gendered Gaze." In A. Lardinois and L. McClure (eds.), *Making Silence Speak: Women's Voices in Greek Literature and Society*. Princeton, 201–22.

Slowikoski, S. 1989. "Alexander the Great and Sport History: A Commentary on Scholarship." *Journal of Sport History* 18: 70–78.

Smith, R. R. R. 1988. *Hellenistic Royal Portraits*. Oxford.

Sonne, W. 1996. "Hellenistische Herrschaftsgärten." In Hoepfner and Brands 1996, 136–43.

Spawforth, A. J. S. "The Court of Alexander the Great between Europe and Asia." In A. J. S. Spawforth (ed.) *The Court and Court Society in Ancient Monarchies*, Cambridge, 82–120.

Stanwick, P. E. 2002. *Portraits of the Ptolemies: Greek Kings as Egyptian Pharaohs*. Austin.

Stephens, S. A. 1998. "Callimachus at Court." In M. A. Harder, R. F. Regtuit, G. C. Wakker (eds.), *Genre in Hellenistic Poetry*. Groningen, 167–85.

———. 2003. *Seeing Double: Intercultural Poetics in Ptolemaic Alexandria*. Berkeley.

———. 2004. "For you, Arsinoe." In Acosta-Hughes et al. 2004, 161–76.

———. 2005. "The Battle of the Books." In Gutzwiller 2005, 229–48.

Strootman, Rolf. 2005. "Kings against Celts: Deliverance from Barbarians as a Theme in Hellenistic Royal Propaganda." In K. A. E. Enenkel and I. L. Pfeiffer (eds.), *The Manipulative Mode: Political Propaganda in Antiquity: A Collection of Case Studies.* Leiden, 101–41.

Svoronos, I. N. 1904. *Ta Nomismata tou kratous ton Ptolemaion.* Athens.

Swinnen, W. 1973. "Sur La Politique Religieuse de Ptolémée I er." In F. Dunand and P. Lévêque (eds.) *Les Syncretismes dans les religions grecque et romaine.* Coloque de Strasbourg (9–11 June 1971). Paris, 115–33.

Tarn, W. W. 1910. "The Dedicated Ship of Antigonus Gonatas." *JHS* 30: 209–22.

———. 1913. *Antigonos Gonatas.* Oxford.

———. 1926. "The First Syrian War." *JHS* 46, 2: 155–62.

———. 1929. "Queen Ptolemais and Apama." *CQ* 23: 138–41.

———. 1934. "The New Dating of the Chremonidean War." *JHS* 54: 26–39.

Thiers, C. 2007. "Le marriage divin des dieux Adelphes dans la stele de mendès (CCiare CG 22183)." *Zeitschrift fur Agyptische Sprache und Altertumskunde* 134: 68–69.

Thompson, D. B. 1955. "A Portrait of Arsinoe Philadelphos." *AJA* 59: 199–206.

———. 1973. *Ptolemaic Oinochoai and Portraits in Faience: Aspects of the Ruler Cult.* Oxford.

Thompson, D. J. 1988. *Memphis under the Ptolemies.* Princeton.

———. 2000. "Philadelphus' Procession: Dynastic Power in a Mediterranean Context." In L. Mooren (ed.), *Politics, Administration and Society in the Hellenistic and Roman World.* Leuven, 365–88.

———. 2005. "Posidippus, Poet of the Ptolemies." In Gutzwiller 2005, 269–86.

Tondriau, J. L. 1948a. "Les souveraines lagides en déesses, au IIIe siècle avant J.-C." *Études de Papyrologie* 7: 1–15.

———. 1948b. "Princesses ptolémaïques comparées ou identifies à des déesses (IIIe-Ier siècle savant J.C.)." *Bulletin de la Société de Archéologie d' Alexandria* 37: 12–33.

———. 1953. "Quelques problèmes religieux ptolémaïques." *Aegyptus* 33: 125–30.

Traunecker, C. 1992. *Coptos: Hommes et dieux sur la parvis de Geb.* Orientalia Lovaniensia Analecta 43. Leuven.

Troxell, H. A. 1983. "Arsinoe's Non-Era." *ANSMN* 28: 35–70.

Troy, L. 1986. *Patterns of Queenship in Ancient Egyptian Myth and History.* Uppsala.

Tunny, J. A. 2000. "Ptolemy 'the Son' Reconsidered: Are There Too Many Ptolemies?" *ZPE* 131: 83–92.

———. 2001. "The Health of Ptolemy II Philadelphus." BASP 38, 1–4: 119–34.

Tyldesley, J. 2012. "Foremost Women: The Female Pharaohs of Ancient Egypt." In R. H. Wilkinson (ed.), *Tausret: Forgotten Queen and Pharaoh of Egypt.* New York, 5–24.

Vatin, C. 1970. *Recherches sur le marriage et la condition de la femme mariée à l' époque hellénistique.* Paris.

Vérilhac, A.-M., and C. Vial. 1998. *Le marriage grec: du Vie siècle av. J.-C. à l'époque d'Auguste.* Paris.

Walbank F. W. 1984. "Monarchies and Monarchic Ideas." *Cambridge Ancient History* Vol. 7.1, 62–100.

———. 1988. "From the Battle of Ipsus to the Death of Antigonus Doson." In Hammond and Walbank 1988, 199–366.

———. 1996. "Two Hellenistic Processions: A Matter of Self-Definition." *Scripta Classica Israelica* 15: 119–30.

Walker, Susan, and Peter Higgs (eds.). 2001. *Cleopatra of Egypt*. Princeton.

Wallenstein, J., and J. Pakkanen. 2009. "A New Inscribed Statue Base from the Sanctuary of Poseidon at Kalaureia." *Opuscula* 2: 155–65.

Waterfield, Robin. 2011. *Dividing the Spoils: The War for Alexander the Great's Empire*. New York.

Weber, G. 1993. *Dichtung Und Höfische Gesellschaft: Die Rezeption von Zeitgeschichte am Hof Der Ersten Drei Ptolemäer*. Hermes Einzelschriften 62. Stuttgart.

———. 1997. "Interaktion, Repräsentation und Herrschaft. Der Königshof im Hellenismus." In A. Winterling (ed.), *Zwischen "Haus" und "Staat." Antike Höfe im Vergleich*. Historische Zeitschrift 23. Munich, 27–71.

———. 1998–99 "Hellenistic Rulers and Their Poets: Silencing Dangerous Critics?" *AncSoc* 29: 147–74.

Wendel, C. 1914. *Scholia in Theocritum veteran*. Leipzig.

Wheatley, P. V. 1995. "Ptolemy Soter's Annexation of Syria 320 B.C." *CQ* 45(2): 433–440.

———. 2003. "Lamia the Besieger: An Athenian Hetaera and a Macedonian King." In O. Palagia and S. V. Tracy (eds.), *The Macedonians in Athens 322–229 BC*. Oxford, 30–36.

Wheeler, E. L. 2010. "Polyaenus: *Scriptor Militaris*." In K. Brodersen (ed.), *Polyaenus. New Studies*. Berlin, 7–54.

White, Eric Walter. 1983. *A History of English Opera*. London.

Whitehorne, J. 1995. "Women's Work in Theocritus, *Idyll* 15." *Hermes* 123: 63–75.

Wikander, C. 1992. "Pomp and Circumstance: The Procession of Ptolemaios II." *Opuscula atheniensia* 19: 143–50.

———. 2002. "Dynasty: The Environment of Hellenistic Monarchs." In K. Ascani et al. (eds.), *Studies Presented to J. E. Skydsgaard*. Rome, 185–91.

Wilcken, U. 1896. "Arsinoe 26." *RE* 2,1: 1283.

Will, E. 1979. *Histoire politique du monde hellénistique*. Vol. 1. 2d ed. Nancy.

Winnicki, J. K. 1994. "Carrying Off and Bringing Home the Statues of the Gods: On an Aspect of the Religious Policy of the Ptolemies towards the Egyptians." *Journal of Juristic Papyrology* 24: 149–90.

Wood, Susan. 2000. *Imperial Women: A Study in Public Images, 40 BC–AD 68*. Leiden.

Wörrle, M. 1978. "Epigraphische Forschungen zur Geschichte Lykiens II: Ptolemaios II und Telmessos." *Chiron* 8: 201–48.

Yardley, J. C. (trans.). 1994. *Justin. Epitome of the Philippic History of Pompeius Trogus*. Atlanta.

———. 2003. *Justin and Pompeius Trogus: A Study of the Language of Justin's Epitome of Trogus*. Toronto.

Zographou, Maire. 2005. *Arsinoe E Philadelphos Ethea Aphrodite tes Ptolemaikes Aigyptou*. Athens.

Index

Page numbers written in italics denote illustrations.

Arsinoë II-Ptolemy (*continued*)
    image-making in, 78–79, 85–87, 88,
        103, 104–05, 107, 127–28, 175n148
    images. *See* images of Arsinoë
    life at court, 83–84
    motivations for, 74–82
    political considerations, 70, 76, 78–79,
        160n75
    as sibling marriage, 1, 70–74, 128–29,
        159n34, 160n62, 175n148–149
    suppression of revolts, 158n33, 160n76
    wedding date, 70–71, 123, 158n32,
        177n13
    See also cults; Ptolemaic dynasty;
        Ptolemy II
Arsinoë IV, 106, 129, 131
Arsinoë Philadelphus (cult). *See thea*
    philadelphus (cult)
Arsinoëum, 106, 108, 129–30, 170n17,
    170n19, 170n23, 174n120
art:
    cameos of paired images, 130, 176n163,
        176n166
    Greek female portraiture, 116–17,
        172n85, 172n87
    Greek male portraiture, 121
    See also images of Arsinoë; statuary
Artabazus, 13, 19
Artacama (Apama), 19
Artemis, 98
Asia Minor:
    invasion by Lysimachus, 34, 45
    invasion by Seleucus, 45–46
Athenaeus, 39, 73, 74, 86, 114–15,
    126, 140
Athens:
    Chremonidean War, 91, 92–93, 141
    cults of, 95, 96
    festival of Adonia, 101, 102, 167
        n151–153, 167n156–157
    statues of Arsinoë and Ptolemy II,
        118
Attalid dynasty, 77
Attica, 95
Augustus, 129

Babylon, 2, 13
Barbantani, Sylvia, 129, 143, 166n130
Barsine, 19

basilissa:
    Arsinoë as, 36, 38, 57, 81, 98, 140,
        156n23, 156n25
    definition, 6, 150n60
    first woman attested with, 96
    Philotera as, 76
Berenice (daughter of Arsinoë I-Ptolemy
    II), 68
Berenice (daughter of Ptolemy III),
    166n124
Berenice I:
    arrival in Egypt, 16, 20
    birthplace, 20
    children by first marriage, 20–21
    children by Ptolemy, 21, 150n64
    cult honoring, 96
    death, 65, 157n2
    deification, 65, 157n3
    eponymous cities, 171n47
    first marriage, 20
    marriage to Ptolemy, 2–3, 16, 20–22,
        23, 150n61
    Olympic chariot racing, 27–29, 30, 89,
        151n92–93, 151n99, 157n2
    parents, 20, 21
    portraits, 122, 123, 124, 174n122, 174n124
    relationship to Antipater, 20, 21
    succession rivalry with Eurydice, 2–3,
        22–27, 41, 53, 81
    See also theoi soteres (cult)
Berenice II, 128, 129, 131, 164n64
Bevan, E., 143
Bilistiche, 126, 127, 175n143
Bioni, Antonio, 131
Burstein, Stanley, 143, 144

Caesar, 129
Caldara, Antonio, 131
Caligula, Emperor of Rome, 130
Callicrates, 79, 85, 87, 97, 99, 118, 142,
    166n139
Callimachus, 67, 101–02, 103, 104, 108,
    141–42, 165n114, 168n192, 169n2
Canopus, 97
Canopus decree, 128
Caria, 12, 42
Cassander:
    and Adea Eurydice, 92
    alliance with Lysimachus, 34, 40

sculpture. *See* statuary

second dynasty, 85

Seleucid Empire, 45, 47, 58, 74, 77

Seleucus:
  campaign against Lysimachus, 32–33, 45–46, 49, 53, 154n67, 154n71
  choice of co-king, 29, 42
  death, 46, 50, 53, 139, 155n4
  Lysandra's flight to, 45, 46, 53
  victory over Antigonus, 34
  wars of Successors, 25, 34, 49–50

Smyrna Eurydicea, 36

sons of Arsinoë II and Lysimachus:
  Arsinoë's ambitions for, 1–2, 43, 44, 46–47, 48, 81–82, 84, 92, 93–94, 125, 144
  birth of, 35
  escape from Ephesus, 48
  impact of Ptolemy II's coregency on, 29
  murder of, 1, 2, 51, 55, 60, 63, 64, 153n21, 155n18, 156n31
  See also Lysimachus (son of Arsinoë II and Lysimachus); Philip (son of Arsinoë II and Lysimachus); Ptolemy (son of Arsinoë II and Lysimachus)

Sotades, 73–74, 159n56

soteres (saviors), 96
  See also theoi soteres (cult)

Sparta, 91, 93

Sprott, Duncan, 132–33

Stanzani, Tomaso, 131

statuary:
  Greek female portraiture, 116–17, 172n85, 172n87
  Greek male portraiture, 121
  in honor of Ptolemy II's mistresses, 126–27
  See also images of Arsinoë

Stephanus Byzantinus, 36

Strabo, 36, 44, 45, 139

Strato of Lampsacus, 17

Successors (Diadochi):
  cults, 4, 6, 95
  Justin's description of, 32–33
  link to Argead dynasty, 4
  marriage alliances, 5–6, 25, 31–32
  naming of cities after female relatives, 110

polygamy, 18, 34, 35, 57

post-Ipsus alliances, 25, 31, 34, 40–41

reversals of fortune, 62

role of royal women, 5, 85, 91

royal titles, 2

succession innovations, 4, 18, 26–27, 42

wars of, 2, 5, 13–15, 16, 19, 25, 32–34, 49–50
  See also specific Successors

Syria, 90

Tacitus, 15

Tarn, W.W., 143, 144

Telmessus, 125

Thaïs, 18–19, 20, 21, 22, 150n63

thea philadelphus (cult):
  Arsinoë's involvement, 100, 107
  canephore office in, 106, 109, 127, 175n144
  dates of, 78, 100, 107, 128
  as dual Egyptian and Greek cult, 107–10
  during Roman era, 130
  festival of Arsinoëa, 106, 109
  image-making function of, 79, 106–10
  linking of Arsinoë with Agathe Tyche, 109, 170n34
  linking of Arsinoë with Aphrodite, 101, 109
  linking of Arsinoë with Isis, 108, 109
  overlap with *theoi adelphoi*, 99
  as posthumous vs. lifetime, 106, 169n2
  success of, 74

Thebes, 95

Theocritus:
  on Arsinoë and Ptolemy II, 67, 79, 101, 103, 123–24, 140, 141, 157n40, 161n96–97
  on Berenice and Ptolemy, 21, 22
  interest in female perspective, 168n189
  Ptolemaic patronage of, 21, 167n165, 168n186

theoi adelphoi (cult):
  Arsinoë's involvement, 76, 88, 100
  Callicrates as first priest, 97, 165n109
  coins issued for, 123, 174n116
  creation of, 71, 77–78, 79, 100, 165n104
  image-making function of, 79, 107
  innovations, 97

Lightning Source UK Ltd.
Milton Keynes UK
UKHW010753201219
355695UK00003B/204/P